WOMEN IN THE CHURCH

RECLAIMING THE IDEAL

CARROLL D. OSBURN

ACU
PRESS

Women in the Church: Reclaiming the Ideal

ACU
PRESS
ACU Station, Box 29138
Abilene, TX 79699

Cover illustration: *Head of a Girl,* Jan Vermeer (1632-1675), used by permission of Royal Cabinet of Paintings, Mauritshuis, The Hague, Netherlands

Printed in the United States of America

ISBN 0-89112-021-1

Library of Congress Card Number **96-84095**

4,5

To LINDA

*whose life as
college co-ed, wife, surgical nurse,
mother, grandmother, friend,
community volunteer,
and committed Christian lady
has inspired my life and this book*

CONTENTS

1. Women in the Church: The Present Quandary 1

2. Extremist Approaches to the Problem 19

    Radical Feminism
    Patriarchalism

3. Moderate Approaches to the Problem 49

    Evangelical Feminism
    Hierarchal Complementarianism

4. Refocusing the Approach 87

5. Genesis 1-3 109

6. Jesus' View of Women 125

7. Gal 3:28—"Neither Male and Female" 131

8. Women in Appointed and/or Assumed Roles 139
    Phoebe (Rom 16:1-2)
    Female Deacons (1 Tim 3:11)
    Priscilla

9. Ephesians 5:21-33—Subjection, Submission
    & Headship 155

10. 1 Cor 11:2-16—Cultural Sensitivity in Worship . . . 173

11. 1 Cor 14:34-35—Disruptive Corinthians 189

12. 1 Tim 2:9-15 207

13. Conclusion 253

Author Index 269

Scripture Index 275

Extremes fuel the fire of every movement. When people push and scream loud enough and long enough, there is revolution. Excessive emotional involvement results in distorted perceptions which inhibit the ability to assess clearly and differentiate accurately. A complete lack of self-criticism reigns. Out of anxiety, criticism often is made only of the other view in terms of stereotypes, such as:

Wives should be kept barefoot and pregnant.
Old Southern Proverb

He seldom errs who thinks the worst he can of womankind.
John Home (1722-1808)

I believe in dragons, good men, and other fantasy creatures.
Bumper Sticker

If God is male, then the male is God.
Mary Daly

Such extremist statements flow like a torrent from radios, televisions, books, speeches, magazines, and movies. Each extreme calls like a Pied Piper and each has many followers. Strong polarization against women by traditionalists naturally generates a vehement reaction by feminists against traditionalists. Each group tends to malign the other with stereotypes and avoid communication.

Not being a woman, I view this battleground through my own "masculine glasses" and offer these observations:

1. Some women are treated badly and have reason to be angry. Physical abuse is all too common and emotional abuse seems to be even more prevalent. Much divorce is attributable to abuse. I have encountered an unusually large number of women who have been abandoned by or forced to leave a husband and make it on their own. Often they must support children, yet have few or no marketable skills.

2. Some women are susceptible to extremist propaganda. When one has had enough abuse, it is easy to question masculinity as authoritative and it is easy to turn to anyone who champions a way out. Mistreatment often creates a rough and militant feminist mentality based upon hate. These women leave relationships with a vengeance! On the other hand, the influence of propaganda is also seen in the subjected wife who confuses submission with bondage to a domineering man. That all-too-common look of low self-esteem, inferiority, even fear, evidences the frustrating delusion that she is adhering to the biblical message. These deluded women stay in relationships . . . yet die inside.

3. Some women try consciously to downplay their female-ness by avoiding all appearance of femininity and adopting so-called masculine dress and traits, such as fierce independence and assertiveness. Much confusion exists about roles of women.

4. The Bible is either disdained as a relic from the past with no valid voice to today's pressing issues, or treated selectively in support of preconceived notions rooted in cultural alternatives.

5. More people than ever are divorcing. When my older daughter was a senior in high school in Santa Monica, CA, she was the only student in her psychology class of a hundred whose parents still lived together. This is not surprising, given the divorce rate of 50%. But when I face those freshmen students in my Honors New Testament class and tell them that their chances of a successful marriage are one out of two, those are not good odds. Something is terribly wrong!

6. More people are choosing not to marry at all because of fear. I understand. How many people do you know who are deeply in love, enjoy living together, affirm one another, enjoy children, maintain sexual fidelity, and are secure in their long-term relationship? Not many. The choice of a single life looks good to many.

The centuries-old model of male dominance has received an overdue challenge. Apparently unaware of much of the sociological basis of their faith and practice, many fundamentalist Christians distort biblical texts in an effort to preserve their view. In vain attempts to defend and preserve this unworthy perspective which inherently de-humanizes both male and female, fundamentalist Christians exhibit a detachment from contemporary society. On the other hand, feminist response has either called for abandonment of biblical authority or has engaged in reading much contemporary viewpoint into the biblical text. In so doing they have fallen into the same pit as their fundamentalist adversaries (although admittedly often with considerably more erudition). So there is the battlefield—each side pitted against the other, hurling insult and invective—while many in the middle ground are caught in the crossfire.

It is a wonder that more women are not crushed by these competing propagandas, but they have taken their toll! All too often, I see arrogant, aggressive, and repulsive independent women who detest the term "submit" in any context, who leave in their wake shattered husbands and confused children, yet who live in frustrated loneliness. Alternatively, all too often I see intimidated women who lack personhood, each slavishly bonded to her house and man—silent, intimidated. Unable to deal with the children leaving home or the death of a domineering spouse, such women face the harsh realities of almost insurmountable obstacles in life. Neither of these extremes has legitimate biblical basis.

On a scale of one to ten, there are ones who dominate and abuse women and there are tens who dominate and abuse men. There are also twos who hold tenaciously to male leadership and female subjection but are not mean-spirited, and there are nines who are strong feminists, but not "man haters." In between are threes through eights who do not feel comfortable with either extreme, but are either ignored in the discussion by extremists or made to fit uncomfortably into an extreme which leaves them ill at ease. It is the modest purpose of this book to recast the discussion in a more productive mode for these in the middle.

Now there are two views in this middle ground which have much in common, but in actuality are as different as oil and water. If these in the middle are to live and work together in families, communities, and churches, it is mandatory that each view make an honest effort to see clearly what is held in common and understand precisely where there is disagreement. If the matter of women can be recast in this way, those who hold different views on women can avoid the pitfalls of extremism and engage in the kind of productive communication that can result in mature acceptance of the other view, with which there will be disagreement—but not make it a test of Christian fellowship.

The writer does not claim to be without bias, presuppositions, or prejudice. However, every attempt will be made to work with an awareness of those so that the discussion can be profitable to readers whose biases, presuppositions, and prejudices are different.

I must express appreciation to Mrs. Lucille Carmichael for her strong interest in making my research possible, and to Ms. Jo Ann Walling Halbert and Mrs. Paula Varner for their assistance in making my research available to a broader audience. While many have made valuable contributions to my thinking on this topic, I am especially indebted to Mrs. Sandra Patterson for the invitation to speak at a ladies' retreat in San Antonio which was the genesis of this book, Mrs. Linda Halbert for her critical assessments of the manuscript at various stages, and especially to Mrs. Charme Robarts, my research assistant, whose rigorous interaction with my thinking has been invaluable. Finally, I am indebted to my Graduate Assistant, Chris Benjamin, and to my student secretary, Ms. Tiffany Touchstone, for their assistance in the preparation of the manuscript.

Carroll D. Osburn

Abilene, Texas
15 February 1994

Preface to the Second Edition

For conservative churches continuing to seek the middle ground between radical feminism on the one hand and an unhealthy patriarchalism on the other, it is useful to discuss existing options. Radical feminism and patriarchalism fail to survive biblical and sociological analysis. Egalitarianism and hierarchal complementarianism must be critiqued in terms of their biblical basis and sociological viability.

In the first edition, subtitled *Refocusing the Discussion*, I made a plea for equitable discussion, a sincere quest for truth and a spirit of mutual respect. We must search for an understanding of egalitarian and hierarchical presuppositions and arguments that will permit men and women alike to become whatever it is that God intended in the beginning. Consensus will not come from making presuppositions into prejudices, nor from repeating various views to the point that they become sacred, but from uncommon reliance upon the biblical text as authoritative and all views being held accountable to the highest standards of critical exactitude.

Because the book has been out of print for some time and numerous people have urged that it be reprinted, this second edition, subtitled *Reclaiming the Ideal*, provides an opportunity to make a few corrections. It also provides an opportunity to respond to several constructive remarks made regarding the earlier volume. Since that study, the second volume of *Essays on Women in Earliest Christianity* has come into print and readers will profit from several references to significant studies in that volume.

I have revised the earlier chapters considerably. The biblical studies section has been completely rewritten and greatly enlarged. The conclusion of the volume has been sharpened. While continuing to stress that those holding both median views must maintain an environment of toleration, I have stated my understanding of a biblically viable view of women in the church. The volume presupposes thoughtful, patient reading. It will be very important to have an open Bible while reading chapters five through twelve.

Preface to the Second Edition

Appreciation must be expressed to Mrs. Linda Halbert, Mrs. Jeanne Wyatt, Mrs. Gayle Turner, and Mrs. Sherrill Blazer, whose observations and patient interaction with this volume have been most instructive. For continuing support of my research and writing, I am grateful to Ms. Jo Ann Walling Halbert, Mrs. Lucille Carmichael, and Mrs. Paula Varner. I am indebted more than a little to my graduate assistants, Victor McCracken (1996-98) and Brent Bates (1998-00), as well as to my student secretaries, Mrs. Paige Martin Reynolds (1996-98) and Kara Jarman (1997-99). I am especially indebted to my research assistant, Mrs. Mandy Hardin Chankin (1998-00), for her diligence and thoughtful interaction with my thinking.

Carroll D. Osburn

Abilene, Texas
4 December 2000

ABBREVIATIONS

ASV	American Standard Version
Cf.	compare
Col	Colossians
Deut	Deuteronomy
E.g.	for example
En	Enoch
Eph	Ephesians
EvQ	*Evangelical Quarterly*
Gal	Galatians
Gen	Genesis
Heb	Hebrews
Isa	Isaiah
Jas	James
JBL	*Journal of Biblical Literature*
JerB	Jerusalem Bible
Jn	John
JSNT	*Journal for the Study of the New Testament*
JSNTSup	*Journal for the Study of the NT Supplement*
Jub	Jubilees
KJV	King James Version
Matt	Matthew
Mk	Mark
LCL	Loeb Classical Library series
Lk	Luke
NASB	New American Standard Bible
NEB	New English Bible
NIV	New International Version
NRSV	New Revised Standard Version
NT	New Testament
NTS	*New Testament Studies*
OT	Old Testament
Phil	Philippians
Rom	Romans
RevEB	Revised English Bible
RQ	*Restoration Quarterly*
RSV	Revised Standard Version
SBLDS	Society of Biblical Literature Dissertation Series
SNTSMS	Society of New Testament Studies Monograph Series

TDNT	*Theological Dictionary of the New Testament*
TEV	Today's English Version
Tit	Titus
1 Cor	First Corinthians
2 Cor	Second Corinthians
1 Pet	First Peter
2 Pet	Second Peter
1 Thess	First Thessalonians
2 Thess	Second Thessalonians
1 Tim	First Timothy
2 Tim	Second Timothy

GLOSSARY

Glossary

Allegory — a type of exegesis that minimizes the literal or plain meaning in favor of an alleged hidden or spiritual meaning

Anthropology — the science concerning the biological origins and cultural behavior of humankind

Antiquarianism — study of matters relating to the life and culture of ancient times

Androcentric — male dominance

Androgynous — having characteristics or nature of both male and female; having traditional male and female roles reversed

Apologetics — a reasoned defense; the attempt to establish certain elements of faith as true

Biblical criticism — a type of historical inquiry that seeks to recover the most trustworthy texts of the Bible, and to understand the origin and sources of the text, the relationship between the books, what the text reveals about the community that used it, and to what degree the historical reports are reliable

Bibliolatry (*biblicism*) — a view which accepts as true all that is to be found in the Bible in its literal meaning

Charismatic — Christian religious movement marked by emphasis on divinely-inspired powers or gifts, such as "speaking in tongues," prophecy, and/or healing

Christology — that part of Christian doctrine concerned with the revelation of God in Christ

Circular lexicography — reading one's view into a word so that its definition is then what one wants the word to mean

Conservative — one who advocates maintaining existing views, conditions, or institutions

Demagoguery — making use of popular prejudices and false claims of promises in order to gain power

Diaconate — deacons or deaconesses, servants

Egalitarian — belief in human equality, especially regarding social, political, and economic rights and privileges

Eisegesis — reading one's views into a text so as to make the text mean what one wants it to mean

Eschatology — theological concern with the final events in the history of the world and mankind; the study of death, judgment, afterlife

Etymology — the study of the history of the use of a word by tracing its development since its earliest known use

Evangelical — in America, a term for one who stresses a personal relationship with God in Jesus Christ by faith defined by theological beliefs about certain issues

Evangelical feminism — an egalitarian view that accepts biblical authority, yet maintains that biblical texts used to place restrictions on women have been misunderstood and misapplied

Exegesis — explanation of a text with intent to recover the author's intended meaning

Existentialism — a 20th century philosophical movement centering on the individual, who is responsible for his or her free will and who has no certain knowledge of what is right or wrong or good or bad

Extremism — going to exaggerated lengths; holding radical views; excessive behavior

Feminism — egalitarian theory of political, economic, and social equality of the sexes

Fundamentalism — evangelical Protestantism marked by literal interpretation of the Bible, militant opposition to modern liberal theologies and to some aspects of secular culture

Gnosticism — a type of religious thought widespread in the Greco-Roman world during the early centuries of the church and regarded as a serious threat to Christianity

Hendiadys — the expression of an idea by the use of two independent words, one of which is subordinate to and comments upon the other

Hermeneutics — the study of presuppositions, methods and principles of interpretation (as, how to study the Bible)

Hermeneutic of suspicion — radical feminist view which rejects biblical authority at the outset

Hierarchal, hierarchical — classification of people according to a perceived standing, especially "God, Christ, man, woman"; brings presuppositions of male dominance to the biblical text and life-style

Hierarchal complementarianism — view that understands the Bible to teach male hierarchy for both home and church, but still views women as full participants in church and civic life, except in the areas of church administration and preaching

Historical-critical scholarship — attempt to locate the meaning of a text in its literary and historical context

Interpolation — the alteration of a text by inserting new or foreign matter

Liberalism — a type of religious thought characterized by 1) eagerness to discard old forms in light of modern knowledge, 2) confidence in human reason, 3) belief in the social nature of human existence, 4) reliance upon critical scholarship

Liberationism — radical restructuring of relations between men and women, as well as reorganization of social structures as a whole

Liberationist feminism — view which holds that the central message of the Bible is human liberation; strong commitment to feminism; rejects masculinity of God

Locus-classicus — a passage generally cited as the best illustration or explanation of a subject

Mechanical dictation — view that the Bible was dictated by the Holy Spirit and that the writers of the biblical books were not actually involved in the composition

Mishna — collection of Jewish traditions compiled and written down about AD 200

Misogyny — having or showing a hatred and distrust of women

Modernism — theological tendency to accommodate traditional religious teaching to contemporary thought; especially to devalue the supernatural and the ancient

Mutual deference — relating to others with respect and esteem

Naturalism — theory denying supernatural significance to an event or object

Paradigm — an outstandingly clear or typical example

Patristics — the study of the life, literature, and thought of the theologians of the early church

Patriarchalism — social organization marked by the supremacy of the father and/or males; restrictions placed on women in home, church, and/or civic life

Philology — the study of speech as the language of literature

Premillennialism — view that the world is headed to doom and that Christ's return will be followed by his 1,000 year reign

Postmillennialism — view that Christ will return only at the end of a 1,000 year period

Proof-texting — citing passages randomly from any part of the Bible without regard for the literary and historical contexts of the passages

Radical feminism — tendency to make extreme changes in existing views, habits, conditions, or institutions relating to women in society

Rationalism — theological or philosophical position which values reason as the ultimate judge of all statements

Renewal — societal change should be based upon biblical intent

Restoration Movement — a "back to the Bible" movement originating in the U.S. with Alexander Campbell and Barton Stone, including Churches of Christ, Christian Churches, and Disciples of Christ

Revisionism — works to minimize differences between men and women

Revivalism — often highly emotional form of Protestantism rooted in 19th-20th century reaction against cultural decline in America, and marked by a strong attempt to fight changes that might displace religion as a major cultural shaping force

Rhetorical coquetry — playing games with words; trying to build a case without substantial basis

Sublimationism — assumes significant differences between men and women and that "masculine" and "feminine" qualities actually exist

Syncretistic —a combination of different forms of belief or practice

Theology — that part of religion having to do with the existence and nature of the divine; the entire range of issues concerning mankind's relationship to God

Traditionalism — staunch adherence to a patriarchal model inherited from the past, characterized by opposition to modernism, liberalism, or radicalism

Transformation — church is to be changed in terms of contemporary society

1

WOMEN IN THE CHURCH:
THE PRESENT QUANDARY

At the outset not much can be said with certainty on the matter, but it can be said with confidence that the topic of women in the church is complex, volatile, and unavoidable.

Prejudices on two extremes have resulted in heated discussions of women, particularly in churches. Diverse views are held with almost fanatical zeal. The mere mention of the topic evokes deep-seated feelings and emotions all across the spectrum of thought. Many turn to the Bible, but with different presuppositions, agendas, and traditional arguments. On both extremes, the complex matter of women in the church has become a matter of belief upon which fellowship hinges. For others, it is a matter of opinion to be researched and discussed. Unfortunately, if one seeks middle ground on this issue, one should be prepared to dive for cover, as shots will be fired from both directions. No more volatile topic exists in the church today.

In recent years, I have received numerous letters and phone calls from people who sincerely want to re-examine Scriptures carefully in search of truth, but who are uncertain about how to sort out what is truly biblical and what is cultural. The topic of women in the church is not solely a religious issue; it is rooted deeply in the culture in which we live.[1] Whether one likes it or not, changes are occurring regarding women in our culture and the impact of those

---

[1]See Barbara Harris and JoAnn McNamara, ed., *Women and the Structure of Society* (Durham, NC: Duke Univ. Press, 1984); Alice S. Rossi, *The Feminist Papers* (New York: Bantam Books, 1974); and the useful essays in John Stratton Hawley, ed., *Fundamentalism and Gender* (Oxford: Oxford Univ. Press, 1994), on fundamentalist views of women in America, Indian Islam, Hinduism, Japanese religions, and Judaism.

changes on churches is significant. Frankly, some of these changes are scary. Fearing these changes, some staunchly hold on to the patriarchal model inherited from the past. They tend to regard any who think otherwise as radicals who are merely letting contemporary culture override their biblical mooring. Now, for obvious reasons the voice of radical feminists is not at all strong in conservative churches. Still, some feel forced to choose between patriarchalism and feminism, reluctantly opt for the latter, and leave the church. However, many are caught in the middle who see problems with patriarchalism on one hand, yet who do not want to be identified with radical feminism on the other. What options exist for them? "Women in the church" is a complex topic. It is an agonizingly unavoidable topic.

I fear that the way we are now addressing the matter can only lead to extremism, chaos, and hardening of attitudes. If we are to investigate the matter afresh, we must find a more productive approach.

The way this question is asked will have much to say about religious identity and how the church is to interact with contemporary culture. To ask what *roles* women can have in the church and its worship is, I think, to ask the wrong question. It is true that the role of women in the church and its public worship are important topics. But what compels me to enter the explosive minefield of "women in the church" does not have to do so much with women handing out communion trays in worship, for instance. I am more concerned with widespread problems of abuse and inequity in our society and, more than I care to admit, in our churches. I am particularly bothered by any view of women that demeans, depreciates, and exploits women as merely tools for man's enjoyment and service. The question is not "What *roles* can women have in the church?" but "*How shall we view women?*"

Although the question of women in the church does not seem to be at the heart of the Christian message, it does surface some very diverse feelings. It is to be expected that some readers will hope to learn quickly in these pages whether I am their ally or their enemy and, having "pigeon-holed" me, find the remainder useless, because I would either confirm their hopes or annoy them greatly. In a way, I feel much like Sisyphus, a mythical king of Corinth who attempted repeatedly to "roll the stone of conversation to the top of the mountain of consensus, only to have it come crashing back down." Couching the question in terms of extreme views only hinders objectivity and conversation. We need to move beyond the impasse created by extremism.

What I would really like to see is more gracious, objective, and balanced discussion of the topic of women in the church. My modest tasks in this book are 1) to couch the question in a more productive way so that genuine communication can take place, and 2) to apply my biblical understandings to church life. Accordingly, while the role of women in Christian worship and administration should be discussed, that discussion can occur only after several significant matters have received clarification—matters concerning not the "*role* of women," but the "*view* of women."

1. *Approaching the Topic Productively*

Discussion of women in the church must avoid several pitfalls—pitfalls such as traditionalism and extremism. To avoid pitfalls, I offer the following suggestions.

First, we need to understand the various views of women that exist and how they came to be. These views did not come about in a religious vacuum apart from society. All of them have been shaped to a great extent by culture. How women are to be viewed is not a peculiarly religious topic, but is basically a human dilemma that must be examined in a wider context.

Second, we need to avoid extremes and concentrate on realistic options. The question of women in the church should be couched in terms of median views rather than in terms of the extreme views of *patriarchalism* and *radical feminism*, which will be discussed and dismissed in chapter two. Neither the extreme views of radical feminists nor the "Archie Bunkers" of this world provide an adequate view of women. Moderate views do exist, however, that will provide adequate understandings of women—*evangelical feminism* and *hierarchal complementarianism.* Now don't be too bothered by these terms. Every field has terms that require a little extra effort to understand, but which make work in that field much easier. Both of these views will be discussed in detail in chapter three. Both have much in common, but there are important differences. It is vital to understand both of these views accurately.

Third, we must cultivate a willingness to rethink the problem. Intellectual honesty often challenges old traditions. Long-standing presuppositions that have become identified with "eternal truth" must be dethroned and reclassified as mere presuppositions. Long-standing arguments that, with the passing of time, have hardened into "sacred truth" must now be dethroned and reclassified as mere arguments. Long-standing practices that have become almost like "the unchangeable law of the Medes and Persians" must now be dethroned and reclassified as cultural preferences. Rethinking means that some change might result. So, we must have an honest willingness to change our views and modify our behavior if necessary.

Fourth, we need to clarify the role and function of the Bible. Instead of rummaging through the Bible to find texts that might support our pre-conceived notions, we must re-examine the biblical text—and we must do so rigorously. Women in the church is a serious topic and it deserves serious study.[2] Now, I am not at all suggesting erudite excursions into intellectual black holes, vortices of endless regression into which scholars sometimes drift, never to be seen again. I am suggesting patient exegesis (getting out of the Bible what the writer meant) as the basis for responsible implementation in contemporary life of ancient biblical principles and values.

---

[2]See Carroll D. Osburn, ed., *Essays on Women in Earliest Christianity* (2 vols.; Joplin, MO: College Press, 1993, 1995).

2. Historical Roots of the Problem

If we are to approach such a complex and volatile topic in a productive manner, we should begin with a historical overview of the problem.[3] The church does not exist in a vacuum, but is a part of society, and during the past century a major cultural shift has occurred in Western society regarding women.[4] Early in our nation's history, the patriarchal family was a "citadel of masculine authority"[5] in which gender roles were carefully set. Manliness was identified with work, physical strength, competitiveness, and dominance as father and husband.[6] Women, on the other hand, were primarily mothers and housekeepers.

Then, industrialization and population shifts from farms to the cities in the 1800s led to major disruption of gender roles and family life. Increasingly, males began to assume roles as breadwinners in the business and industrial worlds. Income replaced property as the sign of successful manhood. A wife who did not work outside the home was a significant indicator of having achieved middle-class status.[7] Women were excluded from the male-dominated spheres of business, labor, politics, and government. The "home" became touted as the sphere of "the virtuous woman," idealized now for her motherhood and moral superiority.[8] Although sexual promiscuity increased, women were placed on pedestals and the four cardinal virtues of "True

---

[3]See Kathy J. Pulley, "Gender Roles and Conservative Churches: 1870-1930," *Essays on Women in Earliest Christianity*, 2:443-483.

[4]See Betty A. DeBerg, *Ungodly Women: Gender and the First Wave of American Fundamentalism* (Minneapolis: Fortress, 1990).

[5]Barbara Berg, *The Remembered Gate: Origins of American Feminism* (New York: Oxford Univ. Press, 1978): 49.

[6]See Peter Stearns, *Be a Man! Males in Modern Society* (New York: Holmes and Meier, 1979).

[7]Willam Chafe, *Women and Equality: Changing Patterns in American Culture* (New York: Oxford Univ. Press, 1977): 22.

[8]Barbara Welter, "The Cult of True Womanhood, 1820-1860," *Dimity Convictions: The American Woman in the Nineteenth Century* (Athens, OH: Ohio Univ. Press, 1976): 21-41.

Womanhood" came into being—piety, purity, submissiveness, and domesticity.[9] The most feminine virtue,
submissiveness, was considered part of the order of the
universe.[10] Religion was viewed as vital for women, but
unimportant for masculine identity.[11] However, when
women pushed the abolition of slavery, they found stiff
opposition, including reactions against speaking in public.[12]

By the 1870s, the changing American scene was
marked by the rise of professions, education, and large
businesses in the East, with women working as hard as men
on the frontier.[13] Women began entering colleges, working
in great numbers, entering professions, and becoming active
in politics.[14] As males had mostly abandoned the churches,

---

[9]Welter, "Cult of True Womanhood," *Dimity Convictions*, 21.

[10]Douglas Carlson, "Discovering Their Heritage: Women and the
American Past," *Gender Matters* (ed. June S. Hagen; Grand Rapids:
Zondervan, 1990): 98.

[11]B. Welter, "The Feminization of American Religion: 1800-
1860," *Clio's Consciousness Raised: New Perspectives on the History
of Women* (ed. M. Hartman and L. Banner; New York: Harper & Row,
1974): 137-57.

[12]Alice Rossi, ed., *The Feminist Papers* (New York: Bantam,
1874): 282-322, notes that the Grimké sisters had discerned some of the
basic dynamics that made slavery destructive to both master and slave.
See Angelina Grimké, "An Appeal to the Christian Woman of the
South," *The Anti-Slavery Examiner* 1 (Sept. 1836). Judith Hole and
Ellen Levine, *The Rebirth of Feminism* (New York: Quadrangle,
1971): 3, note that women protesting slavery were caricatured as having
completely lost their natural feminine character. Billie Pate and Elaine
Dickson, "Birth and Rebirth of Feminism: Responses of Church
Women," *Review and Expositor* 72 (1975): 54, observe that religious
attacks on these women were based on the premise that woman's
subjugation is divinely ordained and any deviation from this secondary
position is a violation of God's will.

[13]See Eleanor Flexner, *Century of Struggle* (New York:
Atheneum, 1971): 157-58; and Beverly W. Harrison, "The Early
Feminists and the Clergy," *Review and Expositor* 72 (1975): 41-52.

[14]See Gerda Lerner, *The Grimké Sisters from South Carolina:
Pioneers for Women's Rights and Abolition* (New York: Schocken,
1971).

it is not surprising that women were quite active in Sunday school teaching,[15] church leadership,[16] and even foreign missions.[17] The Women's Christian Temperance Union became the largest organization in the country.[18] Women worked actively for child-labor reform, prison reform, homes for unwed mothers, and city libraries. The campaign for the right of women to vote upset many people. All this wide-scale activity of women outside the home threatened the whole idea of male domination and female subjection.

Patriarchalism had come to depend heavily on the Victorian sexist stereotype of subordinate wives to reinforce masculine identity. By the turn of the century, though, a new identity began to emerge for women that was at variance with patriarchalism—many educated women chose not to marry, but to become "career girls." The double standard on sexual activity was challenged.[19] Dance halls and movie theaters provided new attractions. The emergence of automobiles enabled unchaperoned dating. Sexual activity

---

[15]See J. W. Carroll, B. Hargrove, and A. T. Lummis, *Women of the Cloth* (San Francisco: Harper & Row, 1983): 24.

[16]See Benjamin T. Roberts, *Ordaining Women* (Rochester, NY: Earnest Christian Pub., 1891); and Frances Willard, *Woman in the Pulpit* (Chicago: Woman's Temperance Pub., 1889). Reactions to women speaking in mixed audiences was more pronounced in the 1870s than had been the case earlier. See Elizabeth Cady Stanton, Susan B. Anthony, and Matilda J. Gage, *The History of Woman Suffrage* (New York: Fowler and Weels, 1881): 1.481ff and 531ff.

[17]Virginia L. Brereton and Christa R. Klein, "American Women in Ministry," *Women in American Religion* (ed. J. W. James; Philadelphia: Univ. of Pennsylvania Press, 1980): 171-90; and Joan Jacobs Brumberg, "The Ethnological Mirror: American Evangelical Women and Their Heathen Sisters, 1870-1910," *Women and the Structure of Society* (Durham, NC: Duke Univ. Press, 1984): 108-28.

[18]See Ruth Bordin, *Women and Temperance: The Quest for Power and Liberty, 1873-1900* (Philadelphia: Temple Univ. Press, 1981): xvi-xvii.

[19]Barbara Deckard, *The Women's Movement* (San Francisco: Harper & Row, 1975): 258, notes that as late as 1900 in many states, if a woman was divorced for adultery, she had to forfeit all property, including her own, but there was no similar penalty for men.

increased dramatically, symbolized by the "flapper," the "modern" woman who bobbed her hair, wore short skirts, danced the Charleston, drank, smoked, and enjoyed sex.[20] Divorce increased markedly. This revolution in morals and conduct created great concern in American society.[21]

In spite of the adoption of the Nineteenth Amendment in 1920 giving women the right to vote, traditionalists countered that women should remain in the home. "Woman has no call to the ballot-box, but she has a sphere . . . she is the divinely appointed guardian of the home."[22] As divorce increased rapidly, the home was singled out as the basic building-block of society. Divorce became "the great American sin."[23] In 1922 the Cable Act was passed by Congress, guaranteeing a woman citizenship independent of her husband. This was followed by a virtual avalanche of argumentation that women are subordinate to men and that husbands and fathers are to *rule* the family.

For men whose gender identity and social domination were at stake due to these major upheavals that threatened patriarchalism, religion was seen as a useful tool. While readily admitting that women possess various talents for church work, men now held that women were not to exercise authority. Women were not to recite Bible verses or pray aloud in public and should have their heads covered in church. Church meetings gave way to "men's business meetings." Texts such as 1 Cor 14:34-35 and 1 Tim 2:11-15

---

[20]William O'Neill, *Everyone Was Brave* (New York: Quadrangle, 1969): 298, notes that before 1890, 87% of women were virgins at marriage, but after 1910 only 32% were virgins.

[21]See Andrew Sinclair, *The Emancipation of the American Woman* (New York: Harper & Row, 1965): 325.

[22]J. M. Williams, "Woman Suffrage," *Bibliotheca Sacra* 50 (1893): 343. Note also O'Neill, *Everyone Was Brave*, 229, that in 1924 an employee of the Office of Chemical Warfare smeared women's groups with a chart purporting them to be directed by Moscow!

[23]See Noah Lathrop, "The Holy Scriptures and Divorce," *Bibliotheca Sacra* 56 (1899): 266-77; and Charles Morgan, "Is Desertion a Scriptural Ground for Divorce?" *Bibliotheca Sacra* 43 (1886): 334.

were stressed to forbid women teaching and preaching in the presence of men. Some even argued that women should not speak publicly either in the church *or elsewhere*,[24] nor should a woman be a church official. So, certain areas (administration; public worship) which long had been areas of extensive participation by women were re-designated "male only" as more and more men began to involve themselves in American religion.

Between 1880 and 1920, male authority began to assert itself vigorously in churches all across America. A call went out for "real men" to become ministers. Virility in the ministry was typified by Billy Sunday.[25] Militant and abusive, his revivals were calculated to attract young men. Rather than "Hark! The Gentle Voice" (Mrs. M. B. C. Slade),[26] he preferred such songs as "The Fight Is On." Engaged in heated conflict with the hated enemy, he reaffirmed traditional masculine identity with bombastic sermons in which he powerfully triumphed over evil. Many young men chose to enter the ministry and imitate Billy Sunday, and many ministers followed this assertive model in their sermons and theological debates.

Rejecting the "feminized" Jesus that characterized much nineteenth-century thought, patriarchalists now reinterpreted Jesus as the manliest of all men, hopefully appealing to men in ways earlier evangelism did not.[27] Aggressive language and military terminology were used against all foes, whether

---

[24]See E. G. Sewell in M. C. Kurfees, ed., *Questions Answered by Lipscomb and Sewell* (Nashville: McQuiddy, 1921): 729-30.

[25]See Douglas Frank, *Less than Conquerors: How Evangelicals Entered the Twentieth Century* (Grand Rapids: Eerdmans, 1986): 256-66.

[26]See Welter, "The Feminization of American Religion," *Dimity Convictions*, 88-90, for discussion of nineteenth-century hymnology of women, e.g., "Nearer My God To Thee" (Sarah Adams), "I Need Thee Every Hour" (Annie Hawks), and "Just As I Am, Without One Plea" (Charlotte Elliott).

[27]E.g., Bruce Barton, *The Man Nobody Knows* (New York: Bobbs-Merrill, 1925), often reprinted.

real or imagined.[28] With World War I, this language and
mentality entrenched itself in pulpits. Ministry came to be
seen as a battleground where truth and error were locked in
deadly combat. Controversy, debate, and "fighting spirit"
became the "manly" way to serve God. While some adopted
a more gentlemanly approach, the tenor for the style of
engaging in issues was set by aggressive men whose strident
voices ridiculed adversaries without mercy.   As Rice put
it,[29]

> Doubtless, thousands of men have been kept out of the
> ministry because the ministry, as it is known to the people,
> does not appeal to the best in strong men. And the churches
> have become so effeminate . . . that they do not appeal
> generally to vital business men, strong, earnest robust men.
> You can be sure that the kind of Christianity that produces
> Aimee Semple McPherson does not at the same time produce
> Spurgeons. . . . Then do you wonder that in the modern
> sissyfied churches the average he-man will have no part?
> There was never any lack of men to hear the gospel under the
> bold, strong preaching of . . . Billy Sunday. And plain, solid,
> masculine preachers with holy boldness and a John the Baptist
> type of ministry, have no trouble getting a hearing among
> men today. The gospel is blood and fire and iron. We need
> more than . . . boy preachers and women evangelists in the
> pulpit if the church is to take its rightful place in society."

Jude 3, "contend for the faith," became the principal proof
text for this behavior. Thus, churches became remascu-
linized in the early twentieth century, and firm arguments
were given for women to be domestic and stay away from
the male sphere.

---

[28]Robert Wenger, "Social Thought in American Fundamentalism,
1918-1933," (Ph.D. diss., Univ. of Nebraska, 1973): 46, argues that
militancy was "inherent in fundamentalism."

[29]John R. Rice, *Bobbed Hair, Bossy Wives and Women Preachers*
(Wheaton: Sword of the Lord, 1941): 58-59, 65. Foy E. Wallace, Jr.,
"Editorial, " *The Gospel Guardian* Oct. 1935): 4, said in condemnation
of J. N. Armstrong, president of Harding College, "There is a time for
soft answers but there is no place for soft preachers. They are a misfit
in the line of defence . . . ."

Against the changing sexual mores of the period, traditionalists attacked dancing, novels, immoral plays, and motion pictures, all of which publicized changes in gender roles. Reacting strongly against "flappers," traditionalists made immodest dress a pivotal topic. Flappers were castigated as coarse, daring, vulgar, and immoral for flouting societal norms.[30] On the basis of 1 Tim 2:9, current fads were seen as offensive: e.g., tight skirts, short skirts, peek-a-boo skirts, rolled hose, sheer hose, rouge and powder, and bobbed hair.[31] Mixed swimming became an issue. There is no doubt that premarital sex increased alarmingly during this period. The double standard for men and women was breaking down, but many feared that "modern" women were leaving their lofty pedestal and coming down to man's coarse and obscene level. It was in this context of changing sexual mores that fundamentalism in American religion rose to prominence in the early twentieth century.

All this modernism gave impetus to a now rapidly changing fundamentalist agenda. Since the publication of Darwin's *On the Origin of Species* in 1859, the relationship between Christianity and the natural sciences had been a matter of heated discussion.[32] In the decade that followed World War I, newer social science disciplines, such as sociology, anthropology, and psychology, began to regard religion as a cultural artifact to be examined scientifically.[33] But, having religious behavior and belief subjected to cold, objective inquiry was more than many could stand. As fundamentalists looked to their Bibles for answers to the

---

[30]A. R. Funderburk, "Serving the God of Fashion," *Moody Bible Institute Monthly* 25 (1925): 500; "Editorial," *Bibliotheca Sacra* 86 (1929): 133-35.

[31]DeBerg, *Ungodly Women*, 106-08.

[32]See Theodore Dwight Bozeman, *Protestants in an Age of Science* (Chapel Hill: UNC Press, 1977).

[33]R. L. Moore, "Secularization: Religion and the Social Sciences," *Between the Times: The Travail of the Protestant Establishment in America, 1900-1960* (ed. W. Hutchinson; Cambridge: Cambridge Univ. Press, 1990): 233-36.

social disruptions going on around them, they were fearful and dismayed at the undermining of trust in the Bible by critical scholarship, especially "higher criticism" of the Bible. They rejected the notion that only scholars can interpret Scripture and worked hard at keeping the Bible in the hands of common believers.[34]

The infallibility of the Bible was defended vigorously, as it was viewed as the only reliable source of stability for churches and society as a whole. Fundamentalists did not establish truth by careful biblical study though. Rather, proof-texting (citing a passage here, another there, randomly from any part of the Bible) was the dominant approach to the text. This approach had great appeal because it appeared to give certainty and to allow people to think for themselves. However, it did not deal with the possibility that those who read the text honestly and prayerfully with this method might come to different understandings about what the Bible meant. This use of the text did not prepare readers to evaluate alternative views. Intolerance led readers to eliminate or ignore other views and to consider deviations from the "obvious" meaning as theological subversion or apostasy. While ideas such as "No creed but the Bible" had taken hold in several popular religious movements, there was a glaring gap between the appeal to end sectarian strife and actual practice that ended in a steady stream of issues, quarrels, and divisions.[35] The principal scandal in this use of the Bible is inconsistency between keeping the Scriptures accessible to ordinary believers, but in the end forbidding readers the freedom to come to any other conclusions than those of their leaders.[36] While belief in biblical inerrancy

---

[34]Timothy Weber, "The Two-Edged Sword: The Fundamentalist Use of the Bible," *The Bible in America* (ed. N. Hatch & M. Noll; Oxford: Oxford Univ. Press, 1982): 111-12. Some even believed that under the direct guidance of the Holy Spirit, the interpretation of a common reader was preferable to that of a trained scholar.

[35]Nathan Hatch, *The Democratization of American Christianity* (New Haven: Yale Univ. Press, 1989): 182-83.

[36]See Mark Noll, "Evangelicals and the Study of the Bible," *Evangelicalism and Modern America* (ed. G. Marsden; Grand Rapids:

was common, most could not prove that doctrine and had to rely on trusted leaders who could. Fundamentalist leaders armed with biblical proof-texts[37] led in militant defense of traditional views in theological debates and sermons. This use of the Bible had the effect of hardening certain arguments and proof-texts into sacred orthodoxy in the minds of their fundamentalist followers.[38]

In view of the lack of consensus among Christians on womanhood, traditionalists reacted to shifting sexual mores and increasingly public roles for women by reverting to a traditional, stereotypical Victorian model of femininity. This reaction was then supported by various biblical proof-texts. For example, concerning 1 Tim 2:11-15, Rice asserted,[39]

> careful observers must admit that women are also easier led into false doctrines and into errors of various kinds. But the argument here in I Timothy 2:14 is that Satan was able to deceive Eve when he could not deceive Adam, and that this is an evidence that women should not be placed in authority in churches and in Christian work. . . . This means that women leaders are more likely to lead into heresy in doctrine and unscriptural practice than men.

Arguing that "God is a masculine God" and that "man is made in the image of God," Rice observes, "on the other hand, a woman is not made so much in the image of God, but in the image and as a mate to man" (68). Continuing (76-77) he notes,

---

Eerdmans, 1984): 103-21, esp. 110, where he calls it the spirit of "demagoguery."

[37]George Marsden, "From Fundamentalism to Evangelicalism," *The Evangelicals: What They Believe, Who They Are, Where They Are Changing* (rev. ed. D. Wells & J. Woodbridge; Grand Rapids: Baker, 1977): 156-57.

[38]George Marsden, *Fundamentalism and American Culture: The Shaping of Twentieth Century Evangelicalism, 1870-1925* (New York: Oxford Univ. Press, 1980): 90-92.

[39]Rice, *Bobbed Hair, Bossy Wives and Women Preachers*, 41.

"If women only knew the charm and beauty of long hair to
intelligent men and the reverence it inspires for godly women,
they would never cut their hair. . . . I remember with what
pride I saw my bride take down her long hair and brush it."

He then refers to Luke 7:37-38, where the sinful woman
wiped her tears from Jesus feet with her hair. "How Jesus
seems to have delighted in having His feet wiped with the
long hair of this woman's head," Rice observes, but "she
could never have given this beautiful mark of her devotion
and surrender and love . . . if she had been a modern woman
with bobbed hair. . . . Yes, the modern . . . bobbed-haired
woman has fallen from her pedestal."

Then came World War II. After Pearl Harbor, some six
million women joined the work force. "Rosie the Riveter"
became the billboard and poster symbol of women who
assembled the airplanes. The war opened to women
economic opportunities previously denied them.[40] Federal
funds were allocated for day care facilities. However, with
the peace-time economy that came with the end of the war,
many women were forced to step aside to make room for
returning veterans. In 1946 funds for day care were cut off.
However, most women, after experiencing economic
advantages, remained in the work force.

After World War II, a rapid social and economic change
swept America and a great upheaval pervaded society in
general.[41] Juvenile delinquency, drugs, situation ethics,[42]
rampant divorce, radical feminism, and even working
mothers refocused attention on the home. The peril of
atheistic communism was a major concern. Two major
social movements widened the gap between values and

[40]See Carlson, "Discovering Their Heritage: Women and the
American Past," *Gender Matters*, 106-07.

[41]Robert Wuthnow, *The Struggle for America's Soul:
Evangelicals, Liberals, & Secularism* (Grand Rapids: Eerdmans, 1989):
33.

[42]See Joseph Fletcher, *Situation Ethics: The New Morality*
(Philadelphia: Westminster Press, 1966).

behavior[43]—the civil rights movement and the anti-war movement, both of which challenged the idea of authority in society by advocating civil disobedience.[44] Selfishness increased dramatically. The civil rights movement, for instance, brought into relief the dilemma of "subscribing to egalitarian values in principle but engaging in racial discrimination in practice."[45] In response, there was a marked increase in church attendance among conservative Christian groups. The wedge was driven deeper between fundamentalists, who opted to concentrate on personal belief (e.g., conversion; revivalism), and liberals who opted for social justice.

In 1963, Friedan's,[46] *The Feminine Mystique*, struck a chord with many women and is viewed as the beginning of the modern feminist movement. That same year, the Equal Pay Act passed and gender was included in Title VII of the 1964 Civil Rights Act. The National Organization for Women was formed on 29 October 1966, with Friedan as its president. Amatniek gave her famous "Funeral Oration for the Burial of Traditional Womanhood."[47] Feminists concluded, "We can't destroy the inequalities between men and women until we destroy marriage. *We must free ourselves. And marriage is the place to begin.*"[48] Women marched and picketed, carrying signs that read, "Don't Cook Dinner—Starve a Rat Today," and "End Human Sacrifice— Don't Get Married." In spite of Friedan's opposition, the

---

[43]See J. Veroff, E. Douban, and R. Kulka, *The Inner American: A Self-Portrait from 1957 to 1976* (New York: Basic Books, 1981); and Harry Girvetz, ed., *Contemporary Moral Issues* (2nd ed.; Belmont, CA: Wadsworth, 1968).

[44]See Kenneth Keniston, *Youth and Dissent: The Rise of a New Opposition* (rev. ed.; New York: Harcourt, Brace, Jovanovich, 1971).

[45]Wuthnow, *The Struggle for America's Soul*, 33.

[46]Betty Friedan, *The Feminine Mystique* (New York: W. W. Norton, 1963).

[47]Kathie Amatniek, "Funeral Oration for the Burial of Traditional Womanhood," *Notes from the First Year* (June 1968).

[48]Robin Morgan, ed., *Sisterhood is Powerful* (New York: Vintage, 1970): 537.

feminist movement attracted many lesbians who demanded equal rights. Although N.O.W. resisted strongly,[49] in 1971 a strongly-worded, pro-lesbian resolution was passed nearly unanimously. In 1972, *Ms.* magazine was begun, and Dekker[50] posits, "There is a female mind-set on those glossy pages slipping into American homes concealed in bags of groceries . . . . Curious girl children will accidentally discover feminism in *Ms.* the way we stumbled onto sex in our mothers' *Ladies Home Journal.*"

Concerning women in the church, evangelicals reacted in two conflicting ways. Bendroth[51] observes, "some reasserted the traditional notions of male and female roles with even greater insistence, while others began to question the very existence of seemingly arbitrary sexual roles." Traditionalism's attempt to reassert the old family ideal (June Cleaver; "Father Knows Best;" *Ladies Home Journal*) was persuasive to many, but many other women no longer paid strict adherence to maternal and domestic tasks and questioned traditional roles.[52]

Among religious fundamentalists, the line of argument shifted to invoke a divine "order of creation" as the rationale for male dominance and female subjection in the church and home. The argument had been in place for a long time, but now sexual hierarchy became outlined in stricter terms and

---

[49]Sidney Abbott and Barbara Love, *Sappho was a Right-On Woman* (New York: Stein and Day, 1973): 112, note that in 1970, after considerable pressure, Rita Mae Brown resigned from N.O.W., saying, "Lesbianism is the one word which gives the New York N.O.W. Executive Committee a collective heart attack." Further, "Womens Lib: A Second Look," *Time* (Dec. 8, 1970): 121, attacked Kate Millet, who had openly declared her bisexuality.

[50]See Kirsten Grimstad and Susan Rennie, ed., *The New Woman's Survival Catalog* (New York: Coward-McCann, 1973): 35.

[51]See Margaret L. Bendroth, "The Search for 'Women's Role' in American Evangelicalism, 1930-1980," *Evangelicalism and Modern America*, 122-34, esp. 122-23.

[52]See now Timothy S. Robinson, "How Women's Minds Have Changed in the Last 5 Years," *Glamour* 85 (Jan., 1987): 224.

with greater insistence.[53]   Instead of basing women's subordination in the Fall and Curse of Gen 3:16, they based it in creation itself: woman was created *after* man, so women must rank *below* men in God's hierarchy. The popularity of this ideology among traditionalists was more than a reaction to secular feminism; it was seen as a vital move in bringing order to a rapidly disintegrating family structure in America.

So, what is the situation today? The shape of things currently might be called "terminal ambiguity."[54] Many challenge the concept of "eternal truth" and advocate pluralism instead.[55] As in earlier times when "things seemed to be coming apart at the seams," fundamentalists react to disturbing changes in Western society by continuing to emphasize traditional Victorian gender roles in the modern era. Under the guise of biblical mandate, biblical proof-texts continue to undergird the protection of "male turf" in churches, especially regarding "leading"—everything from eldership and preaching to praying, reading Scripture in public, and even passing out communion trays and church bulletins. Such fundamentalist views on women in the church are primarily the result of reaction against cultural changes and only secondarily the result of biblical proof-texting. This, basically, is our legacy.

Cultural agendas have dominated both feminist and fundamentalist extremes regarding women and continue to do so. While radical feminists often deny scriptural relevance to the problem or seek radical re-interpretation of texts to make them conform to their agenda, it is to the credit of fundamentalists that they herald the primacy of the Bible.

---

[53]Bendroth, "The Search for 'Women's Role' in American Evangelicalism, 1930-1980," *Evangelicalism and Modern America,* 131. For examples, see Tim LaHaye, *The Battle for the Family* (Old Tappan, NJ: F. H. Revell, 1982), and Larry Christensen, *The Christian Family* (Minneapolis: Bethany Fellowship, 1970).

[54]With Grant Wacker, "The Protestant Awakening to World Religions," *Between the Times,* 274.

[55]See Madan Sarup, *Post-structuralism and Post-modernism* (Athens: Univ. of Georgia Press, 1989).

However, fundamentalists have ignored the obvious ways in which their own agenda is culturally biased. They also are guilty of reading their conclusions into their presuppositions.

This brief survey provides a context and perspective in which to understand better our present dilemma. Women today face vastly different circumstances than those of a century ago. Many of these changes are directly related to changes in society and social structures. Some changes—industrialization and material wealth, reduction of disease, advances in communication and transportation—are generally viewed as beneficial. On the other hand, racism and women's roles still result in controversy and opposition. Yet, more and more women are lawyers, doctors, corporate executives, pilots, etc., and their numbers will likely increase. More women are graduating from college than ever before, and they are living in a different world than previous generations. Divorce is rampant, and more people are choosing not to marry. These changes cannot be ignored.

As we reflect on the historical Christian faith and attempt to relate that thinking to contemporary society, we Christians must face matters of gender. Having recognized the issue, we must avoid being dominated by traditionalism or societal demands. We must understand properly the biblical material and implement those principles responsibly in our world. For instance, although traditionalists once opposed the right of women to vote, they now consider that opposition as unjust and unfair. Though not without difficulty, traditionalists changed. As we investigate matters of gender in our contemporary society, we have an opportunity to learn from how our society has dealt with women's experience in the past. We also must shoulder the obligation to participate intelligently in the resolution of issues concerning women today.[56]

---

[56]Carlson, "Discovering Their Heritage," *Gender Matters*, 109-110.

2

WOMEN IN THE CHURCH: EXTREME APPROACHES TO THE PROBLEM

There are two views of male/female relationships—hierarchical and egalitarian. Now I know that you don't want to be bothered with technical terms, but about a half-dozen are commonly used in discussing women in the church—and, trust me, it is important that one understand these few terms very well. As the dictionary defines it, *hierarchalism* refers to a classification of people according to ability or standing. *Egalitarianism* is the belief in human equality, especially concerning social, political, and economic rights and privileges. We will refer to these frequently.

Egalitarian		Hierarchal	
Radical Feminism	Evangelical Feminism	Hierarchal Complementarianism	Patriarchalism

Radical feminism and *evangelical feminism* are both egalitarian. Both advocate equality of the sexes. Now *radical feminism* places little or no reliance upon the Bible and views Scripture as essentially "masculine" and therefore suspect. *Evangelical feminism*, though, accepts the Bible, yet maintains that texts used to place limitations on women have been misunderstood and those, if properly understood, are not always applicable to current situations.

On the other hand, *patriarchalists* and *hierarchal complementarians* both advocate male authority and leadership. *Patriarchalists* appeal to the Bible for a strict hierarchy in both home and church (male domination and female subjection) and insist upon strict limitations on women in church and civic life based upon a variety of biblical texts. *Hierarchal complementarians*, however, understand the Bible to teach a hierarchy for both home and church, but still view women as full participants in church and civic life, with the exceptions of church administration and preaching.

Now the purpose of breaking down this complex topic into categories is not to label people, but only to try to understand accurately and evaluate meaningfully the various views. In attempting to categorize views, I have tried to avoid oversimplification and unfair classification. Too, I have tried as much as possible to allow each view to speak for itself.

1. *Radical Feminism*

My first encounter with radical feminism was in "The Bitch Manifesto."[1] This feminist from Chicago wrote:

Bitches have some or all of the following characteristics:

1) *Personality.* Bitches are aggressive, assertive, domineering, overbearing, strong-minded, spiteful, hostile, direct, blunt, candid, obnoxious, thick-skinned, hard-headed, vicious, dogmatic, competent, competitive, pushy, loud-mouthed, independent, stubborn, demanding, manipulative, egotistic, driven, achieving, overwhelming, threatening, scary, ambitious, tough, brassy, masculine, boisterous, and turbulent [and] a bitch occupies a lot of psychological space. You always know she is around.

2) *Physical.* Bitches are . . . loud, brash, harsh, awkward, clumsy, sprawling, strident, ugly. Bitches move their bodies freely rather than restrain, refine and confine their motions in the proper feminine manner. They clomp up stairs, . . . and don't worry about where they put their legs when they sit. . . . Bitches are not pretty.

---

[1] Joreen, "The Bitch Manifesto," *Radical Feminism* (ed. Anne Koedt, Ellen Levine, and Anita Rapone; New York: Quadrangle, 1973): 50-59, esp. pp. 50-52. See now Elizabeth Wurtzel, *Bitch: In Praise of Difficult Women* (New York: Doubleday, 1998).

3) *Orientation.* Bitches . . . never *marry* anyone or anything: man, mansion, or movement. . . . They are independent cusses and believe they are capable of doing anything they damn well want to. . . . They . . . are often perceived as domineering.

. . . A woman should be proud to declare she is a Bitch, because Bitch is Beautiful. . . . One does not have to have all of the above three qualities, but should be well possessed of at least two of them to be considered a Bitch. . . . The most prominent characteristic of all Bitches is that they rudely violate conceptions of proper sex role behavior. . . . She incorporates within herself qualities traditionally defined as "masculine" as well as "feminine." Bitches refuse to serve, honor or obey anyone.

Repulsive, isn't it? However, the writer does lament that feminists "can become so hard and calloused that the last vestiges of humanity become buried deep within and almost destroyed" and that they "can be very obnoxious because they never really trust people."[2]

Not all radical feminists are this obnoxious, but unfortunately this callous attitude seems all too descriptive.[3] However, as a male, I am convinced that the hurt, frustration, and anger lying behind such an acrimonious plea are not imagined, but very real. Many women in our society have been victimized and oppressed.[4] Women live in a society in which exploitation of them as mere sex objects is

---

[2]Ibid., p. 56.

[3]Bell Hooks, *Feminist Theory from Margin to Center* (Boston: South End Press, 1984): 33, notes, "In their eagerness to highlight sexist injustice, women focused almost exclusively on the ideology and practice of male domination. Unfortunately, this made it appear that feminism was more a declaration of war between the sexes than a political struggle to end sexist oppression. . . . Their anger, hostility, and rage was so intense that they were unable to resist turning the movement into a public forum for their attacks. . . . It did not strengthen public understanding of the significance of authentic feminist movement."

[4]See Sarah Couper, "Prelude to Equality: Recognizing Oppression," *Gender Matters* (ed. June S. Hagen; Grand Rapids: Zondervan, 1990): 249-63.

all too common.[5] While not all expressions of sexual attraction are correctly termed harassment,[6] Lafferty and Clark[7] observe, "Every female person knows the humiliation of being constantly harassed and solicited by males." Women live in a demeaning pornographic society.[8] Women live in a society where abuse is common and rape an ominous threat.[9] Women live in a society that cultivates a view of them as trivial and weak, leading them to accept their plight timidly or to manipulate men as a means of survival.[10] Women live in a society that scorns them in certain professions,[11] places "glass ceilings" on advancement, and often offers them less pay than men for equal work.[12]

---

[5]See Judith Long Laws, "Woman as Object," *The Second X: Sex Role and Social Role* (New York: Elsevier, 1979): 171-239; and Evelyn Reed, "Cosmetics, Fashion, and the Exploitation of Women," *Problems of Women's Liberation* (New York: Pathfinder, 1970): 77-86.

[6]See Barbara Gutek, "Sexual Harassment: Nature and Frequency," *Sex and the Workplace* (San Francisco: Jossey-Bass, 1985): 42-60.

[7]Jeanne Lafferty and Evelyn Clark, "Self Defense and the Preservation of Females," *The Female State: A Journal of Female Liberation* 4 (1970): 96.

[8]See Vivian Gornick and Barbara Moran, ed., *Woman in Sexist Society* (New York: Basic Books, 1971).

[9]See *Attorney General's Task Force on Family Violence.* (Washington, D.C.; Department of Justice, 1984); Susan Schechter, *Women and Male Violence: The Visions and Struggles of the Battered Women's Movement* (Boston: South End Press, 1982); and Bell Hooks, "Feminist Movement to End Violence," *Feminist Theory* (Boston: South End Press, 1984): 117-31.

[10]David C. McClelland, "Wanted: A New Self-Image for Women," *The Woman in America* (ed. Robert Lifton; Boston: Houghton Mifflin, 1965): 173-92.

[11]See Barbara Deckard, "Professional Women: The Obstacle Course," *The Women's Movement: Political, Socioeconomic, and Psychological Issues* (New York: Harper & Row, 1975): 113-42; and Richard Levinson, "Sex Discrimination and Employment Practices," *Women and Work* (ed. Rachel Kahn-Hut, Arlene Daniels, and Richard Colvard; Oxford: Oxford Univ. Press, 1982): 54-64.

[12]See Barbara Bergmann, "Why Are Women's Wages Low?" *The Economic Emergence of Women* (San Francisco: Harper, 1986): 118-45.

Women live in a society that generates in them low self-esteem and dependence upon others for self-definition.[13]

So, radical feminists have an agenda.[14] 1) They seek equality, opportunity for full expression of talents, and recovery of the full humanity of women.   2) They want to abolish hierarchalism in every form,[15] beginning with the rejection of God,[16] or at least a reconception of God that includes feminine characteristics.[17] 3) They seek sexual freedom, including abortion. The National Organization of Women suggests, "Heterosexual relationships are by their very nature oppressive to women in a male dominated society"[18] and women should be free to choose "heterosexuality, homosexuality, bisexuality, or asexuality without embarrassment."[19] 4) They seek power and control over society. However, feminists are not all alike.

---

[13]See Betty Friedan, *The Feminine Mystique* (New York: W. W. Norton, 1963).

[14]See Deckard, "Current Issues of the Women's Movement," *The Women's Movement*, 376-413.

[15]See Dale Spender, *Man Made Language* (London: Routledge and Kegan Paul, 1980), on language and sexism, especially how perception is shaped by patriarchal terminology. In 1990, the New Revised Standard Version of the Bible published by the National Council of Churches adopted "gender inclusive" language. See now Carol Newsom and Sharon Ringe, ed., *The Women's Bible Commentary* (Louisville: Westminster/John Knox, 1992.

[16]Note Gloria Steinem's, *Saturday Review of Literature* (March, 1973): 30, statement that "By the year 2000 we will . . . raise our children to believe in human potential, not God."

[17]See Elisabeth Schüssler Fiorenza, *In Memory of Her* (New York: Crossroad, 1992; Alix Pirani, ed., *The Absent Mother: Restoring the Goddess to Judaism and Christianity* (London; Mandala, 1991); and Joseph Campbell and Charles Musès, ed., *In All Her Names: Four Explorations of the Feminine in Divinity* (San Francisco: Harper, 1991).

[18] *Declaration of Feminism* (National Organization of Women).

[19]Ibid, p. 8.

Much radical feminism is purely secular.[20] The roots of women's oppression are simply this—*men*. According to radical feminist argument,[21] "women will have to take power away from men in order to establish a truly egalitarian society, because egalitarianism is only possible under matriarchy." Some radical feminists, such as Mary Daly,[22] essentially reject the Bible as a sexist document rooted in a patriarchal culture, so instead they place a premium upon contemporary experience.[23] Assessment of the Christian tradition by radical feminism often casts Jesus as one who, because of his illegitimacy[24] and erotic relationship with Mary Magdalene, tried to do away with discrimination

---

[20]For socialist feminism, see Evelyn Reed, *Problems of Women's Liberation* (New York: Pathfinder, 1970).

[21]Carol S. Robb, "A Framework for Feminist Ethics," *Journal of Religious Ethics* 9 (1981): 48-68, esp. 55.

[22]Mary Daly, *Beyond God the Father: Toward a Philosophy of Women's Liberation* (Boston: Beacon, 1973): 13, says, "The symbol of the Father God, spawned in the human imagination and sustained as plausible by patriarchy, has in turn rendered service to this type of society by making its mechanisms for the oppression of women appear right and fitting," and states (p. 10) that women, "are rising up to castrate not people but *the system* that castrates—that great "God-Father" of us all which indulges senselessly and universally in the politics of rape." She states (p. 10),

A patriarchal divinity and His son are exactly not able to save us from the horrors of a patriarchal world. Rather, only radical feminism can open up human consciousness adequately . . . and reveal sexism as the basic model and source of oppression.

[23]Note the appeal to pragmatism in Rebecca S. Chopp, "Feminism's Theological Pragmatics: A Social Naturalism of Women's Experience," *Journal of Religion* 67 (1987): 241, and idem, *The Power to Speak: Feminism, Language, God* (New York: Crossroads, 1989). A useful summary of the problem with patriarchy is Cullen Murphy, "Women and the Bible," *The Atlantic Monthly* (Aug. 1993): 39-64, esp. 41-45,

[24]See Jane Schaberg, *The Illegitimacy of Jesus: A Feminist Theological Interpretation of the Infancy Narratives* (New York: Crossroad, 1990).

against women. However, it also views Paul as a chauvinist hostile to women. So, Daly[25] put it typically, "Who the hell cares what Paul thought?" This type of thinking reflects the "rejectionist" approach. While Jesus' ideal may have had some value, the Christian tradition itself is hopelessly sinful, corrupt, and unredeemable. In fact, radical feminism often assesses the Bible,[26] but does not permit the Bible to assess feminism.[27] Many give up on the Bible as hopeless.

Haney,[28] for instance, critiques the Judeo-Christian ethic as representing "only a part of Christian and human reality—that of men." She says, "It simply is not liberating if it is done by men only and if it is not profoundly informed by feminist perception and values." So she calls for women to "challenge two thousand years of apparent wisdom, indeed 'inspiration'." "Even those principles from the past—principles of love, justice, and mercy, for instance— to some extent must be redefined or held as suspect," she says, and replaced with "the paradigms of nurture and friendship."[29] Daly notes, "There has been a *theoretical*

---

[25]See Eleanor Humes Haney, "What is Feminist Ethics? A Proposal for Continuing Discussion," *Journal of Religious Ethics* 8 (1980): 116. See also Shirley Chisholm, "Women Must Rebel," *Voices of the New Feminism* (ed. Mary Thompson; Boston: Beacon, 1970): 211, that, "We must reject the thought of St. Paul who said, 'Let the woman learn in silence'."

[26]Fiorenza, "The Will to Choose or to Reject," *Feminist Interpretation of the Bible*, "locates revelation not in biblical texts but in the experience of women struggling for liberation from patriarchy . . ." (p. 136). Rosemary Ruether, "Feminist Interpretation: A Method of Correlation," *Feminist Interpretation of the Bible*, 111, notes, "women's experience is an interpretative key for feminist theology."

[27]Carl B. Hoch, "The Role of Women in the Church: A Survey of Current Approaches," *Grace Theological Journal* 8 (1987): 243.

[28]Haney, *Journal of Religious Ethics* (1980): 116.

[29]Ibid., 116, 121, 118. Penelope Washborne, "Authority or Idolatry? Feminine Theology and the Church," *Christian Century* 92 (29 Oct. 1975): 961-964, calls for an end to the traditional Christian framework and return to "the experience of the demonic and the holy within our particular limited existence" as the basis for theology. For the use of contemporary literature by women as a substitute for

one-sided emphasis upon charity, meekness, obedience, humility, self-abnegation, sacrifice, service."[30] Instead, Andolsen[31] argues, "The virtues which theologians should be urging upon women as women are autonomy and self-realization."

Now certainly feminists are correct in addressing prejudices and abuses against women by stating this, making it public, and seeking support for their cause. However, when feminists combine this worthy goal with prejudices against males, the recovery of the full humanity of women for which they call cannot take place. "Full humanity" involves respectful relationships between the sexes, not hatred. In rejecting men, radical feminists only fuel the fire of the "battle of the sexes."[32] Much feminist literature is steeped in prejudice and no different from the "masculine" literature it tries to counter. A fatal flaw in radical feminism is that it is so negative. One simply cannot form a theory out of hurt and negative experience and then try to claim universal validity for it.[33] In fact, some secular feminists find radical feminism unattractive and counterproductive.[34]

Scripture, see Carol P. Christ, *Diving Deep and Surfacing: Women Writers on Spiritual Quest* (Boston: Beacon Press, 1980).

[30]Daly, *Beyond God the Father*, 100.

[31]Barabara H. Andolsen, Christine E. Gudorf, and Mary D. Pellauer, ed., *Women's Conscience: A Reader in Feminist Ethics* (Minneapolis: Winston, 1985): 74. Valerie Saiving Goldstein, "The Human Situation: A Feminist View," *Journal of Religion* 40 (1960): 100-112, argues that sin has a masculine definition and that women's sin is actually self-negation, for which they need self-assertion.

[32]Susanne Heine, *Women and Early Christianity: A Reappraisal* (trans. J. Bowden; Minneapolis: Augsburg, 1988): 2-3, rightly says, "The battle must be against all prejudices, and not for the imposition of a different, new prejudice."

[33]Ibid.

[34]Naomi Wolf, *Fire with Fire* (New York: Random House, 1993), is disgusted with depressing, hairy-legged, man-hating feminists, in love with their victim status and obsessesd with "political correctness." She proposes a set of principles that vigorously, but non-ideologically, affirm women's rights, including "Women matter as

For example, Mary Matalin[35] writes:

> Mainstream feminists, get a grip. There's a reason 63 percent of those you purport to empower spurn you. We are not victims; our daughters are not infants; our sons are not brutes; our men are not monstrous pigs. The extremists have hijacked your bully pulpit; your hard-earned successes are being mutilated by their excesses. They redefined the last 30 years— don't let them define the next.

Susanne Heine,[36] professor on the Protestant Theology faculty at the University of Vienna, is correct in asserting that,

> I see no other alternative than to attack prejudices, no matter on which side they appear and are brought into play; this is the only possible way of getting out of the vicious circle of each side blaming the other, and also of being able to live with those aspects of reality which seem strange and threatening, so that they can lose their threatening character and be felt as an enrichment.

Feminists are correct in noting that woman was not created to keep man amused, but many seem to miss the point that woman calls man into communication, relationship, and love. While we must not shut our eyes to oppression and abuse of women, neither can we permit negative male-female experiences to shape our theology. We must rise above the level of negative experiences and give primary attention to the ideal. Only where biblical ideals of love, trust, kindness, forgiveness, patience, peace, etc., reign is there hope for shaping newness of life.

---

much as men do" and that feminism "hates sexism without hating men." And Mary Matalin, "Stop Whining!" *Newsweek* (Oct. 4, 1993): 92, says, "Ask any woman why she's not a feminist and she's likely to say: I don't want to emulate men to succeed—I like being a woman; I respect the right of women to stay home; I don't hate men."

[35]Matalin, *Newsweek* (Oct. 4, 1993): 92.

[36]Heine, *Women and Early Christianity*, 4-5.

Some feminists do turn to the Bible, maintaining that it reflects patriarchalism, and that any passage teaching female submission must not be the norm and must be reinterpreted in terms of equality.[37] Liberationist feminism holds that the central message of the Bible is human liberation. They readily admit that they are committed to the feminist cause and assumptions before they even open the Bible. In this vein, Ruether[38] rejects the masculinity of God and the Son, arguing that this leaves women unable to identify with Christianity.[39] So, some feminists refer to God as "Mother."[40] A recent hymn, "Bring Many Names," praises "strong Mother God."[41] In one gathering of feminists,[42] milk was substituted for wine in communion and a prayer was addressed to "Sophia" (Greek for "wisdom," but also

---

[37]For a colloquy between feminism and Christianity, see Denise Lardener Carmody, *Feminism and Christianity: A Two-Way Reflection* (Nashville: Abingdon, 1982. For examination of presuppositions and methods of Ruether and Daly, see Isabel Carter Heyward, "Ruether and Daly: Theologians Speaking and Sparking, Building and Burning," *Christianity and Crisis* 39 (2 April 1979): 66-72. For an extended critique of biblical feminism, see Jack Cottrell, *Feminism and the Bible* (Joplin, MO: College Press, 1992).

[38]Rosemary Ruether, *Religion and Sexism: Images of Women in the Jewish Christian Traditions* (New York: Simon and Schuster, 1974); and idem,"The Female Nature of God: A Problem in Contemporary Religious Life," *Concilium* 143 (1981): 61-66. In the mid-1980s, the National Council of Churches began publishing its multi-volume Inclusive Language Lectionary (Bible readings for Sunday worship) which omits male pronouns for God, which has now sold nearly 100,000 copies.

[39]Daly, *Beyond God the Father*, 19, states, "if God is male, then the male is God," and speaks of "cutting away the Supreme Phallus." See further Catharina Halkes, "The Themes of Protest in Feminist Theology Against God the Father," *Concilium* 143 (1981): 103-110.

[40]See Paul R. Smith, *Is It Okay to Call God "Mother": Considering the Feminine Face of God* (Peabody, MA: Hendricksen, 1993).

[41]See R. G. Niebuhr, "The Lord's Name: Image of God as 'He' Loses Its Soveriegnty in America's Churches," *Wall Street Journal* (27 April 1992): A1, A4.

[42]See Ray Waddle, "Women's meet blasphemous, say opponents," *The Nashville Tennessean* (15 January 1994): 1-2B.

an ancient goddess): "Our maker Sophia, we are women in your image . . . With the hot blood of our wombs we give form to new life . . . ."[43] In its commitment to the destruction of socially-defined sex roles and gender systems, radical feminism disdains as sexist all masculine imagery of God.

It is instructive to survey approaches to the Bible by radical feminists. Typical of the use of the Bible in radical feminism is the anthology *Feminist Perspectives on Biblical Scholarship*.[44] I will briefly survey some of the chapters. Fiorenza[45] favors the use of "historical-critical scholarship while at the same time scrutinizing and contesting its androcentric philosophical-theological presuppositions, perspectives, and goals." Historical-critical scholarship refers to the attempt to locate the meaning of a text in its literary and historical context. Brooten[46] observes that the urgent task of reconstructing a history of women in the

---

[43]On Goddess religion, see N. Goldenberg, *Changing of the Gods: Feminism and the End of Traditional Religions* (Boston: Beacon, 1979).

[44]Adela Yarbro Collins, ed., *Feminist Perspectives on Biblical Scholarship* (Atlanta: Scholars Press, 1985). See also Ann Loades, ed., *Feminist Theology: A Reader* (Louisville: Westminster/John Knox, 1990). See also Carol Newsom and Sharon Ringe, ed., *The Women's Bible Commentary* (Louisville: Westminster/ John Knox, 1992). For radical feminism in Roman Catholicism, see Leonard Swidler and Arlene Swidler, ed., *Women Priests: A Catholic Commentary on the Vatican Declaration* (New York: Paulist Press, 1977); and Carroll Stuhlmueller, ed., *Women and Priesthood: Future Directions* (Collegeville, MN: Liturgical Press, 1978).

[45]Elisabeth Schüssler Fiorenza, "Remembering the Past in Creating the Future: Historical-Critical Scholarship and Feminist Biblical Interpretation," *Feminist Perspectives on Biblical Scholarship*, 43-63. See also, idem, "Toward a Feminist Biblical Hermeneutics: Biblical Interpretation and Liberation Theology," *The Challenge of Liberation Theology* (ed. B. Mahan and D. Richesin; Maryknoll, NY: Orbis, 1981): 91-112.

[46]Bernadette Brooten, "Early Christian Women and Their Cultural Context: Issues of Method in Historical Reconstruction," *Feminist Perspectives on Biblical Scholarship*, 65-91, esp. 69, 81.

biblical period is not to be done by pasting together a collage of historical details that then passes as historical reality, but by "placing the study of women in the NT in a historical, cultural context" that has women as its center rather than what men thought about women. Osiek,[47] notes that due to its limitations and prejudices the historical-critical method can no longer claim to be *the* only method, and that its use must be complemented by a variety of other methods. Collins[48] states that feminism which rejects the Bible is not appealing, nor is a loyalist view which holds that the biblical tradition cannot be dismissed under any circumstance. However, she sees three approaches as viable for integrating Christian faith and feminism: 1) *liberationism*,[49] which calls for radical restructuring of relations between men and women, as well as reorganization of social structures as a whole, 2) *revisionism*,[50] which works to minimize the differences between men and women, and 3) *sublimationism*,[51] which assumes significant differences between men and women and that there are "masculine" and "feminine" qualities.

Approaching the text with a "hermeneutic of suspicion," Fiorenza[52] views Jesus as having attacked traditional social

---

[47]Carolyn Osiek, "The Feminist and the Bible: Hermeneutical Alternatives," *Feminist Perspectives on Biblical Scholarship*, 93-105.

[48]Adela Yarbro Collins, "Introduction," *Feminist Perspectives on Biblical Scholarship*, 8.

[49]For example, Rosemary Ruether, *New Woman/New Earth: Sexist Ideologies and Human Liberation* (New York: Seabury, 1975; idem, *Sexism and God-Talk: Toward a Feminist Theology* (Boston: Beacon, 1983); and Fiorenza, *In Memory of Her*.

[50]For example, Phyllis Trible, *God and the Rhetoric of Sexuality* (Philadelphia: Fortress, 1978).

[51]For instance, Joan C. Engelsman, *The Feminine Dimension of the Divine* (Philadelphia: Westminster, 1979).

[52]Elisabeth Schüssler Fiorenza, "The Will to Choose or to Reject: Continuing Our Critical Work," *Feminist Interpretation of the Bible* (ed. Letty Russell; Philadelphia: Westminster, 1985): 130, advocates a hermeneutic of "suspicion rather than the acceptance of biblical authority."

structures of the Greco-Roman world that limited women in the public sphere and sought to replace those with "a discipleship of equals." Early in the primitive church, women such as Prisca, Phoebe, and the prophesying women of 1 Cor, participated fully in church life. For Fiorenza, then, Gal 3:28 ("no longer male and female") is "the magna carta of Christian feminism." Ruether[53] holds, however, that later on there came to be a strong emphasis on the subordination of females in the church by appealing to texts calling on wives to obey their husbands. The church then became patriarchal in a sense not expected by Jesus. Thus an oppressive hierarchalism emerged from which the church has not been able to free itself.

We might note, as well, that some feminists do seek to maintain the relevance of the Bible. Trible,[54] for instance, professor at Union Theological Seminary in New York, believes that feminism and the Bible can and should critique one another and that feminism should not be put on a pedestal. She does view the Bible as a patriarchal text, but perhaps not so patriarchal as has often been assumed. In seeking to understand both positive and what are considered negative patriarchal attitudes in the Bible, she avoids a major pitfall of feminism, i.e., assuming that all biblical writers are patriarchal. Her concerns for methodological exactness and objectivity are appreciable.[55]

Even so, there is a strong prejudice among many feminists expressed well by Tolbert:[56]

---

[53]Rosemary Radford Ruether, "The Subordination and Liberation of Women in Christian Theology: St. Paul and Sara Grimké," *Soundings* 61 (1978): 168-181.

[54]Phyllis Trible, *God and the Rhetoric of Sexuality*. See also her *Texts of Terror: Literary-Feminist Readings of Biblical Narratives* (Philadelphia: Fortress, 1984).

[55]See the essays by male and female scholars in *"Women Like This"—New Perspectives on Jewish Women in the Greco-Roman World* (ed. Amy-Jill Levine; Atlanta: Scholars Press, 1991).

[56]Mary Ann Tolbert, "Defining the Problem: The Bible and Feminist Hermeneutics," *Semeia* 28 (1983): 103-126, esp. 114.

First, I have a clear commitment to feminism and its critique
of all oppressive cultural structures, including Christianity.
Second, ... Although I am trying to stand within the
Christian tradition, the moral demands of feminism require me
to risk discovering that tradition is no longer viable. . . . The
third bias I must admit to is a bias in favor of the Bible. I
frankly want to claim that text as a continuing resource for
living in the modern age. I wish neither to relinquish its study
to antiquarian motives nor to reject its concerns as unalterably
oppressive. [but] this favorable inclination toward the Bible
must be open to judgment and, if necessary, dismissal.

So, as Tolbert puts it, "Feminist hermeneutics [approach to
interpretation, CDO] stands over against *patriarchal*
hermeneutics," its goal achieved "by small, often unnoticed
acts of subversion. Numerous such incremental changes,
like erosion, will eventually bring down the fortress."[57]

2. *Patriarchalism*

So, what is this "patriarchalism" that is so detestable to
feminists? Well, patriarchy[58] in Christianity (strict hierarchy
of male leadership and female submission) is basic to fundamentalism and is the extreme opposite of radical feminism.
Marsden[59] observes that, "a fundamentalist is an evangelical
Protestant who is militantly opposed to modern liberal
theologies and to some aspects of secularism in modern
culture." The literal interpretation of the Bible is understood
as authoritative in matters of faith and practice.[60] Also,
fundamentalists generally stress strict adherence to standards
emerging from the revivalist tradition, such as avoidance of

---

[57]Ibid., 118, 121.

[58]See Guy B. Hammond, "Patriarchy and the Protestant
Conscience: A Critique," *Journal of Religious Ethics* 9 (1981): 84-102.

[59]George Marsden, "Defining American Fundamentalism," *The
Fundamentalist Phenomenon: A View from Within; a Response from
Without* (ed. N. Cohen; Grand Rapids: Eerdmans, 1990): 22. See also
George W. Dollar, *A History of Fundamentalism in America*
(Greenville: Bob Jones Univ., 1973): p. xv.

[60]See John R. Rice, *I Am A Fundamentalist* (Murfreesboro, TN:
Sword of the Lord, 1975).

alcohol and immodest dress.[61] Few are "charismatic," that
is "speak in tongues," but most are premillennialists, who
view the modern world as heading toward doom and who
are simply awaiting Christ's return. Fundamentalism is
rooted in the nineteenth- and twentieth-century reaction to a
perceived cultural decline in America. It attempted to fight
changes that seemed to be displacing religion as a major
culture-shaping force.[62] Between World Wars I and II, a
split in this camp[63] saw fundamentalists move to the extreme
right, as far away from the radical left as possible, and
conservatism emerged as "middle of the road." This split is
clearly seen in each position's view of women.[64] We will
discuss the conservative position later. First, let's look at
the fundamentalist view of patriarchalism, a view as
offensive as radical feminism, yet which enjoys considerable support in contemporary culture.

Old-line fundamentalist patriarchalism pervades a book
entitled *Bobbed Hair, Bossy Wives and Women Preachers*,
which begins, "the authority of the husband over the wife is
as fundamentally settled as the authority of God over Christ
and the authority of Christ over man."[65] Referring to Gen
3:16, "Unto the woman he said, I will greatly multiply thy
sorrow and thy conception; . . . and thy desire shall be to thy
husband, and he shall rule over thee," Rice concludes,
"Wives must be subject to the rule of their husbands if they
fit into God's order of things." Essential to patriarchalism in

---

[61]George Marsden, *Fundamentalism and American Culture: the
Shaping of Twentieth Century Evangelicalism* (New York: Oxford
Univ. Press, 1980): 3-4.

[62]See Martin E. Marty, "Fundamentalism as a Social
Phenomenon," *Evangelicalism in Modern America* (ed. G. Marsden;
Grand Rapids: Eerdmans, 1984): 56-68.

[63]See Joel A. Carpenter, "From Fundamentalism to the New
Evangelical Coalition," *Evangelicalism in Modern America*, 3-16.

[64]See Margaret L. Bendroth, "The Search for 'Women's Role' in
American Evangelicalism, 1930-1980," *Evangelicalism and Modern
America*, 122-134.

[65]John R. Rice, *Bobbed Hair, Bossy Wives and Women Preachers*
(Wheaton, IL: Sword of the Lord, 1941): 15.

the church is the "order of creation" in which, before the sin of Adam and Eve, God set up an order of authority in the universe:[66]

```
┌─────────────────────────────┐
│                             │
│            God              │
│           Christ            │
│            Man              │
│           Woman             │
│                             │
└─────────────────────────────┘
```

Crucial to this "order of creation" view is Eph 5:22-24, "Wives, submit yourselves unto your own husbands, as unto the Lord. For the husband is the head of the wife, even as Christ is the head of the church: . . . Therefore, as the church is subject unto Christ, so let the wives be to their own husbands in everything." He continues (21-37),

> . . . notice that verse 24 says "in everything." I didn't write that. I even tremble and hesitate to emphasize it. But . . . a wife is to be subject to her husband as if he were Christ. . . . If women do not want to take this meek and submissive attitude toward their husbands, then they sin against God, against their husbands, and against their own future happiness when they marry. This is God's plan. . . . In matters of duty, even to God, the wife is to be subject to her husband. That sounds shocking, . . . [but] so says the law.

Referring to Titus 2:3-5, Rice notes that women are to teach younger women to be "keepers at home, good, OBEDIENT TO THEIR OWN HUSBANDS." And referring to 1 Pet 3:1-2, "wives, be in subjection to your own husbands," he emphasizes, ". . . reverence them, *and obey them!*"

Not limiting the order of creation to the family, but extending it to all dimensions of life, Rice states,[67] "women are not as well fitted for executive authority." Further (65),

---

[66]See Larry Christenson, *The Christian Family* (Minneapolis: Bethany Fellowship, 1970): 17.

[67]Ibid., p. 41.

There are women doctors, and any woman who can pass the medical course is permitted to be a doctor; yet how few men will call a woman doctor! How few business men on a board of directors would elect a woman as general manager of a big company. How few men would hire a woman boss over other men. The truth is that men know that which is so plain in all nature, that God did not intend a woman to be in authority over men. It is unnatural and inefficient.

Kirkpatrick[68] suggested that women are too nervous and high strung to make good surgeons and that women should not be permitted to hold political offices that involve great responsibility. Viewing women as extremely culpable, Rice observes, "women leaders are more likely to lead into heresy in doctrine and unscriptural practice than men," then states, "A woman may teach other women and . . . children," but "no woman . . . is to be allowed to teach a class of men, or to teach a mixed class including men, nor to teach the church in a public assembly including men" (41-43). Some even hold that a woman should not speak in public at all.[69]

True, these represent the 1930's and 40's, but what about today? Would anyone really advocate this today? Christenson[70] makes a strong appeal, using little biblical exegesis. He begins his book assuming "God's Order for the Family," the order being: Christ, husband, wife, children. He posits that the wife is vulnerable physically, emotionally, psychologically, and spiritually—thus needing the protection of a husband (35). Christenson is committed to the principle of women's subordination. He advises:

Wives, rejoice in your husband's authority over you! Be subject to him in all things. It is your special privilege to move under the protection of his authority.

---

[68]C. Kirkpatrick, "The Construction of a Belief Pattern Scale for Measuring Attitudes Toward Feminism," *Journal of Social Psychology* 7 (1936): 421-37.

[69]See E. G. Sewell in M. C. Kurfees, ed., *Questions Answered by Lipscomb and Sewell* (Nashville: McQuiddy, 1921): 729-30.

[70]Larry Christenson, *The Christian Family* (Minneapolis: Bethany Fellowship, 1970).

Elisabeth Elliott's popular book, *Let Me Be a Woman* accepts such hierarchalism.[71] She says, yet with little biblical exegesis, "The notion of hierarchy comes from the Bible" (122). Equality, in her opinion, is not a Christian ideal (125-27).

Tim LaHaye[72] reacts strongly against feminism. He gives six reasons for his negative assessment (135-46):

1. Feminism creates unnecessary competition between husbands and wives.
2. Feminism blurs the distinction between the sexes.
3. Feminism creates unnecessary dissatisfaction with being housewife and mother.
4. Feminism creates insecurity in women.
5. Feminism destroys femininity.
6. Feminism creates insecurity in men.
7. Feminism creates insecurity in children.

His wife, Beverly,[73] writes from this traditionalist viewpoint as well. She detects in feminism hatred of God and authority, disdain for family life, and a rebellious attitude based upon selfishness (53). Viewing feminist "restlessness" as the basis of the breakdown of the family in today's society, she speaks of "the sick ideas espoused by the leaders of the feminist movement" and says, "in a very real sense these women are mentally disturbed" (85-86).

Well, precisely how would this hierarchical view play out in daily life? Goebel Music,[74] a contemporary patriarchalist, puts it this way:

---

[71]Elisabeth Elliott, *Let Me Be a Woman* (Wheaton: Tyndale, 1976).

[72]Tim LaHaye, *The Battle for the Family* (Old Tappan, NJ: Fleming H. Revell, 1982).

[73]Beverly LaHaye, *The Restless Woman* (Grand Rapids: Zondervan, 1984).

[74]Goebel Music, *Behold the Pattern* (Colleyville, TX: Goebel Music Publications, 1991): 533-39, adapting Roy C. Deaver, "Admonitions for Christian Women," *Biblical Notes* 7 (1974): 119-124.

1. Be Mindful of the Power and Influence of the Christian Woman. . . . One of the most powerful influences *for good* is the influence of the *Christian* woman, the *Christian* mother. . . . "The hand that rocks the cradle is the hand that rules the world."

2. Determine That You are Going to be a Real "Help-Meet." . . . The Christian woman will be a real helper. She won't "take over."

3. Recognize and Respect the Divine Arrangement. Memorize and quote often Ephesians 5:22ff. In the family unit, someone has to carry the responsibility of being the head. Someone has to make the final decision. God has placed this responsibility upon the husband. . . . Don't be afraid to be in subjection. This is commanded by the Lord. This doesn't mean that the wife is a slave. This doesn't mean that the wife is inferior. This doesn't mean that the wife has nothing to say about the matter. It does mean obedience, and not just obedience when there is agreement.

4. Don't Ever Allow Yourself to be Placed in a Position of "Having Dominion Over" a Man. Read carefully 1 Timothy 2:12. . . . God made the woman for the home, and it is as a homemaker that her greatest contribution is made.

5. If You Are Married to a Husband Who is Not a Christian, Then Know That Your Greatest Responsibility is to be Faithful to the Lord.

6. Be Determined to Imitate the "Holy Women" Discussed in 1 Peter 3:4-6. . . . the "holy women": Did not place the emphasis upon outward adorning; did adorn themselves in a "meek and quiet spirit, which is in the sight of God of great price"; were characterized by a wonderful *faith* [and] *hope*; were in *subjection* to their own husbands; were *obedient* to their own husbands; were *respectful* to their own husbands.

7. Be Sure to Heed the Instructions of Titus 2:3-5. Paul tells Titus to teach the aged women: to be reverent in demeanor, not to be slanderers, not to be enslaved to much wine, and to be teachers of that which is good. . . . to train the young women: to love their husbands [and] children, to be sober-minded, to be chaste, to be workers at home, to be kind, to be in subjection to their own husbands.

8. Train Your Daughters. . . . Teach them to prepare themselves to be the best possible Christian companion.

9. Learn to Live Within Your Husband's Income. Don't place the emphasis upon material things.

10. Don't be a Thief. I have in mind here the physical side of marriage. . . . In Mark 10:19, the Lord said, "Do not *defraud.*"

So, patriarchalists believe that God instituted a hierarchy that must continue in the home and in the church today. Males are destined to lead and females to follow. A great example of female subjection in patriarchalism, although from the 70's, is *Fascinating Womanhood:*[75]

There is one need which is fundamental, and it is *for her to be loved and cherished by her husband.* . . . This book will teach *the art of winning a man's complete love and adoration.* (6)

---

[75]Helen B. Andelin, *Fascinating Womanhood* (new ed.; Santa Barbara, CA: Pacific Press, 1974). See also Marabel Morgan, *The Total Woman* (Old Tappan, NJ: F. H. Revell, 1973): 94-99, who says:

Never let him know what to expect when he opens the front door; make it like opening a surprise package. You may be a smouldering sexpot, or an all-American beauty. Be a pixie or a pirate—a cowgirl or a showgirl. Keep him off guard. . . . My first costume, the pink baby-doll and boots, was among my more conservative outfits. . . . You may not wish to parade around in nylon net at half-past five with your fifteen-year old son all eyes. But the children will love your costumes. It makes life exciting. Can't you just imagine Junior on the sandlot telling his friends, "I've got to go now, guys. Got to see Mom's outfit for tonight."
. . . Still another gal . . . welcomed her husband home in black mesh stockings, high heels, and an apron. That's all. He took one look and shouted, "Praise the Lord!"

But interestingly, recounting a similar attempt by Anita Bryant that fizzled, she says,

Anita felt chagrined and humbled by the truth. "What does turn you on? she asked. Bob was silent for a moment and then said sternly, "Kindness, Anita."

The first commandment which God gave the woman was, "Thy desire shall be unto thy husband and he shall rule over thee." The Apostle Paul instructed women to *"reverence"* their husbands and said, *"Submit yourselves unto your own husbands."* . . . Men have inherent traits of leadership, tend to be decisive and have the courage of their convictions. Women, on the other hand, tend to vacillate, and lack the qualities of good leadership. (121)

If the man is to be the head of the family, the right to final say is his. . . . This arrangement is neither harsh nor unfair. It is entirely a matter of law and order and compliance with divine command. . . . *The husband is . . . in full command.* . . . Hers is a *submissive role, a supporting role.* (122-24)

Obedience is probably the most important rule in being a good follower. . . . What is important is that you support his office, his authority or his right to decide. (130)

The Domestic Goddess serves faithfully as the understanding wife, the devoted mother, and the successful homemaker. (199-200)

Femininity has great appeal to men. . . . A man has a certain pride in his wife's femininity. . . . The feminine appearance is acquired by *accentuating the differences between yourself and men, not the similarities.* . . . When a woman dresses in womanly clothes it encourages her to act more feminine in the way she walks, her gestures, the way she sits and conducts herself. . . . women should be delicate, tender, gentle and light. . . . Typical of a feminine woman is a cooing quality in the voice. . . . One of the marks of a feminine woman is refinement. (225-30)

Another quality of femininity is submissiveness . . . yielding, obedient, to yield to power or authority or to leave matters to the opinions, discretion or judgment of another. (240)

Feminine dependency is very attractive to men. . . . When a man is in the presence of a tender, gentle, trustful, dependent woman, he immediately feels . . . stronger, more competent, bigger, manlier than ever. . . . In acquiring femininity, you must first dispense with any air of strength and ability, of competence and fearlessness, and acquire instead an attitude of frail dependency upon men to take care of you. (235-38)

If one of the charms of womanhood is feminine dependency, a girl should not center her education around a career, in which she becomes *independent*. . . . The independence which results from the ability to make money can be a dangerous thing for a woman, serving as an escape. (244-45)

One of the greatest threats to a man's position of No. 1 is when his wife earnestly pursues a career. . . . Another threat to the man's position occurs when a woman pursues other interests such as the development of talents. (114)

Although a man may love his wife devotedly, it is not always possible or even right for him to make her Number One. . . . A man's Number One responsibility is to provide. . . . However, if a woman is always careful to keep a man in the Number One position and let him know it, she can usually win his cooperation. . . . when we make a man Number One in our life, we must also make his interests, desires and responsibilities Number One. (114-115)

The center of a woman's happiness in marriage is to be loved—but the center of a man's is to be admired. . . . If you admire only traits which are admirable in both men and women, he will be disappointed. . . . if you admire him because he is kind, thoughtful, helps you with the dishes, is pleasant or well groomed, . . . it will do little to stir his feelings for you. *It is his masculinity that he wants noticed and admired*. . . . Spend less time thinking about your affairs and more about him. (59-61)

. . . *masculine pride is very sensitive*. A man cannot stand to have his masculinity *belittled*, *ridiculed* or treated with *indifference*. . . . This will *cut like a knife*. . . . A woman has a double responsibility to a man in regard to his pride—first, not to injure the man's pride herself and second, to heal the wounds that others inflict. (73, 83)

Perhaps she does give up some of her precious freedom, but when a woman surrenders to her husband his leadership position, relinquishing what may appear to be her rights, she gains every advantage a woman could hope for . . . (299)

Once the principle of male leadership based upon an "order of creation" is granted, there is a definite impact on church life. Questions arise. Can a mother teach her own son after a certain age? Can a wife lead a prayer when her husband is present or in a mixed home Bible study? Can a female read a passage from the Bible in a mixed class or in public worship? Can a woman pass out communion trays or lead singing in worship? On and on and on this list goes.

LaGard Smith[76] observes correctly that searching for absolute rules on such matters is unwise. "I don't mean to cop out on this point," he says (292 [276]), "but it is the main principle about which I am most concerned."   . . . "We can—and indeed *must*—honestly and humbly acknowledge the basic scriptural principle." He continues,

> Changes in church participation seem petty on the surface. If women want to pass the communion or hand out church bulletins, someone might ask, "Why not let them?" If women want to lead public prayers, someone might question, "What harm could it do?" . . . If women want to be recognized as deaconesses, who are we to say that they shouldn't be? And as long as women can fill those roles, what objection could we have to appointing women as ministers and elders as well? (292-293 [276-77])

Good questions. But then Smith shoots his foot!

> . . . Yet you remember the old saying: "For want of a nail the shoe was lost; for want of a shoe the horse was lost; for want of a horse the rider was lost; for want of a rider the battle was lost; for want of a battle the war was lost." *Somewhere* along the line, the biblically mandated principle of male spiritual leadership is eroded. And *somewhere* along the line, the participation of women in the life of the church is contrary to God's way. (293 [277])

> . . . If all we maintain of the principle is male exclusivity at the highest levels of church government, then we not only have created an illogical and unbiblical dichotomy which women would have every right to see as sheer discrimination,

---

[76]F. LaGard Smith, *Men of Strength for Women of God* (Eugene, OR: Harvest House, 1989): 291-99; [republished as *What Most Women Want* (Eugene, OR: Harvest House, 1992).

but we have robbed the church of its broader male strength.
The responsibility of spiritual leadership for *all* Christian men
must never be confused with the exclusive male hierarchy of
just a few. (293 [277])

. . . This is the reason why women participating even in
relatively neutral activities, such as passing the communion or
leading the singing or reading the Scripture, is dangerous—
even if they do not lead ultimately to headship roles. [Smith
omits this sentence in his revised ed.] . . . Crack the door
open in biblically neutral areas of service, and we will soon
find it to be a threshold to the biblically ordained leadership
roles themselves. (294 [278])

. . . Two ideas must be put to rest once and for all. The first
is that the principle of male spiritual leadership was part of a
patriarchal system no longer relevant to our situation—that it
was simply a matter of custom in a culture foreign to our
own. . . . The principle of male spiritual leadership found its
genesis *in* Genesis, before culture or custom began. It was
established in the process of Creation as a part of Creation . . .
. The second idea which must be abandoned is that role
distinctions in the church violate human rights, equality, and
fair play. . . . The church is not a secular organization
governed by an Equal Rights Amendment. (298 [289])

God called men to be the spiritual heads of their wives—to
nurture them, to protect them, and to serve them through the
Word and through lives of personal strength and honor. God
called women to submit to their husband's spiritual leading as
they go about their family-oriented responsibilities and in
everything else they do. (296-297 [288])

. . . we nevertheless are bound by the overarching principle of
male spiritual leadership. Any involvement of women which
threatens that principle is contrary to God's will. (298 [289])

Smith assumes that "male spiritual leadership" was ordained
by God from creation. Making no distinction between the
pre- and post-fall worlds, Smith's unclear understanding of
Genesis results in a typical fundamentalist response to
radical feminism in which patriarchy (or as he puts it "the
principle of male spiritual leadership") counters the feminist
presupposition of "the principle of human equality."

In fairness, patriarchalism has some features that are commendable. 1) Patriarchalists place a premium upon seeking to do the will of God. 2) Patriarchalists place a strong emphasis upon following the biblical text. 3) Patriarchalists have a strong aversion to rampant cultural degradation in society. 4) Patriarchalists place strong emphasis upon the church not accommodating to society, but being "a light set on a hill" for society. 5) Patriarchalists insist on maintaining the differences between male and female. 6) Patriarchalists place strong emphasis upon the home. 7) Patriarchalists emphasize masculine responsibility and, generally speaking, are against repressive and abusive males and husbands. 8) Patriarchalists place emphasis on women being loving, kind, serving, nurturing, etc., which are prominent biblical characteristics.

However, several features of patriarchalism render it questionable and unattractive.

1) Patriarchalists seem oblivious to the cultural influences that have shaped much of their view. Patriarchalists have deluded themselves into thinking that their view of women's issues has been influenced strictly by Scripture while other views are shaped strictly by culture. In fact, that is not the case at all. Much of what is held as "truth" by patriarchalists seems actually to be nothing more than cultural bias.

While the need to control women is not essential to religious traditionalism, it seems an inevitable by-product. Overwhelmed by the modern world, traditionalists tend to respond by isolating themselves from culture. This happened in the past century all over America. A number of forces—contact with the larger world, burgeoning cities, dramatic population increase, industrialization, poverty, nationalism, war, illiteracy, bureaucracy, the theory of evolution, racism, and changing roles for women—converged in the late nineteenth century, resulting in considerable anxiety around the country. It was felt that what was needed was something that could provide focus and security in a world which had become too complicated.

Not unexpectedly, religion came to play a central role in dealing with this stress and providing orientation. As is well-known, gender roles are the basic building blocks of social organization, so traditionalists turned to family structure in search of stability. Now, eternal truths and values must be brought to bear upon constantly changing situations. However, in their quest for something solid, traditionalists isolated and listed all sorts of "truths" to make their religion a solid rock for them in the midst of a shifting world. However, they did not rigorously seek and apply biblical principles. Instead, they merely imposed culturally-generated gender roles into their religion and called that "truth." This imposed view actually provided little flexibility to respond to life's complexities or the challenges of changing times.[77] It only provided a false sense of security. Thus, the view of women that emerged in nineteenth-century America was in reaction to the social upheavals of the day, using so-called biblical and theological "truths" to control what was seen as threatening.

It is precisely this fundamentalist reaction to culture that enabled the adoption of patriarchalism as an assumption that serves as its own presupposition and its own unnecessary conclusion. In spite of extensive appeal to Scripture, the patriarchal view of women is essentially rooted in culture and provides only an apparent security. And that is why it is not surprising to hear some patriarchalists, faced with biblical data, say, "I don't care *what* the Bible teaches, as long as I have anything to say about it, no woman will . . .!"

2) Through "proof-texting," patriarchalists have assigned meanings to biblical texts that cannot stand rigorous analysis. The view of the Bible in patriarchal thought fails to question when or how texts about women are descriptive (what happened in ancient times) or prescriptive (what happened is authoritative for today), and it disregards literary and historical contexts in interpretation. Consequently,

---

[77]See Karen McCarthy Brown, "Fundamentalism and the Control of Women," *Fundamentalism and Gender* (ed. J. S. Hawley; Oxford: Oxford Univ. Press, 1994): 175-201.

interpretations of the Bible that arose from reaction to societal issues have been allowed to become sacred interpretation—unquestionable church law.

Concerning the use of the Bible, Smith, for instance, refuses to admit even the theological seriousness or spiritual motivation of those who view biblical texts differently from himself. As Mitchell observes,[78] Smith's charming style "diverts the reader's attention from the very subjective and idiosyncratic character of Dr. Smith's view about women's role in the church." Biblical examples of women in spiritual leadership (for example, Deborah, Huldah, prophetesses, teachers) might seem to indicate God's approval of female leadership in these cases, but Smith's intuition leads him to conclude that these are not divinely approved examples, but unfortunate and illegitimate usurpation of exclusively male prerogative of leadership.

In Smith's view, anyone but those influenced by feminism or "new hermeneutics" would clearly understand these examples as alterations of God's order of creation. The Fall of Adam and Eve is seen as the result of attempted female leadership; therefore, any female leadership thereafter must be only the unfortunate result of men not accepting their leadership roles adequately. Smith further argues that, being sensitive and spiritually inclined, women make capable leaders in times of male abandonment of leadership, but that males, not so sensitive and spiritually inclined, must not permit women to usurp this leadership—a line of reasoning Mitchell calls "rhetorical coquetry" (22). Further, Smith's strong appeal to bar women from any public activity (even admittedly those not sinful, such as serving communion) because "it makes the wrong statement," assumes that for any woman to participate publicly is to surrender to the feminist agenda.

---

[78]See the insightful review of F. LaGard Smith's, *What Most Women Want, What Few Women Find* (Eugene, OR: Harvest House, 1989), by Lynn Mitchell, *Wineskins* 2 (May, 1993): 21-23.

In typical patriarchal fashion, these views control Smith's interpretation of Scripture and lead him to stress that to come to any other conclusion than his is not to take the Bible seriously.

Let's just take a break from patriarchalism for a moment and talk about the Bible. The real dynamic of the Bible usually does not surface until basic questions are brought to it. The Bible can become *Scripture* for us only if we are honest about the problems we have in reading it—and only if we take it seriously enough to make an honest effort to understand it. "In fact," Keck[79] says, "one can measure its 'Scripturehood' by the degree we are willing to risk hearing what the Bible actually has to say." The Bible is not so much a "heaven-sent answer book" as a historical book produced within and for a historical community—yet it serves as Scripture today because people find themselves accountable to it. That is what makes it Scripture.

The power of the Bible to meet us where we really are requires more than casual, even prayerful, reading. The Bible requires relentless reading. Proper understanding of the biblical text runs deeper than commitment to a purely traditional or denominational understanding, and that means reading the Bible not knowing in advance what the Bible means. It is basic in study of the Bible to stress first, not "what it means today" but, "what the writer meant to say then." A responsible way to learn what the Bible has to say is to read texts in their literary and historical contexts. Now this does not stifle devotional reading of the text, but it does mean that we must seek to know what the ancient writers intended. In this way, we ward off speculation and fantasy. But we must go beyond the historical orientation and get to the heart of the matter—we must ask *why* the text says what it does. That is to say, we must press the ancient writer to surface the rationale of the statements in the text. Having penetrated the text to the point that one knows what a text says and the rationale behind it, another step must be taken if

[79]Leander E. Keck, *Taking the Bible Seriously* (Nashville: Abingdon, 1962): 24.

the text would actually become *Scripture*—and that is, to engage the text in dialogue to ask, "Now that I understand the meaning of this text for today, can I accept this?"

Reading the Bible in this way is no simple devotional exercise in which one supports one's presuppositions. Rather, reading the Bible so as to hear it and respond to it can be a serious struggle in which the stakes are high. Only after coming to understand the underlying intent of the biblical text does one know the meaning of the text, and sometimes those meanings are hard to accept. Indeed, there is a certain danger in reading the Bible—one might have to change. In fact, though, that very threat of change is a basic reason to take the Bible seriously.

Now, back to patriarchalism. It is in this vein that much of the use of the Bible by patriarchalists fails miserably.[80] Smith says, "Where the Bible does *not* speak, no person, no church, nor any creed has the right to impose further doctrine or tradition on anyone" (192). This statement destroys his whole book on women and betrays his essentially unworkable approach to the Bible.

3) Often, in patriarchalism, leadership and submission are actually *domination*, *subjection*, and *manipulation* couched deceptively in language that leads to female degradation. Even if well-intentioned, to insist on female subordination while at the same time insisting that such subordination does not imply inferiority seems pure nonsense. Patriarchalists present an unbalanced view of both masculinity and femininity. On one hand, males are depicted as strong leaders, but on the other are depicted as having 1) weak egos that require support, 2) sensitive pride that requires women to "walk on eggshells," and 3) a lack of impression with characteristics such as love, kindness, sensitivity, and nurturing. Patriarchalism essentially presents a view of man that robs him of his full humanity.

---

[80]See the critique of hermeneutic in F. LaGard Smith, *The Cultural Church* (Nashville: Twentieth Century Christian, 1992), by Gary D. Collier, *Image* (May/June, 1993): 23-24.

The view of women as intellectually inferior, emotionally unstable, incompetent, and spiritually culpable is demeaning. It seems odd that women would be presented as more easily led into heresy, yet still be entrusted with teaching the children (!). It is not at all surprising that many women in a patriarchalist environment resort to manipulation in order to cope with their stress.

4) Implementing patriarchalism creates an environment for emotional and physical abuse. Certainly not all patriarchalists are abusive, but it has been my experience that there seems to be a disproportionately large problem in this area.

3. *Summary*

Consequently, it is evident that both radical feminism and patriarchalism have some good questions and some good answers. However, since both patriarchalism and radical feminism proceed in reactionary ways from a basically cultural agenda, it is unlikely that contemporary Christianity will profit significantly from either perspective. Both views are steeped in prejudice and are essentially extremist. Both views are essentially isolationist. In using the Bible, both views are influenced tremendously by cultural bias, radical feminism acknowledging the bias, but patriarchalism deludedly evasive on the matter. Both views tend to ignore passages that do not support their presuppositions and stress those that do, or with some adjustment might. Working principally with stereotypical views of the other position, each overstates its case and promotes a charged emotional atmosphere in which objectivity seems impossible and critical evaluation of its own essence entirely avoidable. There is much that is both blatantly and subtly offensive in each of these views. So, while neither view provides needed balance and perspective, each should be incorporated into the discussion to the extent possible, as each view has something valuable to contribute. To continue to couch the question in terms of these two extremes as the viable options, however, is unproductive. We must look elsewhere for a responsible Christian view of women.

3

WOMEN IN THE CHURCH:
MODERATE APPROACHES TO THE PROBLEM

Two moderate approaches, *evangelical feminism* and *hierarchal complementarianism*, seem to be more responsible Christian views of women. Now these are a couple of unfamiliar terms, but we must make a serious effort to understand each. Both views share common commitment to the authority of the Bible. Both views share commitment to a responsible literary and historical investigation of the biblical text. Both views share a commitment to serious analysis of contemporary culture and responsible application of ancient biblical principles to current life. Both views theoretically share a commitment to rigorous analysis of their own positions and interaction with other views.

However, these two views differ significantly in what they bring to the biblical text, one bringing egalitarian (human equality) presuppositions, the other hierarchical (male leadership) ones. Present are the valid concerns of *radical feminism* and *patriarchalism*, but extremist attitudes and divisiveness are not as strong.

1. *Evangelical Feminism*

The long-standing feminist movement, reestablished in the 1960s, has become so prominent in secular thinking that it is forcing all our institutions, including the church, to rethink views and attitudes towards women, womanhood, manhood, and sexuality.[1] It may be that many younger Christians who are pressing for change have simply grown up in an era where feminist concerns and thinking have

---

[1] Shirley Dex, "The Church's Response to Feminism," *The Baptist Quarterly* 31 (1986): 320.

become taken-for-granted, without stopping to reflect upon the biblical basis for their views. On the other hand, it may be that the older generation's opposition to feminist concerns evidences an uncritical acceptance of gender roles that have become equated with, but which are not necessarily, Christian.

The support for and opposition to feminist concerns in the church is easy to understand. On one hand, our society tends to place men in positions of domination in which women are dependent, exploited, vulnerable, passive, and manipulated. Many find this view of women intolerable. Feminists are critical of the role the church has played in fostering this view of the sexes. On the other hand, the church correctly reacts negatively to *heavy-handed* feminist demands for women's rights. The church rightly opposes feminist attacks on motherhood and the family. Some Christian men react defensively to derogatory feminist views of males. Some feel threatened by the loss of a traditional view of headship and authority. There exists a wide range of responses among Christians, both by those sympathetic with feminist concerns and by those who oppose them.

Feminism, as we have said, comes in different forms.[2] Many Christian women are uneasy about biblical statements concerning women, as traditionally understood and applied in the church. Some have presumed only two choices: either to regard Paul as authoritative and accept his view as one that conflicts with women's liberation, or to dismiss him either in part or wholly.[3] However, another choice has presented itself that views some traditional understandings of Paul as the result of superficial and careless reading of biblical texts. When interpreted according to responsible exegesis, views emerge which differ from the traditional understandings.

---

[2]See Josephine Donovan, *Feminist Theory: The Intellectual Traditions of American Feminism* (New York: Ungar, 1985), for discussion of different types of feminism.

[3]See Barbara Hall, "Church in the World: Paul and Women," *Theology Today* 31 (1974): 50-55.

Evangelicalism, too, comes in different forms.[4] While evangelicals have rarely viewed evangelical feminists as allies, there is indication that each is willing now to take seriously the other's concerns and work.[5] In view of the hard lines drawn between fundamentalists and modernists in the early twentieth century, the growing number of persons who are both evangelicals and feminists constitutes an interesting hybrid that seeks to work out a theology that combines both viewpoints: the critical analysis of the Bible and the acceptance of egalitarianism.[6] Difficult decisions must be made concerning what in the conservative religious tradition is primary and what is culturally biased, as well as what can be accepted from the feminist agenda without compromising the essence of conservative faith.

Evangelical feminists differ with other feminists regarding the authority of Scripture.[7] Yet while honing their exegetical skills in order to establish biblical bases for women's equality, evangelical feminists seek theoretical insights and social support from other strands of feminism—but rarely work with other feminists to face common

---

[4]See Robert Webber, *Common Roots* (Grand Rapids: Zondervan, 1978), suggesting no less than fourteen different types of evangelicals. George Marsden, "The Evangelical Denomination," *Evangelicalism and Modern America* (ed. G. Marsden; Grand Rapids: Eerdmans, 1984): vii-xix, however, views evangelicalism as a single movement, despite its diversities.

[5]For instance, David Scholer, "Feminist Hermeneutics and Evangelical Biblical Interpretation," *Journal of the Evangelical Theological Society* 30 (1987): 407-420; and Katharine Doob Sakenfeld, "Feminist Perspectives on Bible and Theology: An Introduction to Selected Issues and Literature," *Interpretation* 42 (1988): 5-18.

[6]See Carolyn De Swarte Gifford, "American Women and the Bible: The Nature of Woman as a Hermeneutical Issue," *Feminist Perspectives on Biblical Scholarship* (ed. Adela Yarbro Collins; Atlanta: Scholars Press, 1985): 11-33, on biblically-based feminism in American history.

[7]See George Marsden, "From Fundamentalism to Evangelicalism: A Historical Analysis," *The Evangelicals* (ed. D. Wells and J. Woodbridge; Grand Rapids: Baker, 1975): 159, on the centrality of biblical authority among evangelicals.

concerns.[8] For instance, evangelical feminists share with other feminists an understanding of the common roots of oppression and an emphasis upon individualism and appreciation for experience as a major element in the discussion, as well as concern for power and control and for justice beyond feminist issues. However, significant differences in focus and concern exist, especially concerning what sources are to be authoritative (for example, women's experience or Scripture), what is to be considered as sin (social or individual), and the role of eschatology (realities of today or the immanence of God).

A. *What is Evangelical Feminism?*

Evangelical feminism actually began with the work of Letha Scanzoni and Nancy Hardesty,[9] both free-lance writers, but the scholarly work of Paul Jewett at Fuller Theological Seminary is the real watershed of evangelical feminism. In an initial abstract, Jewett presents his thesis:[10]

> I take the position that the "woman question" is a "man/woman" question which has its roots, theologically speaking, in the doctrine of the *imago Dei* [image of God] . . . The major portion of the study is devoted to the question of a hierarchical view of the man/woman relationship. My own conclusion is that the case for hierarchy, in the last analysis, requires one to argue not only for the priority but also the superiority of the male. The classical statement of the argument plainly affirms as much: the woman is subordinate to the man because she is inferior to him. . . . The entire case for sexual hierarchy becomes a *non sequitur* which may be summarized as follows: (a) the woman is in no way inferior to the man, (b) yet she is different from him, (c) therefore she is subordinate to him. This argument is not compelling. The

---

[8] See Esther Byle Bruland, "Evangelical and Feminist Ethics: Complex Solidarities," *Journal of Religious Ethics* 17 (1989): 139-160, esp. 144-145.

[9] Letha Scanzoni and Nancy Hardesty, *All We're Meant to Be: A Biblical Approach to Women's Liberation* (Waco: Word, 1974).

[10] Paul K. Jewett, *Man as Male and Female* (Grand Rapids: Eerdmans, 1975).

difference between the sexes does not entail a relationship of super- and subordination.

I therefore reject a hierarchical model of the man/woman relationship in favor of a model of partnership. According to the creation ordinance, man and woman are properly related when they accept each other as equals whose difference is mutually complementary in all spheres of life and human endeavor. . . . I place great weight upon the exegetical possibilities of the Genesis account of human origins and especially upon the way in which Jesus related to women. The contrast between the data of Scripture . . . and the view of woman stemming from the patriarchal culture of Old Testament Israel is carefully reviewed, as both these strands of redemptive history meet in the apostle Paul, the supreme interpreter of the revelation of God in Christ. The question of Paul the former rabbi versus Paul the apostle of Christ is explored with the help of the distinction between his perception of the truth and his implementation of it in the Greco-Roman world of the first century, the world in which the Christian church was born. Appealing to the issue of slavery as illustrative of this distinction, I make the plea that the church today should canonize, not the implementation, but the insight of the apostle into the manner in which the man/woman relationship is redeemed in Christ.

For Jewett, Pauline arguments for the restriction of women are inconsistent with the larger views expressed elsewhere in his epistles. Jewett's suggestion that Paul's vision was sometimes limited by his rabbinical training seemed to some to challenge biblical infallibility. In fact, Lindsell,[11] editor of *Christianity Today*, accused Jewett of denying biblical inerrancy, which is heresy, but Carl Henry[12] correctly points out the lack of scriptural documentation and the presence of overstatement in Lindsell's negative assessment. F. F. Bruce,[13] professor of NT at the Univ. of Manchester, England, concludes fairly,

---

[11]Harold Lindsell, *The Battle for the Bible* (Grand Rapids: Zondervan, 1976): 117-21.

[12]C. F. H. Henry, *The New Review of Books and Religion* (September 1976): 7.

[13]F. F. Bruce, *Evangelical Quarterly* (1976):

"Dr. Jewett interprets Paul with the respect which his
apostolic authority requires, but in so doing he vindicates
Paul's title to be acknowledged as the patron saint not only of
Christian liberty in general but specifically of women's
liberty."

Later Jewett argued[14] that on the basis of the Christian
ideal of the partnership of the sexes, women ought to share
fully with men the privileges and responsibilities of church
ministry. Elisabeth Tetlow[15] also used a feminist approach
to the Bible to underscore the importance of allowing women
into the ministry. However, Elaine Storkey,[16] Lecturer in
sociology and philosophy at Oak Hill College in London,
observes, "It has often been supposed that a discussion of
women and the Church is, in the end, about the ordination of
women. . . . (but) the issues are more complex than that"
(53). Storkey, an evangelical feminist, fears that an indig-
nant reaction against the women's movement might result in
failure to deal with substantive feminist issues. Others, she
fears, might become so preoccupied with feminist issues that
Christian distinctiveness is lost, and genuine feminist
concerns are dominated by radical feminist theology.

Typical of evangelical feminists is Mollenkott,[17]
professor of English at William Paterson College in New
Jersey. She defines evangelicalism as "a mind-set
emphasizing biblical authority and personal conversion
through faith in the atoning work of Jesus Christ," and
feminism as "willingness to implement the political,
economic, and social equality of the sexes." In this vein
Mollenkott underscores that, "Evangelical feminists insist,
however, that the real hope for humanity lies not in

---

[14]Paul Jewett, *The Ordination of Women: An Essay on the Office
of Christian Ministry* (Grand Rapids: Eerdmans, 1980).

[15]Elisabeth Meier Tetlow, *Women and Ministry in the New
Testament: Called to Serve* (New York: Paulist, 1980).

[16]Elaine Storkey, *What's Right with Feminism?* (Grand Rapids:
Eerdmans, 1985).

[17]Virginia Ramey Mollenkott, "Evangelicalism: A Feminist
Perspective," *Union Seminary Quarterly Review* 32 (1977): 95.

discarding the Bible but in coming to a more profound understanding and implementation of it," and further, "Like all evangelical feminists I know, I am just as concerned with furthering the best interests of men and boys as of women and girls." In approaching the topic, she assumes that, "the idea that one category of persons must submit to the authority of another category is the root concept not only of sexism, but racism, economic exploitation, and imperialism." It follows that she views sexism as "the most pervasive and profound expression of the egocentric nature that is hostile to genuine godliness." She forthrightly views patriarchalism as a "Christian heresy."

Mollenkott[18] understands "God as a woman not only carrying us in her womb and bringing us to birth in creation and redemption, but also as suckling." On the other hand, Achtemeier[19] acknowledges the problem of discrimination against women in the church for centuries and the misuse of the Bible in that regard, but contends that alteration of language *about God* by feminists in reality exchanges "the true God for those deities which are 'no gods,' as Jeremiah put it (2:11)." She argues 1) that the God of the Bible has no sexuality, 2) the few instances of female imagery for God in the Bible take the form of simile, not metaphor, and 3) the Bible uses masculine language for God because that is the language with which God has revealed himself.[20]

---

[18]Virginia Ramey Mollenkott, *The Divine Feminine: The Biblical Imagery of God as Female* (New York: Crossroad, 1991): 20.

[19]Elizabeth Achtemeier, "Feminist God-talk in the Church," *Christianity Today* (16 Aug. 1993): 17-23.

[20]See also Pamela Dickey Young, "Christianity's Male Savior— A Problem for Women?" *Touchstone* 4 (1986): 13-21, who says, "As Christians we must deal with Jesus—and Jesus was a male. Yet we must also recognize that the maleness of Jesus has been and can be used as an instrument for the opposition of women" (p. 17), and ". . . one cannot dismiss Christianity as an inherently sexist and patriarchal religion simply because it has a male savior. . . . Although Jesus is a male figure from a very patriarchal environment, there is, surprisingly enough, nothing in the Gospels to suggest that he regarded women as in any way inferior to men" (p. 19).

So, evangelical feminism accepts in theory the authority of the Bible, but underlying much of their exegesis is the assumption that the Bible must support an egalitarian view.[21]   Often Gal 3:28, "neither male and female," functions presuppositionally in the interpretation of other texts, and this creates more than a few problems.

B. *Problems with Evangelical Feminist Reinterpretation of Texts*

Evangelical feminism rescues the Bible from the oblivion to which much radical feminism would assign it, holds that the Bible presents a viable view of women, and places firm emphasis upon Jesus as model.[22] However, as Kathy Pulley,[23] professor of religion at Southwest Missouri State, observes, serious questions exist in critical scholarship regarding the carefulness and accuracy of evangelical feminist exegesis. Certainly this approach has not been able to free itself from suspicion that it has been manipulative of biblical texts in support of its own assumptions.

Catherine Clark Kroeger, an adjunct professor at Gordon-Conwell Theological Seminary, is exemplary of evangelical feminists who maintain the importance of the Bible in discussion of women in the church, but whose application of rigorous literary and historical controls in the use of the biblical text is unsatisfactory. For instance, in 1 Tim 2:12 the verb *authenteo* (which occurs only here in the

---

[21]A non-evangelical feminist, such as Rosemary Radford Ruether, *Womanguides: Readings Toward a Feminist Theology* (Boston: Beacon, 1985): ix, can write, "Feminist theology must create a new textual base, a new canon. . . . Feminist theology cannot be done from the existing base of the Christian Bible." However, evangelical feminists do not seek a new feminist canon, but stress the need to reinvestigate existing texts.

[22]See, for instance, Aída Bensançon Spencer, *Beyond the Curse: Women Called to Ministry* (Nashville: Thomas Nelson, 1985).

[23]Kathy Pulley, "Women in the Church in Recent Discussion," *Essays on Women in Earliest Christianity* (ed. Carroll D. Osburn; Joplin, MO: College Press, 1993): 23.

NT) means "have authority, domineer"[24] and "to control, to domineer,"[25] and is translated "usurp authority" (KJV), "have authority over" (NIV, NRSV), and "domineer" (NEB). Attempting to locate an alternative rendering, Kroeger[26] suggests that *authenteo* in 1 Tim 2:12 is actually an erotic term referring to ancient female teachers in 5th century BC Athens who offered sex to their students after class. Kroeger says that it is that practice which is being forbidden by this text. Needless to say, this rather peculiar proposal was quickly countered by an avalanche of criticism from the scholarly world.[27] Not a single classical text cited by Kroeger supports her view of a sexual connotation to this verb.

It is not at all surprising, then, that in a recent study of this text a different view is presented.[28] The Kroegers' new view is that the verse only prohibits women from teaching the gnostic heresies that women were created before men, that women were the source of all wisdom, and that bearing children was dishonorable. The Kroegers' treatment of this text purports to be an attempt to observe high standards of

---

[24]Walter Bauer, *A Greek- English Lexicon of the New Testament and Other Early Christian Literature* (trans. W. F. Arndt and F. W. Gingrich; 2nd ed. rev. Gingrich and F. W. Danker; Chicago: Univ. of Chicago Press, 1979): 121.

[25]Johannes P. Louw and E. A. Nida, *Greek-English Lexicon of the New Testament Based on Semantic Domains* (New York: United Bible Societies, 1988): 1.474.

[26]Catherine Clark Kroeger, "Ancient Heresies and a Strange Greek Verb," *The Reformed Journal* 29 (1979): 12-15, a view popularized uncritically by such writers as Kari Torjesen Malcolm, *Women at the Crossroads* (Downers Grove, IL: InterVarsity Press, 1982): 78-80, and though not accepted, is mentioned as "an interesting idea" by Spencer, *Beyond the Curse*, 87, n. 15.

[27]See, for example, A. J. Panning, "ΑΥΘΕΝΤΕΙΝ—A Word Study," *Wisconsin Lutheran Quarterly* 78 (1981): 185-191; and Carroll D. Osburn, "ΑΥΘΕΝΤΕΩ (1 Timothy 2:12)," *Restoration Quarterly* 25 (1982): 1-12.

[28]Richard Clark Kroeger and Catherine Clark Kroeger, *I Suffer Not a Woman: Rethinking 1 Timothy 2:11-15 in Light of Ancient Evidence* (Grand Rapids: Baker, 1992).

scholarship, including both philological and historical elements. The passage is viewed as refuting a specific heresy at a specific time and place, and should not be read as a universal restriction on women in the church. However, in support of their current suggested translation, that woman is not to "represent herself as originator of man" (103), the Kroegers do not succeed philologically or historically.

The Kroegers seem oblivious to proper word-study methodology.[29] In arguing that *authenteo* should be translated "represent oneself as originator of," they ignore the fact that this verb is rendered "domineer" in NT times. They appeal to outdated sixteenth-century Greek lexicons for a meaning that they then project back into Greek texts of the fourth and fifth centuries AD.[30] While they cite much secondary literature, they repeatedly misunderstand the sources they cite,[31] and selectively omit recent literature that would oppose their view.[32] They continue to repeat the misinformation that *authenteo* means "to murder" in ancient Greek. Now this meaning does occur for the noun form, but not for the verb form until the tenth century AD. While

---

[29]See James Barr, *The Semantics of Biblical Language* (Oxford: Oxford Univ. Press, 1961); and John F. A. Sawyer, *Semantics in Biblical Research* (Studies in Biblical Theology, 24; Naperville, IL: Alec Allenson, 1972).

[30]See the extensive and scathing review of Albert Wolters in *Calvin Theological Journal* 28 (1993): 208-213. In addition, the Kroegers' interpretation takes the *oude* (negative) in v. 12 as a hendiadys (expression of an idea with two independent words connected by *and* [e.g., nice and warm] rather than a word and modifier [nicely warm]), making *authenteo* here function as an infinitive of indirect discourse. This vital grammatical point, however, is not supported with grammatical analysis, but simply with a reference to Philip Barton Payne (pp. 83-84), and this in spite of a negative response to Payne's view that they were aware of and quoted on p. 21.

[31]The Latin quote from Guillaume Budé on p. 102 (230, n. 27) is completely misunderstood, as is their mistranslation of a German citation on p. 101.

[32]L. E. Wilshire, "The TLG Computer and Further References to Αὐθεντέω in 1 Timothy 2:12," *New Testament Studies* 34 (1988): 120-134.

leaving the impression of engaging in scholarly investigation of the term (36-37, 84-102), in reality the Kroegers are merely scavenging the philological arena for an alternative to the traditional reading of the text.   A review by Wolters concludes ominously:[33]

> ... the Kroegers have conspicuously failed to make their case. No doubt the book will have considerable influence in the evangelical world, but it is very doubtful whether any serious commentary on 1 Timothy will ever adopt its basic thesis. . . its argumentation is a travesty of sound scholarship.

Historically, the Kroegers fail miserably.[34] There is no evidence that a Gnostic sect such as they postulate ever existed in first-century Ephesus, or anywhere else.   The supposed Gnostic sect, which is the historical key to their view of 1 Tim 2:12, is nothing more than a hypothetical composite derived from various features of pagan religion in Ephesus and Asia Minor, and from some considerably later Gnostic texts.   In simply "proof-texting" ancient sources, the Kroegers evidence uncritical methodology and their treatment of secondary sources is careless, to say the least. For instance, in their effort to locate sexual issues "under every stone" in Ephesus, they appeal to Vermaseren[35] to set the problem in 1 Timothy in a context of supposed widespread influence of the cult of Cybele in Ephesus. However, the Kroegers mention over "seventy inscriptions" honoring Cybele, but only twenty exist and most of those are from a much later period—the ones that do exist were found at one small shrine, which does not constitute proof of "widespread influence."   Examples of such careless historical work abound in the Kroegers' work.   Further, failure to treat extensive ancient sources that do refer to the late-first century church in Ephesus (the fourth gospel, Polycarp, Ignatius, Papias)—none of which evidences the

---

[33]Wolters, *Calvin Theological Journal* (1993): 213.

[34]See the insightful, negative review by Richard Oster in *Biblical Archaeologist* 56 (1993): 225-227.

[35]M. J. Vermaseren, *Corpus Cultus Cybelae Attisdique* (Leiden: Brill, 1987): 1.184-203.

kind of Gnostic sect at Ephesus the Kroegers suggest—
damages their case beyond repair.[36] Oster, professor of NT
at Harding Graduate School of Religion, concludes:[37]

> . . . irrespective of one's sympathy for the pain and frustration
> of women who have been oppressed by "the traditions of
> men," . . . this publication does not present a cogent and
> defensible way to circumvent or neutralize 1 Tim 2:11-15. A
> judicious use of historical and archaeological data may
> someday help the Christian community to see 1 Tim 2:11-15
> in a better way, but if and when that is accomplished, it will
> have to be done using better evidence and superior research
> methods to those found in this work.

The Kroegers' work might appear promising at first glance,
filled as it is with ancient references, but improper
methodology and manipulation of data render their work
unusable.

Exemplary of grammatical manipulation in support of
feminist assumptions is Bilezikian's[38] (Willow Creek Community Church and teacher at Wheaton College) fabricated
rule on the Greek particle ἤ (pronounced like the letter *a*) in
1 Cor 14:36. Odell-Scott[39] took the first word in v. 36,
"or," as a disjunctive particle meaning "What!" resulting in
v. 36 being a *response* to the *Corinthian* view that women
must be silent in vv. 34-35. In this way, vv. 34-35 are not a
Pauline command, but a Corinthian view! In an effort at
grammatical proof, Bilezikian (286-288) argues that this
word commonly introduces statements counter to preceding
material, and that this is characteristic of 1 Corinthians.

---

[36]See Thomas A. Robinson, *Orthodoxy and Heresy in Western
Asia Minor in the First Christian Century* (Ph.D. dissertation at
McMaster Univ., 1985), esp. chapter 2 on Ephesus.

[37]Oster, *Biblical Arachaeologist* (1993): 227.

[38]Gilbert Bilezikian, *Beyond Sex Roles* (2nd ed.; Grand Rapids:
Baker, 1985): 286-288.

[39]D. W. Odell-Scott, "Let the Women Speak in Church: An
Egalitarian Interpretation of 1 Cor 14:33b-36," *Biblical Theology
Bulletin* 13 (1983): 90-93.

However, Carson, [40] professor of NT at Trinity Evangelical Divinity School, notes correctly regarding vv. 34-35 that,

> in every instance in the New Testament where the disjunctive particle in question is used in a construction analogous to the passage at hand, its effect is to reinforce the truth of the clause or verse that precedes it.

In truth, not a single passage cited by Bilezikian demonstrates the grammatical "rule" he proposes! As Robertson[41] said in his grammar, "It is the commonest grammatical vice for one to make a conjectural translation into English and then to discuss the syntactical propriety of the Greek . . . on the basis of this translation."[42] Bilezekian's work adds nothing to this discussion.

C. *Positive Contributions of Evangelical Feminist Exegesis*

The concerns of evangelical feminists regarding women being dependent, vulnerable, passive, oppressed, exploited, and manipulated are legitimate.[43] Among evangelical feminists, biblical authority is held in high regard. Yet, influencing much evangelical feminist exegesis is the prejudice of egalitarianism. Presuppositions, as we shall discuss later, are unavoidable. This particular assumption, however, unfortunately distorts much of their work and

---

[40]D. A. Carson, "'Silent in the Churches': On the Role of Women in 1 Corinthians 14:33b-36," *Recovering Biblical Manhood & Womanhood: A Response to Evangelical Feminism* (ed. J. Piper and W. Grudem; Wheaton: Crossway, 1991): 151.

[41]A. T. Robertson, *A Grammar of the Greek New Testament in the Light of Historical Research* (Nashville: Broadman, 1934): 821.

[42]See Carroll D. Osburn, "Interpreting Greek Syntax," *Biblical Interpretation: Principles and Practices* (ed. F. Kearley, E. Myers, T. Hadley; Grand Rapids: Baker, 1986): 234-243, for similar examples of distorted appeals to "the Greek" by zealous, but misinformed, persons.

[43]See Elaine Storkey, *What's Right with Feminism* (Grand Rapids: Eerdmans, 1985).

renders it suspicious. Susanne Heine,[44] professor at the
Univ. of Vienna, discusses new insights brought by feminist
scholarship to the study of the Bible and early Christian
literature. At the same time, she issues a strong appeal for
feminists to become open to analysis and correction. What
is needed, she says, is more rigorous application of
scholarly methods to "counter prejudices through criticism,
and negative experiences through active hope" (13).

An example of a more substantive contribution from an
evangelical feminist perspective is that of Craig Keener,
professor of NT at Hood Seminary.[45] Focusing on four
crucial texts from Paul's epistles (1 Cor 11:1-16, 14:34-35;
1 Tim 2:9-15; and Eph 5:18-6:9), Keener discusses the
background behind each text,[46] concluding that Paul's
seemingly restrictive view of women is not surprising. He
reasons that the women of Paul's time were mostly
uneducated and were thus prone to fall prey to heresy (84).
"If Paul does not want the women to teach in some sense,"
says Keener, "it is not because they are women, but because
they are unlearned" (120). Paul's directive, then, is not only
for uneducated women but also for equally uneducated
men.[47] Paul is not addressing those women and men who
are well-versed in Scripture. Contrary to the cultural norms
of his day, Paul calls on husbands to recognize the wives'
"need to know" (1 Cor 14:34-35) and to be responsible for
their being informed (84-85).

Keener also addresses women's role in the family.
From casual reading of the text, it may appear that Paul
adopts traditional Greco-Roman attitudes in this regard (Eph

---

[44]Susanne Heine, *Women and Early Christianity: A Reappraisal*
(trans. J. Bowden; Minneapolis: Augsburg, 1988).

[45]Craig Keener, *Paul, Women & Wives* (Peabody, MA:
Hendrickson, 1992).

[46]Cf. A. C. Perriman's critique of Keener, in *Themelios* 19.2
(Jan 1994): 27-28, for not engaging in a more extensive discussion of
the hermeneutical difficulties involved.

[47]Cf. John Pryor's review of *Paul, Women & Wives*, in *Journal
of Religious History* 1994 (18): 98-99.

5:18-6:9). In actuality, according to Keener, Paul places more emphasis on the mutual submission that is to characterize all Christian marriages (168-72). Thus, Paul is not necessarily advocating the patriarchal family structure of his day. Rather, Paul is calling all Christians to live the Christian life within the leadership framework of their own culture (209-211). In essence, Paul's call for mutual submission is the principle that is to characterize familial relationships. How that principle is played out will vary, depending on cultural expectations.

Keener's work demonstrates careful historical study and good analysis of 1 Cor 11, as well as of the Christian family in Eph 5, and his discussions of 1 Cor 14 and 1 Tim 2 are very useful.

Another example of evangelical feminist exegesis not dominated by prejudice is that of Scholer.[48] Scholer's commitment to responsible, contextual interpretation of Paul's statements in 1 Tim 2:9-15 and consistent application of this text in the life of the church are commendable. For Scholer, biblical authority is a crucial matter.

First, Scholer discusses this difficult text exegetically. He notes at the outset that often vv 11-12 are highlighted in discussion, but that vv 9-10, and especially v. 15, are often slighted. He critiques the misuse and neglect of v. 15 by various hierarchalists,[49] and engages in a lively and rigorous analysis of v. 15 in its context. Scholer views 1 Tim 2:15 as the climax of the entire section that begins in v. 9. It provides a positive conclusion to the negative statements in vv. 2:2-14. Unless v. 15 is correctly understood, he says, there is no legitimate understanding of vv. 9-14.

---

[48]David Scholer, "1 Timothy 2:9-15 & the Place of Women in the Church's Ministry," *Women, Authority & the Bible* (ed. Alvera Mickelsen; Downer's Grove, IL: InterVarsity, 1986): 193-224.

[49]Susan Foh, *Women and the Word of God: A Response to Evangelical Feminism* (Grand Rapids: Baker, 1980): 128, says of v. 15, "The last verse in this section is a puzzle and a sort of non sequitur."

Whereas the NIV translates v. 15 as, "Women will be kept safe through childbirth," Scholer argues that rather than coming through childbirth safely, Paul must certainly have had theological salvation in Christ in mind (196). Now the problem here hinges on the verb "will be saved" (Gk. *sothesetai*) being singular, but the second verb "remain" (Gk. *meinosin*) being plural. He notes,

> This demonstrates the obvious connection between verse 15 and 2:9-14—Eve (v. 13) represents woman (v. 14) /women (vv. 9, 10, 11); thus, the grammatically natural shift in verse 15 from the singular (woman as womankind) to the plural (individual women) (196).

Thus, the conclusion to Paul's discussion of women in this context means that women find their theological salvation (assuming continuing faithfulness) in the maternal and domestic roles understood in that ancient culture to be proper for Greco-Roman women.

This concern for propriety in v. 15 occurs also in v. 9 at the beginning of this paragraph, where stipulations are made regarding women's dress and adornment that are also in line with expectations of decency and propriety in Greco-Roman society.

Such concerns in 1 Timothy clearly suggest to Scholer that a challenge to propriety among the women was being made. This challenge is evidently related to the opposition that Paul is encouraging Timothy to confront and counter (1:3ff). It is specified in 4:3 that certain individuals are forbidding marriage. Their assault on marriage and proper conduct in society poses a major problem. So Paul stresses proper conduct in marriages in 1 Tim 2, as well as in 5:9-15. Church leaders must be individuals whose homes and family life are commendable (3:4-5, 12). Further, in 3:7 he stresses that "a good reputation with outsiders" is important, and in 5:14 says that they must "give the enemy no opportunity for slander." The rationale for good behavior is stated in 2:2-4, that such behavior should result in "quiet and peaceful lives in all godliness and holiness."

Scholer's understanding coheres with the literary context of the letter of 1 Timothy. From 1:3-7 it is clear that the sinister influence of certain individuals must be countered, and the letter concludes in 6:20-21 with a strong concern about this false teaching. This opposition is mentioned throughout the letter (1:18-20; 4:1-8; 5:16; 6:3-10). Thus Scholer stresses that it is within this purpose of 1 Timothy that 3:14-15 should be understood, "I am writing you . . . so that . . . you will know how people ought to conduct themselves in God's household."

Scholer disagrees with Knight[50] and Hurley,[51] who see 3:14-15 as *the* purpose of 1 Tim. It is, Scholer says, presumptious to take 3:14-15 out of its context of the opposition in Ephesus and use it to make 1 Tim out to be a "church manual" for all time. Instead, 1 Tim should be seen as directed to the specific occasion mentioned in the letter, which involves Timothy countering the influence of this improper teaching and life-style, part of which has resulted in women abandoning traditional values of marriage and conduct in society (200).

Scholer then concentrates on 2:9-10, stating that "2:9-10 is clearly as serious a set of injunctions in the context as 2:11-12" (201). Vv. 9-10 are similar to v. 15 in affirming high standards of conduct in opposition to the teachings of the adversaries. He argues from both Jewish and Greco-Roman cultures that modesty in those ancient times involved avoidance of expensive clothing, jewelry, etc., which when worn in public evidenced a certain disrespect for husbands. Not only was extravagance at stake, but sexual fidelity as well, in dressing in this way.

The discussion in 2:9-15 then moves from womens' adornment to conduct in public worship. Scholer concludes, "In view of this unity of 2:9-12 and the conclusion in 2:15,

---

[50]George W. Knight, III, *The New Testament Teaching on the Role Relationship of Men and Women* (Grand Rapids: Baker, 1977): 29-30.

[51]Hurley, *Man and Woman*, 195-97.

there is no exegetical, historical or hermeneutical basis to
regard 2:9-10 as normatively different from 2:11-12" (202).
However, some take vv. 11-12 as a mandate to place
limitations on women in worship, but take the injunctions in
vv. 9-10 to be culturally relative and do not take them to be
applied literally today. This is unacceptable for Scholer . If
vv. 11-12 are to be taken literally, he asks, then why not
also take 9-10 literally?

The injunctions in vv. 11-12 correspond with accepted
Greco-Roman norms of behavior for women, as do vv. 9-10
and v. 15. These statements, he says, "are thus ad hoc
instructions intended for a particular situation in Ephesus"
(203). They are "not to be understood as universal
principles encoded in a suprasitutional 'church order manual'
that limit women in ministry in all times and places" (203).
Instead, vv. 11-12 are directed to certain women who have
been influenced or captivated by the teachings about which
Paul is concerned in 1:3-7. Vv. 11-12, "occur within a
specific paragraph, the climax of which (2:15) already
indicates a specific situation" (204).

Scholer notes that *authentein* in v. 12 has been understood in a sense of "to domineer." Thus v. 12 applies
specifically to those women who are dominating the leaders
and teachers in the church at Ephesus (205).[52]

Turning to 2:13-14, Scholer concludes that the allusions
to Gen 2-3 are explanatory illustrations rather than universal
injunctions. In this respect, Paul selects data from Genesis to
explain 2:11-12.

---

[52]Scholer, *Women, Authority & the Bible*, 206-07, rejects the
view that two levels of authority are involved, 1) one level (see Rom
16:1-16, Phil 4:2-3) is not prohibited by 1 Tim 2:11-12, and 2) another
level prohibited in that text. However, two levels of authority are never
indicated in the writings of Paul. He also rejects the view that
prophecy is permissible, but teaching is not. D. Aune, *Prophecy in
Early Christianity and the Ancient Mediterranean World* (Grand Rapids:
Eerdmans, 1983), among others, has established that prophecy did
function as authoritative among Paul's churches.

D. *Summary: Biblical Egalitarianism*

Rejecting the extreme stances of radical feminism, evangelical feminists have heralded the importance of the biblical text regarding women in the church, but claim that traditional exegesis has assigned improper meanings to certain texts. Proper exegesis can lead to meanings being attached to texts that are somewhat different from traditional understandings. That much is good. However, the very term "feminist" carries with it so much baggage that it might be preferable for responsible exegesis to be termed "biblical egalitarianism."

2. *Hierarchal complementarianism*

In response to evangelical feminism, other evangelicals have taken a position that, while not entirely the same as the traditional patriarchal view, still maintains a very strong view of male leadership and female submission. One must view complementarianism as essentially a hierarchal reaction against evangelical feminism.

A. *Reactions Against Evangelical Feminism*

The opening response to evangelical feminism was that of George Knight, professor of NT at Covenant Theological Seminary in St. Louis, interacting in *Christianity Today* with Scanzoni, Hardesty, and Jewett. Knight is

> distressed that some who have written on the subject seem to be abandoning the inerrancy of Scripture and the authority of God and his Word, seem willing to appeal to the passages in Scripture that support their position and to minimize other passages or declare them to be either wrong or only culturally relative and not normative, even when these passages themselves claim to be normative and not culturally relative.[53]

---

[53]George W. Knight, III, "Male and Female Related He Them," *Christianity Today* 20 (9 April 1976): 710.

Knight's reaction to evangelical feminism centers on the following topics: 1) order of creation, 2) effects of the fall, 3) relation of slavery to women's issues, 4) subordination or submission and equality, and 5) whether Paul's view of Gen 2 reflects an unacceptable rabbinical view.

Concentrating on men and women in the teaching and ruling offices and functions in the church, in public worship, and in the home, Knight addresses in book-length treatment the *role relationship* where the question of authority, headship, or leadership is in view.[54] Knight views the relationship between men and women as a "role relationship . . . that is ordained by God for all cultures, societies, and times" (9). While not every relationship among men and women is one in which headship or authority is in question, Knight argues that biblical teaching is clear regarding church office and the home. A basic contention is Knight's view that, "Equality and role differences are compatible" (14). In marriage, while men and women are both equal and bear the image of God to the same degree as in Gen 1:27, masculinity and femininity reflect God's image in different and complementary ways as in 2:18-25 (20-21). This does not mean, according to Knight, that submission of wives necessitates acceptance of slavery or government by kings (21-27).

Concerning submission and headship, Knight concludes that in creation God ordained different roles and functions for men and women and that this results in the exclusion of women from the ruling-teaching office and functions in the church, yet allows praying, prophesying, diaconal service and teaching of women and children (29-53). Knight insists that, analogous to the Trinity where the Son is subordinate to the Father yet not inferior, so it is with the relationship between man and woman (55-60). Knight concludes with a reminder that male headship requires love and service, not tyranny, and specifies, "Elders and husbands are heads not because they are inherently

---

[54]Knight, *The New Testament Teaching on the Role Relationship of Men and Women*

superior—for they exercise their functions among and with equals—but because they have been called by God to their tasks" (59).

In the same vein as Knight, Foh,[55] a graduate of Westminster Theological Seminary, categorizes the leading evangelical feminists, such as Scanzoni and Hardesty, Jewett and Mollenkott, as rejecting a trustworthy Bible. She notes that they "see irreconcilable contradictions in the Bible's teaching on women" (6). In castigation, Foh asserts, "A doctrine of Scripture which admits error eventually results in apostasy or heresy. The feminist movement is a vivid illustration of departure from the truth." (21). This strong statement counters the equally strong view of Mollenkott that patriarchalism is a "Christian heresy." Challenging feminist hermeneutics, Foh argues that literary and historical contexts do illuminate the text, but also that Scriptures are verbally inerrant, form a coherent unity, and can only be understood by the spiritually regenerate (20-24). She addresses some of the difficult passages, but not always extensively. Regarding the topic of God as male and female, Foh concludes, "masculine terminology has significance because God has given the man authority in the family (husband) and in the church (elder), rather than to the woman" (163). Discussing submission of wives, Foh dismisses the "pink baby doll pajamas and white boots" of Morgan's *The Total Woman*, but advocates Morgan's principles of "submission" as biblical (193-197).

In view of these strong responses to evangelical feminism, one might be surprised at Robbins'[56] negative review of the hierarchalism of Knight and Foh. Robbins, founder and president of The Trinity Foundation, is a traditionalist who attacks traditionalists for not defending hierarchalism in strong enough terms. He praises Knight for his respect for the Bible, but says that his principles of

---

[55]Susan Foh, *Women and the Word of God: A Response to Biblical Feminism* (Grand Rapids: Baker, 1981).

[56]John Robbins, *Scripture Twisting in the Seminaries, Part I: Feminism* (Jefferson, MD: Trinity Foundation, 1985).

interpretation are wrong, as are some of his conclusions. In review of Foh, Conn[57] criticized her heavily-biased approach, saying that, "She has not really seen the cultural woods for the egalitarian trees." Robbins, though, is considerably more blunt in assessing Foh's work. He claims that Foh reads the Bible "through feminist glasses" (49). Foh's "lame response" to feminism, he says, is unacceptable at several points. He criticizes Foh's view of certain "tensions" in the text as denying the harmony of Scripture, impugning the rationality of God, and preventing proper understanding of the texts in question (47). Where Knight holds that women are prohibited from teaching men, Robbins counters that they are prohibited from teaching in the church—period (35)! When Knight and Foh distinguish between preaching and prophesying, thus permitting women to prophesy, Robbins responds that Paul "will not let a woman speak in church, even to ask questions, let alone to prophesy" (36; 47-48). Knight's admission that women prayed in public Corinthian worship draws the stinging rebuttal that "Paul wants the women to be silent and the men (Gk. *andres* "males") to pray" (38; 48). "What these passages forbid," Robbins says, "is *all* teaching, praying, prophesying, preaching, question-asking, and exercising authority by a woman in a church meeting" (39). Knight's view that the position of deacon is for men only but that women are to be involved "in the diaconal area" is met with

> The New Testament, of course, entertains no nonsense about women deacons—or deaconesses—nor about women disciples, apostles, prophets, missionaries, evangelists, and elders. Not a single example is given (41; see also 44).

Robbins certainly disagrees with Knight's urging that "women teach other women in the church" (Tit 2:3-5), holding that the words "in the church" are not in the text and that Knight "exhibits here a mild form of feminism" instead of accepting at face value the biblical command for women not to speak at all in church (42).

---

[57]Harvie M. Conn, "Evangelical Feminism: Reflections on the State of the 'Union'," *TSF Bulletin* (Nov.-Dec., 1984): 22.

On a separate page before the introduction, Robbins quotes Benjamin Warfield, the old Princeton "war horse," that anyone who "modifies the teachings of the Word of God" is "already in principle, a heretic.

B. *The Case for Hierarchalism*

It is unfortunate that popular opinion on hierarchalism is formed often, not by careful biblical exegesis, but by forceful pleading. An example of this is Vanauken's[58] widely-acclaimed chronicle of his departure from feminism to hierarchalism. His reasoning is simply that since Jesus did not appoint any female apostles, clearly there can be no women priests. He does not believe that men are superior to women, but stresses that they are different—equal in importance, but as different as a nut and a bolt.[59] Vanauken, however, does not develop an argument, but tells the story of his developing love for his wife—including idyllic afternoons on their boat, marriage, becoming believers through conversation with C. S. Lewis in Oxford, mysterious illness—and his shift to a patriarchalism more in line with that of Lewis. Comments on the dust jacket of *Under the Mercy* give insight into how powerfully this sort of writing influences its readers—"Touched me so deeply that the book, finally, was like an essay in self-under-standing," and "I wept as I read."

Ronald and Beverly Allen[60] give their interpretation of key biblical texts supporting hierarchalism in one brief chapter, "without," as they put it, "getting bogged down in exegesis." After criticizing Mollenkott for avoiding the Bible and Jewett for denying the inspiration and authority of the Bible, they offer their opinions on various texts. They simply assert on one-half page that Gal 3:28 does not deny distinctions between male and female (Gen 1:27), but in a

---

[58]Sheldon Vanauken, *A Severe Mercy* (New York: Harper and Row, 1977), and idem, *Under the Mercy* (Nashville: Nelson, 1985).

[59]Vanauken, *Under the Mercy*, 214.

[60]Ronald and Beverly Allen, *Liberated Traditionalism: Men & Women in Balance* (Portland: Multnomah, 1985).

world of superiors and inferiors, there exists a new world where whoever you are you are one with all other Christians (135). 1 Cor 11 gets slightly more attention—part of two pages. This text, they say, depends upon hierarchy for Paul's argument to work, but his stress upon mutuality is impressive and must not be overlooked (145-46). In two pages, they admit correctly that the problem in 1 Cor 14 was disruptive women in the worship. However, they conclude incorrectly that the actual problem was women "chattering." Although they can find no passage in the Torah that says "women are to be silent," they conclude curiously that Paul surely must be referring to the "general teaching of biblical Torah" (147). On the other hand, while 1 Tim. 2:9-15 might seem to demand categorical prohibition of women speaking in any teaching role in the church, they suggest correctly that the context implies controls upon "certain women teachers, whose dress and demeanor were suspect and whose teaching was heretical" (148). Lack of exegetical insight is apparent.

Fortunately, the patriarchal case from an evangelical perspective is stated fairly and better by Hurley in a book based upon his doctoral dissertation at Cambridge.[61] Basic to Hurley's discussion is his assumption that all "real" authority is that of "appointive male headship." To put it differently, the subordination of women is a God-ordained pre-Fall matter. This one notion controls virtually all of his argument. Hurley documents from law codes in the ancient Near East the dominant male role, but concludes that subordination of women did not necessarily involve woman's intrinsic inferiority. Gen 1-3, of course, is pivotal for Hurley's view of male/female relationships. For instance, Adam's naming of the woman in Gen 2 is clear demonstration of female subordination. Giving somewhat more attention to Jewish views on women than to Greco-Roman views, Hurley posits that Jesus' views of women contrast with contemporary views in four crucial areas:

---

[61]James B. Hurley, "Man and Woman in 1 Corinthians," (unpublished Ph.D. dissertation, Cambridge Univ., 1973). His *Man and Woman in Biblical Perspective* (Grand Rapids: Zondervan, 1981) was written on a sabbatical leave at Tyndale House in Cambridge.

marriage, divorce, celibacy, and lust. Nevertheless, while recognizing the liberating behavior of Jesus toward women, Hurley does not rely upon Jesus' role model in discussing male/female relationships. While women played active roles in the early church, Hurley finds no evidence that they functioned in leadership roles. Within the marriage relationship, it is normal and necessary for there to be male dominance and female submission. He views Gal 3:28 not as the *locus classicus* of Paul's teaching on women, but with reference to one's status before God. The idea of "mutual submission" in Eph 5:21 is dismissed by applying the text to the congregation rather than to husband/wife relationships. In his discussion of "head" (*kephale*), he reads authoritarian notions into the term.

Regarding worship, Hurley treats the two primary texts: 1 Cor 11:2-16 and 14:33-36. The background for 1 Cor 11 is Paul's concept of man as "head" in Eph 5. The problem in 1 Cor, according to Hurley, is that the "Corinthian women are 'letting their hair down' to show that marital patterns no longer applied, that they were no longer subordinate to their husbands" (168-71). He posits that a conservative Jewish element was imposing veils upon women in the Corinthian church. Thus, Paul's directives were aimed at Christian wives who reject male headship, evidenced by their refusal to wear veils at worship. In 1 Cor 14, the problem involved women "examining the prophets," which Hurley finds incompatible with women's subordination (185-94). He finds no prohibition of women participating vocally in worship or from using spiritual gifts, such as prophecy (see 11:3-4). According to Hurley, 14:33-36 does not address preaching and teaching, but disruption within the service. The text only prohibits women judging the prophets and does not mandate the silence of women in public worship.

Hurley's discussion of church administration treats 1 Tim 2:8-15, 3:1-13; and Rom 16:1, 2. 1 Tim 2:8-15 is taken to prohibit women being "authoritative teachers in the church" (199-200), a task perfomed rather by an "overseer." A woman might bring "a word of instruction" to the church in public assembly, if authorized by an "overseer." While he excludes women from role of "overseer," he approves women serving in the non-authoritative, serving role of deacon. In actuality, Hurley uses 1 Tim 2:8-15 as the basic normative text in terms of which all other texts must be read and understood.

By way of critique, it must be noted that while Hurley insists upon subordination of women as a divine, pre-Fall matter, he has drastically reduced the instances where this applies.[62] Clearly, Hurley is challenging the abuses within hierarchalism. However, he has protected his principal thesis that male dominance is a God-ordained, pre-Fall structure and has not permitted it to be examined. In fact, when Hurley insists that man's superiority over the woman is evident in his "naming" her (Gen 2), he does not interact with Trible,[63] whose work on Genesis 1-3 is significant. Trible has argued successfully that a distinction must be made between the pre-Fall situation in which man recognizes the woman as part of himself, and the post-Fall situation in which man's dominance over woman is one of the sinful conditions of fallen humanity. Hurley has read his prejudice regarding Gen 1-3 into the text, and this is the "Achilles heel" of his thesis. Through this flawed lens, other texts are read with predictable outcomes.

For instance, Hurley both assumes and argues that the instructions about women in 1 Tim 2:11-12 are "timeless" and apply to any and every situation. But this cannot be merely assumed—it must be established by exacting argument. To the contrary, several evangelical and other scholars have made a solid case that the problem addressed in this text has to do with a limited problem of heresy in Ephesus.

---

[62]See Linda Mercadante's review of Hurley, *Man and Woman in Biblical Perspective* in *TSF Bulletin* (Jan-Feb 1983): 21-22.

[63]Phyllis Trible, *God and the Rhetoric of Sexuality* (Philadelphia: Fortress, 1978).

C. *The Emergence of "Hierarchal Complementarianism"*

Whereas Knight and Foh merely reject evangelical feminism, the volume edited by Piper and Grudem[64] presents hierarchal complementarianism more positively. Piper earned a doctorate in theology from the University of Munich and is senior pastor of Bethlehem Baptist Church in Minneapolis. Grudem, with a Ph.D. from Cambridge, is professor of theology at Trinity Evangelical Divinity School. They acknowledge that traditional arguments do not fully answer many detailed and persuasive arguments of evangelical feminists. They do admit with evangelical feminists that selfishness, irresponsibility, and abuse are often altogether too characteristic of patriarchalism. Whereas patriarchalists would denounce evangelical feminists as having abandoned the faith, Piper and Grudem treat evangelical feminists as within the faith—yet challenge their view by presenting a detailed alternative. They argue,

> We are uncomfortable with the term "traditionalist" because it implies an unwillingness to let Scripture challenge traditional patterns of behavior, and we certainly reject the term "hierarchicalist" because it overemphasizes structured authority while giving no suggestion of equality or the beauty of mutual interdependence.[65]

However, this "complementarian" view of women is a distinctly hierarachal view. It purports to take the Bible seriously while avoiding the "feminist blurring of God-given sexual distinctions."[66]   Complementarians view women as fully equal to men in status before God, and in importance to the family and the church. This opens the door to countless women's ministries closed to them in patriarchalism. Neveretheless, it maintains strong affirmation of biblically mandated male leadership in the home and in the church.

---

[64]John Piper and Wayne Grudem, ed., *Recovering Biblical Manhood and Womanhood: A Response to Evangelical Feminism* (Wheaton: Crossway, 1991).

[65]Ibid.

[66]Ibid., xiv.

Piper[67] is stunned at Jewett's statement that there may be no way ultimately to understand "what it means to be created as man *or* woman." [68] Piper responds,

> When the Bible teaches that men and women fulfill different roles in relation to each other, charging man with a unique leadership role, it bases this differentiation not on temporary cultural norms but on permanent facts of creation. . . . in 1 Cor 11:3-16 (esp. vv. 8-9, 14); Eph 5:21-33 (esp. vv. 31-32); and 1 Tim 2:11-14 (esp. vv. 13-14). In the Bible, differentiated roles for men and women are never traced back to the fall of man and woman into sin [but to] . . . the way things were in Eden. . . . Differentiated roles were corrupted by the fall, not created by the fall. They were created by God.

Piper responds with his own definition of "mature" manhood and womanhood:

> At the heart of mature masculinity is a sense of benevolent responsibility to lead, provide for and protect women in ways appropriate to a man's differing relationships (35).

> At the heart of mature femininity is a freeing disposition to affirm, receive and nurture strength and leadership from worthy men in ways appropriate to a woman's differing relationships (36).

So, hierarchal complementarianism is depicted as follows:[69]

> Men and women, as God created us, are different in hundreds of ways. Being created equally in the image of God means at least this: that when the so-called weakness and strength columns for manhood and for womanhood are added up, the value at the bottom is going to be the same for each. And when you take those two columns and put them on top of each other, God intends them to be the perfect complement to each other.

---

[67]Piper, "A Vision of Biblical Complementarity," *Recovering Biblical Manhood and Womanhood*, 35.

[68]Jewett, *Man as Male and Female*, 188.

[69]Piper and Grudem, "An Overview of Central Concerns," *Recovering Biblical Manhood and Womanhood*, 73.

Piper speculates on complementarity as the way God intended it to be before there was any sin in the world:

> sinless man, full of love, in his tender, strong leadership in relation to woman; and sinless woman, full of love, in her joyful, responsive support for man's leadership. No belittling from the man, no groveling from the woman. Two intelligent, humble, God-entranced beings living out, in beautiful harmony, their unique and different responsibilities.[70]

Piper[71] specifies,

> *Biblical headship* for the husband is the divine calling to take primary responsibility for Christlike, servant-leadership, protection and provision in the home. *Biblical submission* for the wife is the divine calling to honor and affirm her husband's leadership and help carry it through according to her gifts. . . . The realities of headship and submission in marriage have their counterparts in the church. . . . *authority* refers to the divine calling of spiritual, gifted men to take primary responsibility as elders for Christlike, servant-leadership and teaching in the church. And *submission* refers to the divine calling of the rest of the church, both men and women, to honor and affirm the leadership and teaching of the elders and to be equipped by them for the hundreds and hundreds of various ministries available to men and women.

However, the hierarchal complementarian approach to recovering the "biblical pattern of mature manhood and womanhood" is not without problems, especially with regard to "implied meanings" in biblical texts. For instance, Ortlund,[72] professor of OT at Trinity Evangelical Divinity School, correctly states, "We see neither the words "male-female equality" nor "male headship" here or anywhere in Genesis 1-3." However, he observes, "What Moses does

---

[70]Piper, "A Vision of Biblical Complementarity," *Recovering Biblical Manhood and Womanhood*, 52.

[71]Ibid., 52-53.

[72]Raymond C. Ortlund, "Male-Female Equality and Male Headship—Genesis 1-3," *Recovering Biblical Manhood and Womanhood*, 98-99.

provide is a series of more or less obvious hints as to his doctrine of manhood and womanhood" and ". . . God's naming of the race 'man' whispers male headship." On this basis, he continues, "He called us 'man,' which anticipates the male headship brought out clearly in chapter two." Further, he notes that one "can feel intuitively the importance of distinct sexual identity." Now Gen 1-3 is a vital text, but clearly more than "more or less obvious hints," "whispers," and intuitive feelings are needed to substantiate one's understanding of the text.

Later, while discussing woman as man's "helper," he asks, "Doesn't this striking fact suggest that manhood and womanhood are distinct and non-reversible?" On the basis of this argument, he concludes, "A man, just by virtue of his manhood, is called to lead for God. A woman, just by virtue of her womanhood, is called to help for God" (102-104). By following imprecise methodology in word study, Ortlund falls into the error of "circular lexicography," i.e., reading conclusions into presuppositions.[73]

Similarly, Ortlund posits that in naming all creatures, thereby bringing them under his dominion, "This royal prerogative extended to Adam's naming of his helper." He notes Ramsey's study[74] which concludes that the naming of Eve in Gen 2 is not an act of domination, but of discernment, but then dismisses all argumentation with the passing remark that the naming of the woman "makes sense as an act of headship and that it does not make sense in any other way."

It is difficult to conclude other than that, in his eagerness to locate "the very foundation of Biblical man-

---

[73]See James Barr, *The Semantics of Biblical Language* (London: Oxford Univ. Press, 1961), and John F. A. Sawyer, *Semantics in Biblical Research* (Studies in Biblical Theology, 24; Naperville, IL: Allenson, 1972).

[74]George W. Ramsey, "Is Name-Giving an Act of Domination in Genesis 2:23 and Elsewhere?" *Catholic Biblical Quarterly* 50 (1988): 24-35.

hood and womanhood" in Gen 1-3, his assertion of "male-female equality" is redefined by prejudice of male hierarchy. He asks, "So, was Eve Adam's equal?" and concludes, "Yes and no. She was his spiritual equal . . . [but] she was not his equal in that she was his 'helper'" (102). Quite rightly, he stresses that we must not resolve the issue of equality or headship based upon reaction to bad experiences. However, it must be observed that neither is it to be resolved by reading preconceived notions into pertinent texts. The view of woman in Gen 1-3 must be understood on some basis other than Ortlund's essay.

Whereas paternalists often selectively omit reference to biblical texts which might be viewed as militating against their view, Piper and Grudem are to be congratulated for treating a wider array of texts. However, the "exegetical analysis" of Gal 3:28 by Johnson,[75] minister at Believers' Chapel in Dallas, does not establish the meaning of the phrase "neither male and female." It consists solely of a reaction against the interpretation given by F. F. Bruce![76] Hence, his following critiques of Jewett[77] and Snodgrass[78] are not based upon sound exegesis, but upon his own presuppositions. Giving instead the "historic orthodox argument," he concludes, "The creeds of the church . . . are more important than the views of individuals. We should begin our discussions with the assumption that *the church is probably right*, unless exegetical and theological study compel us otherwise." In this essay, however, Johnson has not engaged in either exegetical or theological analysis, but has merely allowed his prejudices to become his conclusions.

---

[75]S. Lewis Johnson, Jr., "Role Distinctions in the Church— Galatians 3:28," *Recovering Biblical Manhood and Womanhood*, 154-164.

[76]F. F. Bruce, *Galatians* (Grand Rapids: Eerdmans, 1982).

[77]Jewett, *Man as Male and Female.*

[78]Klyne Snodgrass,"Galatians 3:28: Conundrum or Solution?" *Women, Authority and the Bible* (ed. A. Mickelsen; Downers Grove, IL: InterVarsity Press, 1986): 174-75.

In another essay crucial to hierarchal complementarian thought, Moo,[79] professor of NT at Trinity Evangelical Divinity School, addresses 1 Tim 2:11-15, which has since the early days of the church been thought to place restrictions on the ministry of women. He begins appropriately enough by establishing the historical setting with four observations: 1) false teachers sowed dissension (1 Tim 1:4-6; 6:4-5); 2) false teachers stressed asceticism as a means of spirituality (4:1-3); 3) false teachers had persuaded many to follow them in their doctrines (5:15); 4)

> The false teachers were encouraging women to discard what we might call traditional female roles in favor of a more egalitarian approach to the role relationships of men and women. This is not stated explicitly as a plank in the false teachers' platform anywhere in the pastoral epistles. Nevertheless, it is an inference with a high degree of probability. . . .

Of the four, however, it is this last which serves as the basis for his entire exposition, though it is only hypothetical. In this vein, Moo also postulates,

> These women *had probably picked up* the disputatious habits of the false teachers, and Paul must therefore warn them to accept without criticism the teaching of the properly appointed church leaders. But there is *probably more to the problem* than this. *There is good reason to think* that the underlying issue in verse 11 is not just submission to the teaching of the church but the submission of women to their husbands and, *perhaps*, to the male leadership of the church. (italics mine)

Accordingly, it is not surprising that Moo takes rather predictable routes in his exegesis, which is only a slightly updated version of his earlier article on the subject in response to Payne's critique.[80]   For instance, in his

---

[79]Douglas Moo, "What Does It Mean Not to Teach or Have Authority Over Men?—1 Timothy 2:11-15," *Recovering Biblical Manhood and Womanhood*, 179-193.

[80]Douglas J. Moo, "1 Timothy 2:11-15: Meaning and Significance," *Trinity Journal* 1 (1980): 62-83; Philip B. Payne, "Libertarian

discussion of what it means to "learn in silence" (2:11), he notes that the term for "silence" could refer to absolute silence or to "quietness, peaceableness."[81] "There is good reason," he says, "to think that the word should be translated 'silence' in this context, since its opposite is 'teaching'" (183). Yet, he disregards Payne's earlier critique of his view which suggests that "silence" be paired with "submission" in v. 11 rather than with "teaching" in v. 12.[82]

Similarly, while Moo admits that "teach" can be defined more broadly to include teaching that all Christians do (as in Col 3:16), he says that "teach" in the NT is used "mainly to denote the . . . authoritative proclamation of God's will" and that "the activity usually designated by *teach* is plainly restricted to certain individuals who have the gift of teaching" (as in 1 Cor 12:28-30).[83] Although presenting this caveat, Moo's working axiom is actually, "Paul expressly limits 'teaching' to a restricted number who have the gift of teaching" (184)—in spite of the fact that this understanding of the passage is not inherent in the text. Moo presents no textual argument for his view, but only a presupposition that any teaching of the Bible or doctrine constitutes an exercise of "authoritative teaching"—hence, he concludes, women can teach other women, but cannot teach the Bible or doctrine to men either in the church or elsewhere (186).

Given this view of "teaching," it comes as no surprise that Moo prefers "have authority" rather than "domineer" for the Greek term *authentein* in v. 12. However, his statement that, "the occurrences of this word—the verb—that are

---

Women in Ephesus: A Response to Douglas J. Moo's Article, '1 Timothy 2:11-15: Meaning and Significance,'" *Trinity Journal* 2 (1981): 169-197.

[81]Moo, "What Does It Mean Not to Teach or Have Authority Over Men"? *Recovering Biblical Manhood and Womanhood*, 183.

[82]Payne, *Trinity Journal* (1981): 175.

[83]Moo, "What Does It Mean Not to Teach or Have Authority Over Men"? *Recovering Biblical Manhood and Womanhood*, 185.

closest in time and nature to 1 Timothy mean 'have authority over',"[84] is curious for the two such instances closest to 1 Tim do not substantiate his view.   Both from the first-century BC, a papyrus in Berlin clearly has the meaning of "to domineer,"[85] as does Philodemus, who mentions "dominating masters."[86] If "exercise authority" had been meant, Paul likely would have used *exousiazo* here instead. Moo's counter that the vocabulary of 1 Tim is different from that of Paul's vocabulary in other epistles is unconvincing because one only has to note 1 Cor 6:12, or perhaps 7:4, to see that if "exercise authority" was meant, Paul certainly knew and used the usual term *exousiazo*.

Predictably, for Moo, the two verbs "teaching" and "having authority over" should not be rendered as one thought—"teaching in a domineering manner," but two tasks—"teaching *or* exercising authority." Moo rejects taking the second term as a modifier of the first, reasoning that this "would eliminate entirely the second prohibition (against having authority over a man)." To substantiate why "We do not, however, think this interpretation is likely," he states that *oude* ("neither," "nor") does not usually join together words that are mutually interpreting (187). However, this is to fabricate a rule in Greek for the purpose of theological argument.   What is needed is a careful examination of this grammatical relationship in Greek literature.   No textual necessity exists for Moo's view that two activities are meant here, rather than one.

There are altogether too many "implied meanings" of this sort in *Recovering Biblical Manhood and Womanhood.* While its aim of presenting complementarianism in its best light is solid, the volume fails to deliver what it promises. If

---

[84]Ibid. 186.

[85]*Aegyptische Urkunden aus den koniglichen Museen zu Berlin: Griechische Urkunden* (Berlin: Wiedmann, 1892-1937): No. 1208. See Carroll D. Osburn, "ΑΥΘΕΝΤΕΩ (1 Timothy 2:12)," *Restoration Quarterly* 25 (1982): 1-12, esp. 4-6.

[86]S. Sudhaus, *Philodemi: Volumina Rhetorica* (Leipzig: B. G. Teubner, 1896): 133.

this book is its classic statement, hierarchal complementarianism must default due to incompetent use of the biblical
text and mistaking prejudices for conclusions—the very two
problems these writers find with evangelical feminism!

Another analysis of 1 Tim 2:9-15[87] from the heirarchal
point of view appeared in 1995. In several essays,
Köstenberger, et al, attempt an analysis of the text according
to ancient linguistic usage and cultural milieu. They argue,
with Moo, that *authenteo* does not mean "domineer," but
"exercise authority," and that "teach" and "exercise
authority" are two separate items. However, they are not
convincing as they fall into some of the same pitfalls as Moo
and the Kroegers. This is true not only linguistically, but in
terms of culture as well. Their chapter on Ephesian culture
is dominated by hierarchical presupposition and does not
provide an accurate description of the scene. I have decided
not to include a review of the volume at this point because
such a review should really be followed and countered by a
carefully developed exegesis. The volume of Köstenberger,
et al, is rather technical and involved, and it will be reviewed
and critiqued carefully in chapter 12 where the exegesis of
1 Tim 2:9-15 is undertaken.

D. *Summary*

While views of evangelical feminism and hierarchal
complementarianism have significant differences, they also
share major matters in common that make them more
compatible with each other than each would be with either
extreme.

It is significant that both views place prominence on the
existence of the supernatural. Both remain committed to
working out a view of women within the historic Christian
faith. Both view the Bible as authoritative. Both work in
terms of the ancient manuscript tradition lying behind the

---

[87]A. J. Köstenberger, T. Schreiner, and S. Baldwin, ed., *Women
in the Church: A Fresh Analysis of 1 Timothy 2:9-15* (Grand Rapids:
Baker, 1995), a year after Osburn, *Women in the Church*, appeared.

biblical text and both approach exegetical work in terms of
strict literary and historical controls on interpretation. Both
attempt to understand the Bible in terms of its cultural milieu.
Both understand that culture has influenced the church, both
past and present. Both presuppose equal value of the sexes.
Both acknowledge discrimination and oppression of women,
both in society and in the church. Both theoretically find
radical feminism and male domination unacceptable. Both
theoretically have a willingness to evaluate their own view
and to interact with other views.

On the other hand, major differences exist that create no
little tension. The presuppositions of "God-ordained
hierarchalism" for these complementarians and of "God-
ordained egalitarianism" for some evangelical feminists
influence strongly both the selection of Scriptures used to
support arguments and the exegetical conclusions of each
group. The reality of false objectivity emerges here. Each
view, with its strong presuppositions, has a problem in
being objective regarding the interpretation of Scripture.

Another unresolved issue is the definition that each
group has of inerrancy of Scripture. On one hand, Knight
accuses some evangelical feminists of "abandoning the
inerrancy of Scripture" (see p. 46 above). Foh goes further,
implying that one who holds another view on these texts
must be among the unregenerate and headed toward apostasy
(p. 47). On the other hand, Mollenkott questions the
sincerity of one professing belief in inerrancy when one
claims not to know and seems "not to care" what Galatians
3:28 means.[88] In a bold statement regarding evangelicals as
a whole, Dunn, formerly professor at the Univ. of Durham,
England, whose appreciation among British evangelicals is
well known, concluded that the commonly-held evangelical
concept of biblical inerrancy is "exegetically improbable,
hermenuetically defective, theologically dangerous, and

---

[88]Virginia Mollenkott,"Evangelicalism: A Feminist Perpsective,"
Union Seminary Quarterly Review, 32(1977): 100-101.

educationally disastrous."[89] Stott,[90] former Rector of All Souls Church in London, states that inerrancy cannot be made an indispensable criterion of evangelical orthodoxy.

In view of these differences, it is not unexpected that some "positioning" of each group against the other would occur. However, what we do not need is a hardening of attitudes, premature judgments, irrational applications of convictions which have not been carefully researched, drawing lines of fellowship, or questioning others' motives or faithfulness. What is greatly needed is clear under-standing of each view, biblically and culturally, and a keen awareness of the influences at work in each view.

It is to be expected that both groups will co-exist in evangelical churches. Rather than engage in open warfare, however, what is needed is accurate reflection on both views and responsible interaction. It must be remembered that "women in the church" is not the primary element in the Christian faith, but an important matter of discussion that needs to occur in a context of mutual tolerance.

The quest to find a genuinely Christian view of women is a matter of renewal. This will be discussed in the next chapter. Discomfort with change or the lack of change is not license for unchristian behavior toward those seeking the same goal.

---

[89]J. D. G. Dunn, "The Authority of Scripture According to Scripture," *Churchman* 96 (1982): 104-22, esp. 118.

[90]John Stott, "The Authority of the Scriptures: A Response," *Evangelical Essentials: A Liberal-Evangelical Debate* (Downers Grove, IL: InterVarsity Press, 1989): 101.

4

WOMEN IN THE CHURCH:
REFOCUSING THE APPROACH

Altogether too much discussion of women in the church is conducted with the two opposing extremes of *patriarchalism* and *radical feminism* as the alternatives. This unfortunately results in reinforcing prejudices rather than enhancing communication and balanced thinking. The question is larger than what women can do in worship. The question is, what view of women shall we have? If we are to make progress, we must recast the discussion with more balanced options between these two extremes. *Evangelical feminism* and *hierarchal complementarianism* are viable options deserving further consideration.

There are two agendas in treating the topic of women requiring clarification. *Transformation* and *renewal* have to do with how culture and the church relate. In this connection, we must also discuss precisely how we are to use the Bible and how culture figures in that discussion.

1. *Transformation* or *Renewal?*

A. *Transformation*[1]

Viewing Christianity as a movement that is both informed and changed by its cultural environment, some see the church's task to be that of responding to the contemporary situation, just as the early church did in its own time. That is to say, society is to transform the church. Transformationists assume that knowledge now exists about matters such as sexuality and gender that was unavailable to

---

[1]See discussion in John B. Cobb, Jr., "Revisioning Ministry for a Revisioned Church," *The Spire* 15 (Fall 1992): 14-18.

biblical writers. So, they contend that current Christian thought should adapt to, or be transformed by, this new insight from our culture. Transformationists view sexuality as a God-given gift that must be used responsibly, but they do not feel compelled to accept what biblical writers offer as a definition of responsible sexuality. In this view, both biblical teachings and Christian practice should be evaluated by the new cultural situation.

Obviously, transformation has great appeal to those who feel damaged by patriarchy. Unfortunately, transformationists often allow feminist identity to replace Christian identity. An attack on patriarchy is the dominant focus of transformation—all else is secondary to that agenda. Transformation is fundamental to radical feminism.

It is not surprising, then, that transformation thinking receives much criticism. If biblical norms of Christ and the early church are adjusted by current thought, how are we to identify what is distinctively Christian?   Evangelical feminists assert that contemporary understandings are vital to anyone rethinking the view of women, but caution that transformation without a strong biblical base is in grave danger of soon ceasing to be Christian.

B. *Renewal*

Others think the church should not engage in wholesale accommodation to what is going on in society at large. Instead, society should be renewed in terms of ancient biblical intent.   However, rather than just arbitrarily enforcing selected rules from the past, Christianity should be responsible for implementing biblical principles and values in culturally-responsible ways. While patriarchy has created much suffering, the sexual revolution also has created considerable agony. The answer to the sexual revolution, though, is not found in the rules of traditionalism, but in distinctively Christian principles and ideals.[2]

---

[2]See Monroe Hawley, *The Focus of Our Faith: A New Look at the Restoration Principle* (Nashville: 20th Century Christian, 1985).

The approach of renewal meets the needs of many who turn to the church for perspective and support. It reaffirms much that has been challenged and offers refuge in the midst of agonizing change and confusion in society. Careful research can help the church to sort out what is truly biblical and what is merely cultural in its beliefs and practices. Deeply committed to the search for truth, unswerving in its reliance upon the biblical text, and using credible method with impartial rigor, renewal finds in the Bible an approach to sexuality and gender very different from that of the sexual revolution—an approach with demanding ramifications for church life and homes.

It is my belief that we must subject deeply entrenched beliefs and practices to the rigors of biblical analysis. As not all preferred views and practices will withstand the close scrutiny of honest biblical analysis, this is not an easy task. It demands uncommon integrity in following biblical norms. It also demands that we cease to mandate practices and customs that derive from mere traditionalism. Certainly, intellectual honesty demands that the search for reassurance in times of change not be at the expense of integrity. If the church is to follow biblical principles, true renewal may well demand profound reversal in certain areas.

2. *The Role and Function of the Bible and Culture*

David Wright,[3] professor of Near Eastern and Judaic Studies at Brandeis University, put it succinctly:

> One of our most urgent tasks is the elaboration of a satisfactory doctrine of Scripture for an era of biblical criticism . . . . In particular, we have to work out what it means to be faithful *at one and the same time both* to the doctrinal approach to Scripture as the Word of God *and* to the historical treatment of Scripture as the words of men.

---

[3] David Wright, review of James Barr, *Fundamentalism* (Philadelphia: Westminster, 1977), in *Themelios* 3 (1978): 88. See also Bernard Ramm, *After Fundamentalism: The Future of Evangelical Theology* (San Francisco: Harper and Row, 1983): 101-115.

While it might seem easy enough, agreeing on the approach
to Scripture is no small task for evangelicals. It is no secret
that evangelicals disagree on a variety of topics—free will,
baptism, communion, church administration, to name only a
few. It is their shared idea of the sacredness of Scripture
that seems to hold evangelicals together. Still, there is major
disagreement on whether one should use the Bible to
undergird doctrines in a "proof-texting" way, or whether one
should allow doctrine to emerge from understanding texts in
their literary and historical contexts. Certainly, these
differing views of Scripture lie behind differing views of
women in the church.[4]

The legacy of American evangelicals includes many
good things—evangelism, missions, social service.
However, there is also a deeply-rooted tradition of religious
extremism. In recent evangelical history, this tendency to
extremism has never been far from the surface—particularly
regarding evangelical approaches to Scripture.[5] Particular
approaches to biblical interpretation are held with such vigor
that the examination of alternatives becomes practically
impossible. Noll[6] states, "This spirit, which at its worst
shades over into demagoguery, has not been limited to the
uneducated or the uniformed. . . . It exists wherever blanket
condemnations take the place of respectful attention to
careful study." Extremism stifles fresh examination of
biblical texts and hinders dialogue and communication by
restricting the boundaries of discussion.

---

[4]Significant differences exist among evangelicals regarding the
inspiration, inerrancy, infallibility, and authority of Scripture. See
Mark A. Noll, "Evangelicals and the Study of the Bible," *Evangelicalism and Modern America* (G. Marsden, ed.; Grand Rapids:
Eerdmans, 1984): 198-199.

[5]See Carroll D. Osburn, "The Exegetical Matrix of the Quest for
the Non-Sectarian Ideal," *The Peaceable Kingdom: Essays Favoring
Non-Sectarian Christianity* (Abilene, TX: Restoration Perspectives,
1993): 53-70.

[6]Noll, "Evangelicals and the Study of the Bible," *Evangelicalism
and Modern America*, 110.

As I see it, complementarians and evangelical feminists are both concerned about contemporary cultural matters. Neither can avoid being shaped by those concerns. As Bendroth[7] put it, while a doctoral candidate at Johns Hopkins, "Disparaging but not rejecting an earlier fundamentalist pattern of retreat from 'worldliness,' evangelicals have vacillated between nostalgia for a less secular past and a yearning for social relevance in the present." Certain ideas about women are rooted in nineteenth-century Victorianism. Other prominent ideas are rooted in the philosophy and goals of modern feminism. Often both are embraced rather uncritically—resulting in ideological poles that have set limits of creative discussion among evangelicals.

Much of the animosity and emotional explosiveness among traditionalists regarding the topic of women is because this is not merely a religious topic, but touches a deep and sensitive cultural nerve as well. Both evangelical feminists and complementarians seem to have interpreted the Bible to fit their own agendas. Both too often allow their prejudices to become unquestioned, sacred decrees. It is important for the reader to be aware of the indebtedness to societal concerns in each approach—that is to say, how cultural influences sometimes prejudice viewpoints.

A. *Complementarianism: Its Biblical and Cultural Heritage*

Quebedeaux,[8] campus minister at the Univ. of California at Santa Barbara, correctly protests that "For too long it has been the fault of Ecumenical Liberalism to lump together with pejorative intent all theological conservatives into the worn Fundamentalist Category." Complementarian thinking does emerge from a restrictive fundamentalism,[9]

---

[7]Margaret L. Bendroth, "The Search for 'Women's Role' in American Evangelicalism, 1930-1980," *Evangelicalism and Modern America* (ed. G. Marsden; Grand Rapids: Eerdmans, 1984): 123.

[8]Richard Quebedeaux, *The Young Evangelicals: Revolution in Orthodoxy* (New York: Harper and Row, 1974): 19.

[9]John Stott, "The Authority of the Scriptures: A Response," *Evangelical Essentials: A Liberal-Evangelical Dialogue* (ed. David L.

but is really more evangelical[10] in nature than fundamentalist. It is the curious mix of evangelical and
fundamentalist features that gives this view its distinctive
character.[11] The distinction is important, however, because,
"In general, Evangelicals resent being called Fundamentalists, and Fundamentalists likewise do not usually
appreciate the Evangelical designation."[12]

One must distinguish between complementarianism,
which is a moderate view of hierarchalism, and patriarchalism, which is an extreme view. For instance, complementarians prefer to examine texts in their literary and
historical contexts, whereas patriarchalists prefer the old
method of "proof-texting." Complementarians, unlike patriarchalists, are willing to reassess biblical texts, and have
arrived at very different interpretations of certain passages
regarding women's service roles. Complementarians have
questioned old paradigms and redefined areas of authority,
concluding that some matters are not matters of "leadership,"
but "service," and that women can and should serve in these
capacities. Patriarchalists, on the other hand, restrict

Edwards and John Stott; Downers Grove, IL: InterVarsity Press, 1989):
90-91, lists eight tendencies of the fundamentalist mind-set: 1) general
suspicion of scholarship and science, which sometimes degenerates into
a thorough-going anti-intellectualism, 2) mechanical-dictation theory of
biblical inspiration, 3) reverence for KJV translation of the Bible, 4)
literalistic interpretation of Scripture, with insufficient recognition of
genre, 5) separatist ecclesiology, 6) cultural imprisonment, 7) denial of
social implications of the gospel, and 8) premillennialism.

[10]L. Harold DeWolf, *Present Trends in Christian Thought* (New
York: Association Press, 1960): 45-47, lists characteristics of
evangelicalism: 1) the Bible is authoritative, but not inerrant, 2)
biblical texts must be studied in their literary and historical context
from the original languages, 3) a strong concern for social problems.

[11]See Gordon Harland, "Evangelicalism and Fundamentalism,"
Touchstone 5 (1987): 26-42; George Marsden, "From Fundamentalism
to Evangelicalism: A Historical Analysis," *The Evangelicals* (ed. D.
Wells and J. Woodbridge; Grand Rapids: Baker, 1975).

[12]Quebedeaux, *The Young Evangelicals: Revolution in
Orthodoxy*, 19.

women's roles. Complementarians recognize problems regarding views of women in our society beyond those of patriarchal concern. They also emphasize mutuality in male/female relationships more than do patriarchalists. They deal with single women in the church more than do patriarchalists. So, while complementarians advocate hierarchy, they are considerably unlike patriarchalists.

Still, with hierarchalism as the controlling principle, both complementarians and patriarchalists staunchly maintain traditional interpretations of certain texts having to do with male *authority* in the home and the church. The view of women among both patriarchalists and complementarians is shaped largely by the assumption that there is a divinely-ordained hierarchical order in creation—God, Christ, man, woman. However, the hierarchical model of complementarians is, as Pulley[13] puts it, "a less structured and certainly less demeaning hierarchy than the traditional model of male domination and female subjection, which cannot under any circumstances be considered Christian."

The complementarian view is shaped largely by reliance on the Bible. Noticeably absent is any stated support for "proof texting" of Scripture that is so common among patriarchalists. Their attention to literary and historical context does not differ theoretically from evangelical feminists. It is not unexpected that there are tremendous differences in interpretation from the paternalists, but given their method of interpretation one might expect an appreciable degree of similarity with evangelical feminist exegesis. In fact, a remarkable similarity does exist in the interpretation of many texts. However, on all texts treating authority or public worship there is massive disagreement between complementarians and evangelical feminists.

In response to contemporary cultural concerns, complementarians have rid themselves of patriarchal control

---

[13]Kathy Pulley, "Women in the Church in Recent Discussion," *Essays on Women in Earliest Christianity* (ed. Carroll D. Osburn; Joplin, MO: College Press, 1993): 9.

in many dimensions of public life, emphasized differences in the sexes, and stressed equality. It is more than interesting that the complementarian view created authority as necessary in the home and church, but not in society. This means that, other than in the church and home, women can have authority over men in various spheres of life. Even public roles for women in the church are emphasized considerably more than among patriarchalists. However, hierarchical assumptions demand restriction of preaching and church administration to men. Generally, women are not permitted to teach Bible or doctrine to men. Concerning the church and home, then, complementarians have inherited from their fundamentalist past an aspect of hierarchalism from which they cannot let go— and which is at the very center of the current debate. In the early twentieth century, the ancestors of today's evangelicals responded typically to shifting sexual mores and increasingly public roles for women by perpetuating a traditional, Victorian model of femininity and an even older view of hierarchalism rooted in centuries of tradition in "believers' churches."[14]

While denouncing feminists for permitting culture to become their authority instead of the Bible, complementarians are influenced by culture more than they would appear to admit. They support traditional hierarchalism without question, yet complementarians pronounce judgment against contemporary culture without performing the embarrassing task of also proclaiming judgment against their own traditionalist *status quo*. It is good that complementarians herald the importance of Scripture. However, one must recognize the influence of tradition upon complementarianism lest another profound instance occur of culture setting the agenda for the church rather than vice versa.

---

[14]See pp. 6-17 above, as well as Bendroth, "The Search for Women's Role," *Evangelicalism in Modern America*, 122. George Marsden, *Reforming Fundamentalism* (Grand Rapids: Eerdmans, 1987): 123, observes that, "keeping women in their place, though honoring them there, had become part of the fundamentalist ethos." See also Donald Dayton, *Discovering an Evangelical Heritage* (New York: Harper and Row, 1976): 22.

B. *The Dual Heritage of Evangelical Feminism*

Evangelical feminism also emerges from the patriarchal legacy and retains some of its features, such as acceptance of the authority of the Bible. Biblical authority, long a defining criterion among evangelicals, is crucial in distinguishing major feminist approaches.[15] Accepting biblical authority, evangelical feminists are involved in biblical interpretation and application.[16] Evangelical feminists reject "proof-texting" and use the historical-critical method in exegesis.[17] Storkey,[18] lecturer at Oak Hill College in London, says that evangelical feminists "hold tenaciously to the authority of the Scriptures, although [they] challenge many attitudes and ideas which people claim to have derived from them."

In strong reaction against the patriarchal legacy, evangelical feminists have accepted certain features of the feminist legacy. Egalitarianism becomes their controlling principle. So, in application of the literary-historical critical method, there is a willingness—even eagerness—to reexamine texts having to do with women, certainly those involving service, but especially those having to do with *authority*. Evangelical feminists believe that the Bible, when properly understood, supports their egalitarian view.

Evangelical feminism is, by its own admission, shaped largely by the assumption that oppression in any form is ungodly and would not be commended by the Bible. Quite rightly, evangelical feminists have highlighted major societal problems involving the view and treatment of women. Evangelical feminists draw extensively upon the work of

---

[15]See Elaine Storkey, *What's Right With Feminism?* (Grand Rapids: Eerdmans, 1985).

[16]See Esther Byle Bruland, "Evangelical and Feminist Ethics: Complex Solidarities," *Journal of Religious Ethics* 17 (1989): 139-160.

[17]See further, Mark Noll, *Between Faith and Criticism: Evangelicals, Scholarship, and the Bible in America* (San Francisco: Harper and Row, 1986).

[18]Storkey, *What's Right With Feminism?* 121.

other feminists[19] and attempt to integrate feminist concerns
and perspectives into Christian theology and ethics.
Egalitarianism is definitely shared as a controlling principle.
However, the relationship between evangelical feminists and
other feminists is an uneasy one. Evangelical feminists are
disenchanted with radical feminism, for whom "the entire
Christian tradition is overwhelmingly sexist. The gospel is
bad news and there is no way of recovering any part of it for
women."[20]   On the other hand, while radical biblical
feminists (such as Letty Russell and Elisabeth Schüssler
Fiorenza) still regard the Bible as significant, they differ with
evangelical feminists as to *how* the Bible is authoritative.
So, while they seek theoretical insight and social support
from other types of feminism, evangelical feminists often
face challenges to their positions and commitments by other
feminists. As biblical feminists, evangelical feminists face
challenges in discerning what they can borrow from other
strands of feminism without compromising their basic
biblical views and commitments.

To its credit, evangelical feminism is also strongly
shaped by the biblical text. They have rightly called for
responsible reinvestigation of Scriptures that might have
acquired meaning in patriarchal circles merely through
custom and tradition rather than through patient and
controlled exegesis. The appeal to the Bible by
complementarians and evangelical feminists does not differ
substantially in exegetical method, but rather in preconceived
notions brought to the text. It is important to remember this
commonality in the approach to biblical exposition, and to
center attention on their different presuppositions.

However, the theory is better than the practice.
Altogether too much evangelical feminist exegesis is colored
by the lens of egalitarianism through which texts are
examined. A balance between feminism and evangelicalism

---

[19]See Josephine Donovan, *Feminist Theory: The Intellectual
Traditions of American Feminism* (New York: Ungar, 1985), on
various strands of feminism.

[20]Storkey, *What's Right With Feminism?* 121.

would be difficult to maintain under any circumstance. Still, while denouncing others for permitting traditional culture to function authoritatively instead of the Bible, evangelical feminists have fallen into a basic contradiction by unwittingly permitting contemporary culture to function authoritatively for them as well.

It has been noted that the largely unquestioning support evangelical feminists gave to the philosophy and goals of secular feminism allowed them "to pronounce judgment on traditional culture without making them perform the embarrassing task of proclaiming God's judgment on the new *status quo*."[21] Also Liftin[22] points out even more directly that, "Since the New Testament seems to . . . be the alleged rather than the real impetus for the movement, . . . the true impetus behind evangelical feminism is not the spirit of the New Testament, but rather the spirit of the present age." Quebedeaux[23] concludes, "the emergence of evangelical feminism presents a clear example of the influence of trends in the wider culture on contemporary evangelical Christianity—a profound instance of the world setting the agenda for the church, rather than vice versa."

3. *Presuppositions in Biblical Study*

If both have respect for biblical authority and advocate rigorous biblical analysis, why do conclusions of complementarians and evangelical feminists differ?

Although some appeal for an allegedly neutral, unbiased approach, presuppositions are involved at every level of

---

[21]John Alexander, "Are Women People?" *What You Should Know About Women's Lib* (ed. Miriam G. Moran; New Canaan, CN: Keats, 1974): 33. Cf. similar critique of complementarians on p. 94.

[22]A. Duane Liftin, "Evangelical Feminism: Why Traditionalists Reject It," *Bibliotheca Sacra* 136 (1979): 267.

[23]Richard Quebedeaux, *The Worldly Evangelicals* (San Francisco: Harper and Row, 1978): 126.

biblical exegesis. As Stanton[24] of the Univ. of London observes, "presuppositions are far more influential in New Testament scholarship than disagreements over method." Church history, in fact, may be explained to a large extent by the presuppositions adopted in different times and various circumstances.[25]

Bultmann,[26] the most prominent NT writer of the century, chided, "Every exegesis that is guided by dogmatic prejudices does not hear what the text says, but only lets the latter say what it wants to hear." However, "prejudice" and "presuppositions" are not the same thing and demand careful distinction. Stanton[27] observes correctly that one must

> distinguish between the personal factors which affect the judgment of the interpreter (prejudices) and the philosophical or theological starting point which an interpreter takes and which he usually shares with some others (presuppositions).

Of course, prejudice occurs in all areas of life. Regarding biblical study, Flatt,[28] professor at Harding Graduate School of Religion in Memphis, TN, illustrates

---

[24]Graham M. Stanton, "Presuppositions in New Testament Criticism," *New Testament Interpretation: Essays in Principles and Methods* (ed. H. Marshall; Grand Rapids: Eerdmans, 1977): 60.

[25]See G. Ebeling, *The Word of God and Tradition* (London: Collins, 1968): 11-31. See also F. F. Bruce, "The History of New Testament Study," *New Testament Interpretation*, 21-59. Carl E. Braaten, *History and Hermeneutics* (Philadlephia: Westminster, 1966): 52, notes that, "Today, hermeneutical philosophy has made exegetes self-conscious about their presuppositions."

[26]Rudolf Bultmann, "Is Exegesis Without Presuppositions Possible?" *Existence and Faith: Shorter Writings of Rudolf Bultmann* (ed. and trans. J. Smogden; New York: Meridien, 1960): 290.

[27]Stanton, "Presuppositions in NT Criticism," *New Testament Interpretation*, 61.

[28]Bill Flatt, "The Function of Presuppositions and Attitudes in Biblical Interpretation," *Biblical Interpretation: Principles and Practices —Studies in honor of Jack Pearl Lewis* (ed. F. Kearley, E. Myers, T. Hadley; Grand Rapids: Baker, 1986): 61.

> A husband, for example, may have a dominant attitude toward people in general. By nature, he either leads, dominates, or is inflexible. He may then come to a biblical text on family leadership, read it through his domineering glasses, and conclude that he has a biblical mandate to boss, to push, to coerce his wife, even to the point of 'commanding' her love.

If one's prejudice is so deep-seated that one reaches a conclusion before the evidence is considered, then prejudice renders the accurate understanding of a text impossible.

Presuppositions, on the other hand, are pre-understandings that are neutral regarding historicity and prejudice.[29] It is possible to be aware of and work carefully with one's presuppositions. However, it is not possible to analyze a text without approaching it from some particular angle. Certain presuppositions lie behind that initial viewpoint out of which one addresses the text.[30] For instance, Stanton[31] suggests these presuppositions: 1) knowledge of the history of exegesis provides a framework for careful analysis, 2) the historical-critical method keeps assumptions in check, and 3) willingness to allow one's pre-understandings to be modified or even completely reshaped by interaction with the text itself allows the text to be authoritative. While these particular presuppositions are not accepted universally, presuppositions cannot be avoided. However, they must not be allowed to dominate the text, but to serve as guiding principles that are continually adjusted in terms of interaction with the text.

---

[29]E. D. Hirsch, Jr., *Validity in Interpretation* (New Haven: Yale Univ. Press, 1967): 261. See Peter Cotterell and Max Turner, *Linguistics & Biblical Interpretation* (Downers Grove, IL: InterVarsity Press, 1989): 90-97; and Anthony Thiselton, "The New Hermeneutic," *A Guide to Contemporary Hermeneutics: Major Trends in Biblical Interpretation* (ed. D. K. McKim; Grand Rapids: Eerdmans, 1986): 90-97.

[30]Stanton, "Presuppositions in NT Criticism," *New Testament Interpretation*, 66, notes, "The attempt to interpret the New Testament from a neutral detached standpoint with methods which were assumed to be strictly scientific has largely been abandoned."

[31]Ibid., pp. 68-69.

For example, among the presuppositions to biblical study common to both evangelical feminists and complementarians are the following:

1. Religion is rooted in history rather than just in human experience. What happened in the past is authoritative for contemporary faith and practice. As a philosophical base, existentialism (which disregards history) is not acceptable.

2. The biblical text should be approached with faith rather than doubt, realizing that further information might require adjustment of one's understanding. One accepts a biblical statement unless data require unbelief, rather than not believing the text unless certain data require belief. As a starting point for reflection, skepticism is not acceptable.

3. The supernatural exists and God is ultimate. While some believe that a finite mind cannot prove the existence of the supernatural, it can assess the possibility and probability of the supernatural and conclude through available evidence that to believe in the supernatural is credible. Atheism is not acceptable.

4. Though the human mind has limitations in its ability to comprehend, some truth is objective and can be known. While it is true that some truth is relative to a given time or place, not all truth is relative. Relativism is unacceptable.

5. God has revealed Himself in history. Naturalism is not acceptable.

6. The Bible is a record of part of that revelation. While written by various individuals using their own language, emotions, experiences, etc., the Bible is authoritative. "Mechanical dictation of Scriptures" and bibliolatry are unacceptable.

7. One should consider all the Bible, lest distortion result from undue selectivity. A "canon within the canon" is unacceptable.

8. One should understand each text in terms of the historical circumstances at the time of its composition, its author and the readers for whom it was intended, the intellectual milieu from which it originates, and its relation to the developing Judeo-Christian heritage. Casual intuition is an unacceptable basis for interpretation of texts.

9. One must read each text according to appropriate method that recognizes literary and historical contexts. The task of exegesis is to discover the author's intended meaning in a given text and to set that text clearly into the context of the early church. Only when one understands what a text *meant* will one be able to understand with clarity what are its implications for the present. Both "proof-texting" and deconstruction attempt to read texts apart from their historical setting and are unacceptable.

10. The task of Christianity is to create a viable life-style in which biblical principles and values are lived in culturally responsible ways. Antiquarianism is unacceptable.

With such presuppositions, both evangelical feminists and complementarians share common ground. Such presuppositions are, in fact, at the base of the *conservative* mind-set.[32] On such bases, both viewpoints find common rejection of the quite different presuppositions of radical feminists that are more *liberal*[33] in nature, as well as those of patriarchalists which are decidedly *fundamentalist*.[34]

---

[32]See, among others, I. Howard Marshall, *New Testament Interpretation: Essays on Principles and Practice* (Grand Rapids: Eerdmans, 1977); Gordon D. Fee, *New Testament Exegesis* (Philadelphia: Westminster, 1983); and, at the very practical level, Fee and Douglas Stewart, *How to Read the Bible for All Its Worth* (Grand Rapids: Zondervan, 1982). See also Roger Nicole and J. Ramsey Michaels, *Inerrancy and Common Sense* (Grand Rapids: Baker, 1980). For the shift from fundamentalism to conservatism, see Richard Quebedeaux, *The Young Evangelicals: Revolution in Orthodoxy* (New York: Harper and Row, 1974).

[33]See W. G. Kümmel, *The New Testament: The History of the Investigation of Its Problems* (trans. S. McL. Gilmour and H. C. Kee;

However, evangelical feminists and complementarians differ in one major way that accounts for the differences in their understanding of texts pertaining to women: the former presuppose egalitarianism and the latter hierarchalism. While each would like to see its view as the *conclusion* of biblical investigation, it is mandatory that each understand that not only is the other view a presupposition, *but so is its own*! In other words, differences between evangelical feminists and complementarians should be addressed, not in terms of differing understandings of biblical texts, but in terms of prejudices of egalitarianism and hierarchalism that are brought to the text masquerading as presuppositions. Each group, reading the text through the "colored glasses" of its own preconceived prejudices, concludes what it already believes. The discussion is at an impasse. How shall we continue?

4. *Reassessing Hermeneutics*

Both complementarians and evangelical feminists take the Bible seriously. A question exists, though, whether exegesis in either perspective is "objective" or "subjective." Each group views its exegesis as objective and reality-oriented, but brands the other as subjective *eisegesis* that reads its views into the text. It is true that vested interests of a given perspective can distort the actual meaning of the text. In a sense, however, all readings of the text are influenced by the interests and concerns (both conscious and unconscious) of the interpreter—a fact well known in the history of biblical scholarship. There is no such thing as an

---

New York: Abingdon, 1972); W. Schmithals, *An Introduction to the Theology of Rudolf Bultmann* (2nd ed.; trans. J. Bowden; Minneapolis: Augsburg, 1967); J. Macquarrie, *An Existentialist Theology: A Comparison of Heidegger and Bultmann* (London: SCM, 1955); Joseph Fletcher, *Moral Responsibility: Situation Ethics at Work* (Philadelphia: Westminster, 1967).

[34]See R. A. Torrey and A. C. Dixon, ed., *The Fundamentals* (4th ed.; Los Angeles: Bible Institute of Los Angeles, 1917); J. G. Machen, *Christianity and Liberalism* (Grand Rapids: Eerdmans, 1923); Harold Lindsell, *The Battle for the Bible* (Grand Rapids: Zondervan, 1976).

unbiased interpreter who looks with pure objectivity on centuries of data and pronounces definitive interpretations. Rather, public evidence, logical argument, reasonable hypotheses, and intellectual assessment form the basis of a consensus regarding what is acceptable and what is unacceptable.

In view of the bristling controversy surrounding women in the church, it would be folly to assume that all any well-intentioned reader need do is open the Bible, gather the pertinent texts, and draw obvious conclusions. An important concern emerges when competent scholars who are genuinely committed to the Christian faith draw from the Bible incompatible positions.

> That evangelicals, all claiming a common Biblical norm, are reaching contradictory theological formulations on many of the major issues they are addressing suggests the problematic nature of their present understanding of theological interpretation. To argue that the Bible is authoritative, but to be unable to come to anything like agreement on what it says (even with those who share an evangelical commitment), is self-defeating.[35]

Is it possible to arrive at a consensus? For some, the impasse is desirable and comfortable. For others, moving beyond the impasse is necessary, but requires two things: 1) egalitarianism and hierarchalism must be dismissed as prejudices that limit biblical interpretation, and 2) they must be replaced by a method of interpretation based upon responsible presuppositions.

While other approaches may have some usefulness, this writer agrees with Hirsch[36] that the historical-critical method is a useful tool for the correct interpretation of ancient texts.

---

[35]Robert K. Johnston, *Evangelicals at an Impasse: Biblical Authority in Perspective* (Atlanta: John Knox, 1979): vii-viii.

[36]See E. D. Hirsch, *Validity in Interpretation* (New Haven: Yale Univ. Press, 1967).

The historical-critical method also has certain limitations.[37] Stuhlmacher,[38] professor at Tübingen, who advocates the method, stresses its limitations and laments that it is conducted all too often apart from Christian faith. Nevertheless, proper biblical interpretation must begin with and be guided by the original, historical, contextual meaning of the text.[39] Even so, the ancient meaning is not an end in itself, but must be brought to bear upon contemporary culture in a responsible way. Let's look at this approach more carefully.

A. The "meaning" of a text is the meaning intended by the author within a particular literary and historical setting. Although not without difficulty on occasion, it is possible to recover such meaning(s) with reasonable success. This approach does "call into question any hermeneutical approach—existential, devotional, experiential, literary, psychological, structuralist, post-structuralist, or theological—that would argue that the primary locus of meaning for a biblical text is other than in the text itself."[40]

Recognizing that biblical texts were written in and to particular historical situations, it is necessary that one engage in historical-critical exegesis.[41] Swartley,[42] professor at a Mennonite Seminary in Elkhart, IN, says one is more likely to hear the intended meaning on controversial issues when:

---

[37]See discussion in Peter Rhea Jones, "Biblical Hermeneutics," *Review and Expositor* 72 (1975): 139-147, esp. 142-145; and E. F. Scott, "The Limitations of the Historical Method," *Studies in Early Christianity* (ed. S. J. Case; New York: Century, 1928): 3-18.

[38]Peter Stuhlmacher, *Historical Criticism and Theological Interpretation of Scripture: Toward a Hermeneutic of Consent* (Philadelphia: Fortress, 1977).

[39]David M. Scholer, "Issues in Biblical Interpretation," *Evangelical Quarterly* 88 (1988): 10.

[40]Scholer, *Evangelical Quarterly* (1988): 8-9.

[41]See Edgar Krentz, *The Historical-Critical Method* (Philadelphia: Fortress, 1975).

[42]Willard M. Swartley, *Slavery, Sabbath, War & Women: Case Issues in Biblical Interpretation* (Scottdale, PA: Herald Press, 1983): 23.

1. The historical and cultural contexts of specific texts are considered seriously.

2. Diversity within Scripture is acknowledged, thus leading to a recognition that intra-canonical dialogue must be heard and assessed.

3. The basic moral and theological principles of the entire Scripture are given priority over statements which stand in tension with these principles or with other specific texts on the subject.

Conversely, according to Swartley,[43] one is less likely to discover the intended meaning when:

1. Numerous texts, occurring from here and there, are strung together with disregard for their cultural and historical particularity.

2. The interpreter assumes a "flat view" of biblical authority in which all texts, regardless of their original context, must be harmonized into one, rational, propositional truth.

3. Specific texts are used legalistically.

Since Christianity is a historical religion, it matters greatly what a statement meant in its original setting.[44]

---

[43]Ibid.

[44]See Donald K. McKim, ed., *A Guide to Contemporary Hermeneutics: Major Trends in Biblical Interpretation* (Grand Rapids: Eerdmans, 1986). The approach common throughout the past century in Restoration use of the Bible to locate "commands, necessary inferences, and approved examples" is inappropriate. Certain commands, of course, are determinative; however, some [veils, holy kiss] are culture-specific. Inferences are not always trustworthy, due to the fallibility of the one doing the inferring, and there are many approved examples in the Bible that are commonly agreed not to be binding examples. See Michael W. Casey, *The Development of Necessary Inference in the Hermeneutics of the Disciples of Christ/Churches of Christ* (Pittsburgh: Univ. of Pittsburgh Press,

B. Today's interpreters are enmeshed in their own particular
historical and cultural contexts that differ in certain ways
from the ancient settings.   How significantly one's
theological, ecclesiastical, social, economic, and cultural
experiences shape one's biblical interpretations cannot be
overestimated.[45] It simply will not do to hope that somehow
a strong belief in the authority of the Bible will guarantee an
objective, correct, or authoritative interpretation.   There
exists no absolute way to prevent one's subjectivity from
overwhelming one's objectivity—but it is possible to
monitor and control prejudices, biases, and the cultural
conditionedness of interpreters.   Scholer, now of Fuller
Theological Seminary, proposes these steps:[46] 1) the
historical meaning of the text provides the boundaries of
contextual exegesis, 2) the interplay between the historic
Christian faith and contemporary society provides controls
over interpretations, 3) identification of specific historical,
theological, sociological, and ecclesiastical factors in the
experience of the interpreter creates opportunity to evaluate
those factors and whether they facilitate respect for the
integrity of the text or create misreadings, and 4) each
generation must examine texts afresh lest uncritical
acceptance and undue influence of past traditions become
more determinative than the biblical texts themselves.

Even then, one must ask whether the imperative of a
passage is directed toward a specific situation in the ancient
setting that is not directly relevant for contemporary
Christians.[47]   How, then, does one distinguish between
matters that may be culturally relative and those which have
universal normativity?   Scholer[48] posits these useful
guidelines:

1986); idem, "The Origins of the Hermeneutics of the Churches of
Christ," *Restoration Quarterly* 31 (1989): 75-91 and 193-205.
    [45]Scholer, *Evangelical Quarterly* (1988): 11.
    [46]Scholer, *Evangelical Quarterly* (1988): 13.
    [47]Lyle Vander Broek, "Women and the Church: Approaching
Difficult Passages," *Reformed Review* 38 (1985): 225-231.
    [48]Scholer, *Evangelical Quarterly* (1988): 19-20.

1. The further one moves from the central message of the Bible, the greater the possibility of cultural relativity. [Compare resurrection with holy kiss.]

2. Assess the relative amount of emphasis given to a topic. The possibility of cultural relativity increases as the amount of treatment decreases. [Compare baptism with footwashing.]

3. One should distinguish normative teachings from descriptive narratives that must always be assessed in terms of normative teaching. [Compare 1 John 3:17 (whoever has possessions must help others) with Luke 12:33 (command to sell all possessions).]

4. Note when a teaching on a particular point has a uniform and consistent witness and when there are differences. Different terminology, emphases, or structure increase the likelihood of cultural relativity. [Compare biblical teaching on love with the location and format of early Christian worship.]

5. Distinguish between principles and applications. A culturally-relative application may be supported by an absolute principle, yet the application may not be absolute. [Note 1 Pet 2:18-21, submission of slaves to masters is supported by the principle of suffering for good, yet slavery not condoned nor condemned.]

6. Within the canon, reversal may indicate cultural and/or historical relativity. [Compare the commission in Matt 10:5-6 (to go to Jews only) with 28:16-20 (to go to the entire world).]

7. The degree to which a writer agrees with a cultural situation in which there is only one option increases the possibility of cultural relativity. [Note statements on homosexuality (prominent in society but not shared by all) involve principle; however, statements on slavery (a cultural norm providing only one frame of reference) likely involve more cultural relativity.]

8. Compare the biblical setting with our own cultural
setting. Significant differences may uncover
culturally-limited applications of biblical texts.
[Compare prohibitions against eating meat offered to
idols (1 Cor 8-11) with our own culture today.]

Certainly, attempts to provide a "safe" hermeneutic that
"boxes" the Bible into convenient categories have been the
"Achilles heel" of much fundamentalist exegesis. In
abandoning their fundamentalist past, evangelicals must, as
Wright[49] put it (p. 89 above), "work out what it means to be
faithful *at one and the same time both* to the doctrinal
approach to Scripture as the Word of God *and* to the
historical treatment of Scripture as the words of men."

The two opposing views of evangelical feminists and
complementarians form the context of evangelical debate on
the role of women. With equal sincerity, each view charges
the other with worshipping the Baals of culture rather than
the God of Scripture.[50] If these two views are to avoid
unnecessary polarization, this theological stalemate requires
a redefined discussion that works in terms of significant
areas of agreement and the salient unresolved issues.

A keen awareness of the influence of presuppositions
and cultural prejudice and the rigorous application of
exegetical methodology are mandatory. There is no room
for exegetical or hermeneutical oddities. We are not
acultural. Strong feelings exist about what is "right." Still,
changes are occurring in our culture. The question is not
"Will we change?" but "How shall we change?" The church
can, and should, have a meaningful message to contemporary culture regarding the Christian view of women. For
this to happen, there must be a genuine willingness to
investigate and to think, as well as to admit and clarify
presuppositions and cultural biases that affect interpretation.

---

[49]David Wright, review of Barr's *Fundamentalism*, in *Themelios*
3 (1978): 88.

[50]Bendroth, "The Search for Women's Role," *Evangelicalism in
Modern America*, 134.

5

GENESIS 1-3

One already interprets a text through "cultural glasses" as soon as one reads from the Bible—especially from one of the English translations.[1] It may well be that the most important factor in biblical interpretation is the role of culture both for the ancient biblical writers and for the modern interpreter. As Noll[2] observes,

> It is all too easy to allow forms of thought which appear to be only common sense in our century, but which are largely foreign to the world of Scripture, to dictate interpretations of what the biblical writers must have intended. But it is also a temptation for scholars to let the valid fruits of their empathetic research languish for fear of upsetting the dearly held commonsensical opinions of the wider evangelical community.

Far from being foolproof, the attempt to understand texts in their ancient literary and historical settings is still basic to interpreting the Bible. In this connection, we cannot permit prejudices to determine biblical interpretation. We must, however, work with the principles in mind that we have just discussed. So open your Bible and let's reexamine principal biblical texts having to do with women in the church.[3]

---

[1]See Gordon D. Fee and Douglas Stewart, *How to Read the Bible for All Its Worth* (Grand Rapids: Zondervan, 1982): 15-27.

[2]Mark Noll, "Evangelicals and the Study of the Bible," *Evangelicalism and Modern America* (ed. G. Marsden; Grand Rapids: Eerdmans, 1984): 118.

[3]See Carroll Osburn, ed., *Essays on Woman in Earliest Christianity* (2 vols.; Joplin, MO: College Press, 1993, 1995), for detailed discussion of most of the biblical and early Christian texts.

A Re-examination of Genesis 1-3

One might get the impression from current literature that the principal texts pertaining to women in the church are Gal 3:28, 1 Cor 14:34-35, and 1 Tim 2:13-14. However, there are other principal texts. How one understands Gen 1-3, for instance, is crucial in discussion of this topic. As might be expected, the opening chapters of Genesis are understood variously, and differences in views on this text between evangelical feminists and complementarians are of great significance.

1. *Genesis 1-3—The Evangelical Feminist Perspective*

Evangelical feminists[4] suggest that God's intent for the relationship between men and women centers on Gen 1-2 and Jesus Christ. Gen 1:26-31 reveals the pattern God used in creating men and women, their work and responsibilities, and God's response to them. Both men and women are made "in his own image."[5] God gave to both men and women the same responsibilities and commands. "Women like men were to have 'dominion'. . . . Women like men, were to 'subdue' the earth."[6] The term translated "man" in Gen 1:26-27 comes from the Hebrew *'adam* (Adam) and refers to "mankind." In Gen 2, the term is also translated "man," but refers to one specific male who in most trans-lations of Gen 3 is named Adam. In Gen 5:2, the term (translated "man") refers to both the first man and the first woman—Adam and Eve.

Gen 2 relates a separate creation story. God placed man in a garden and told him to work the garden and to name the

---

[4]See Alvera and Berkeley Mickelsen, "Male and Female in the Garden of Eden," *The Standard* (1983): 32, 34.

[5]Paul K. Jewett, *Man as Male and Female* (Grand Rapids: Eerdmans, 1975): 21, 33-40. Aída Besançon Spencer, *Beyond the Curse—Women Called to Ministry* (Nashville: T. Nelson, 1985): 20-23, concludes, "The image of God is a double image."

[6]Mickelsens, "Male and Female . . .," *The Standard*, 32.

animals.[7] However, man's incompleteness soon becomes
apparent. The purpose of parading the animals before Adam
was to demonstrate that no lower form of life would
adequately complete him.[8] So God says in 2:18, "I will
make a helper suitable for him." Taking some of man's own
body, God "built" the woman. Gen 2:23 reads, "she shall
be called Woman (Heb., *ishah*) because she was taken out of
man (Heb., *ish*)." Made of the "same stuff," she was the
equal that God knew man needed to share in the
responsibilities. These two individuals would "become one
flesh" (marriage). Nothing suggests that "helper" indicates
woman was created as "secondary" to man in a hierarchy.[9]
"Helper" (Heb., *ezer*) often refers to God as "helper," but
one cannot infer from this that God is "under the authority
of" or "secondary" to humans. "Helper" rather denotes
"precision" in fitting the needs and deficiencies in man.[10]

How, then, did the sinful world that followed arrive at a
male dominance that pervades nearly every non-Christian
religion and much of Christianity and which has brought
incalculable suffering to women through the centuries? This
becomes clear in Gen 3, where sin enters God's created
world—damaging the relationship between God and humans
and between male and female. Driven from the garden, and

---

[7]Scott E. McClelland, "The New Reality in Christ: Perspectives
from Biblical Studies," *Gender Matters—Women's Studies for the
Christian Community* (ed. J. S. Hagen; Grand Rapids: Zondervan,
1990): 55-56, argues that priority of creation does not denote
superiority, for animals preceded humans, but are not said to be
superior, and that when Paul used an "order of creation" argument in
1 Cor 11:8-9, he quickly added a point to assert the mutuality of man
and woman in vv. 11-12.

[8]Gretchen Gaebelein Hull, *Equal to Serve: Women and Men in
the Church and Home* (Old Tappan, NJ: F. H. Revell, 1987): 154-155.

[9]See Mary J. Evans, *Women in the Bible* (Downers Grove, IL:
InterVarsity Press, 1983): 14-17; and Spencer, *Beyond the Curse*, 23-
29, for argument that Gen 2 focuses on the mutuality of the two sexes
as co-sovereigns.

[10]Hull, *Equal to Serve*, 180-183; Jewett, *Man as Male and
Female*, 24-40.

thus from God's presence, the harmony God intended
between man and woman becomes disharmony. Male
domination enters the picture.

Although hierarchalists assume that Satan approached
Eve because of her weakness and gullibility, one must
remember that God gave the original prohibition concerning
the tree to Adam, not Eve (Gen 2:17). However, hierarchalists believe that Eve's inadequate understanding led her
to doubt the prohibition. Adam, though, seems not to have
hesitated for a moment (Gen 3:6), and Paul holds Adam
responsible for the entrance of sin into the world (Rom 5:12-
14; 1 Cor 15:21-22). Rather than not asserting his
"headship," evangelical feminists argue that the problem is
that Adam improperly taught the prohibition to Eve.[11]

The essence of the first sin in Eden is the desire for
power (Gen 3:5). Nothing suggests that they violated some
so-called "divine order of male dominance"—rather, their sin
was disobedience and wanting to be like God (3:5-6, 11).
The desire for dominance over others is the root of much
moral evil—war, slavery, murder, theft, cruelty, etc. "He
shall rule over you" (Gen 3:16) comes as a result of the Fall
and was not part of God's original intention.

According to evangelical feminists, Christ came to free
humankind from all such bondage. No separate moral
principles, commands, rewards, or promises are given for
men and women. All are called to servanthood and to be
submissive to one another. Gen 1-2 clearly teaches that
every person is made in the image of God, and shares the
same commands and responsibilities in this world. Christ
came to redeem people from the curse of sin that began in
Gen 3. Evangelical feminists, then, say that Gen 3 is
"descriptive" of the human dilemma, an unfortunate result of
the fall of humanity and not at all designed by God.

---

[11]McClelland, "The New Reality in Christ," *Gender Matters*, 57-
58, further argues that Adam's sin was not in "listening to his wife" as
a female (Gen 3:17), but in "listening" to the *content* of what she said.

2. *Hierarchal Complementarian View of Gen 1-3*

Piper[12] contends that inherent in maleness and female-
ness are different responsibilities of leadership. By virtue of
maleness, men have greater responsibility for leadership in
relation to women than women do to men (Gen 1-3).[13]
While Gen 1:27 indicates that man and woman are both
created in God's image and neither is a lesser being,[14] Gen
2-3 shows God's pre-Fall intent was that man should
provide leadership and woman should honor that leadership
as man's submissive helper.[15]

Ortland argues first that man was created before woman
(Gen 2:7; see 1 Tim 2:13).[16] Second, God gave man moral
instruction that was not repeated for Eve, leaving Adam
responsible for providing leadership (Gen 2:15-17). Third,
woman was created as a "helper," a suitable assistant in the

---

[12]John Piper, "Satan's Design in Reversing Male Leadership
Role," *The Standard* (1983): 33, 35.

[13]Raymond C. Ortlund, Jr., "Male-Female Equality and Male
Headship—Genesis 1-3," *Recovering Biblical Manhood and Womanhood* (Wheaton: Crossway, 1991): 102.

[14]Susan T. Foh, *Women and the Word of God* (Phillipsburg, NJ:
Presbyterian and Reformed Pub. Co., 1979): 51, 59. Ortlund, "Male-
Female Equality and Male Headship—Genesis 1-3," *Recovering
Biblical Manhood and Womanhood*, 98, detects "hints" and "whispers"
of male headship in Gen 1, but James B. Hurley, *Man and Woman in
Biblical Perspective* (Grand Rapids: Zondervan, 1981): 206, notes, "The
interpreter may not seek to read into the text any implications about the
headship, subordination, or equality of the sexes. To make Genesis 1
speak about such issues is a matter of projection of prejudice rather than
of extraction of textual meaning."

[15]Ortlund, "Male-Female Equality and Male Headship—Genesis
1-3," *Recovering Biblical Manhood and Womanhood*, 95, says, ". . . as
Genesis 1-3 go, so goes the whole Biblical debate."

[16]Foh, *Women and the Word of God*, 61, argues that "though the
woman's being created second and from and for the man does not
indicate inferiority, it does indicate a difference in the way they are to
function. The woman is created to be a help to her husband; her
function is dependent upon him." See also Hurley, *Man and Woman in
Biblical Perspective*, 207-209.

garden—implying man's leadership (2:20). Fourth, man
"names" woman (Gen 2:23), implying male leadership.[17]
Fifth, Satan's temptation of the woman involved urging her
to usurp the role of spokesman and leader (Gen 3:1), and
further that the man was present during the temptation, but
abdicated his role as leader. So, it was not so much the
content of her thinking that is the issue, but that she was
assuming the role of leadership that was specifically his
(Gen 3:17).[18] Sixth, the curse of Gen 3:16, "your desire
shall be for your husband, and he shall rule over you," is
explained in terms of Cain subduing Abel in Gen 4:7—i.e.,
the curse is neither woman's sexual desire for man nor her
personal desire for companionship, but rather her desire to
subdue man.[19]

So, Gen 1-3 does not support the notion that male
leadership is an evil result of the Fall.[20] Rather, Gen 2
presents man as leader and woman as helper, follower, and
subordinate.[21] When sin came, both roles were corrupted

---

[17]Ortlund, "Male-Female Equality and Male Headship—Genesis
1-3," *Recovering Biblical Manhood and Womanhood*, 100, says woman
"found her own identity in relation to the man . . . *by the man's
definition.*" See also Hurley, *Man and Woman in Biblical Perspective*,
210-214, that naming demonstrates control. Piper, "Satan's Design in
Reversing Male Leadership Role," *The Standard* (1983): 33, cites Gen
32:28, where God names Jacob.

[18]Foh, *Women and the Word of God*, 64, mentions "usurpation
of authority." See also Ortlund, "Male-Female Equality and Male
Headship—Genesis 1-3," *Recovering Biblical Manhood and
Womanhood*, 107-108; and Hurley, *Man and Woman in Biblical
Perspective*, 214-216.

[19]Foh, *Women and the Word of God*, 67-68; Hurley, *Man and
Woman in Biblical Perspective*, 216-219; and H. Wayne House, *The
Role of Women in Ministry Today* (Nashville: T. Nelson, 1990): 27.

[20]Ortlund, "Male-Female Equality and Male Headship—Genesis
1-3," *Recovering Biblical Manhood and Womanhood*, 109; George W.
Knight III, *The New Testament Teaching on the Role Relationship of
Men and Women* (Grand Rapids: Baker, 1977): 43-44.

[21]Piper, *The Standard* (1983): 35. Foh, *Women and the Word of
God*, 61, stresses that 1 Cor 11:8-9 and 1 Tim 2:13 demonstrate convincingly the order of creation in Gen 1-3, as does House, *The Role of*

by pride and self-sufficiency. Men abdicate their responsibility of leadership either in silence or by belittling and/or abusing women. Male brutality is a post-Fall matter. Women debase themselves by feigning subservience or rejecting male leadership altogether.[22] Hierarchal complementarians, then, advocate a "prescriptive" view of Gen 3 in which God intended hierarchalism from the very beginning.

While Jesus evidenced a very high view of women, complementarians do not view him as overturning the divine order of creation. Thus, with Jesus, the roles of headship and submission are not obliterated, but returned to their original purity. One can see this continued, they say, in Paul's statement, "Wives, be subject to your husbands as to the Lord. For the husband is head of the wife as Christ is the head of the church" (Eph 5:22-23).

3. *Critique*

Several similarities exist in these two views of Gen 1-3. For instance, Gen 1:27 is understood as stating clearly that both man and woman are created in the image of God and that no superiority is attached to maleness, nor is any inferiority attached to femaleness. Both views understand from Gen 2:19-20 that man was incomplete (lonely), and that woman was created to complete or complement man. Both view Adam and Eve as present at the temptation by Satan and understand the primal sin to involve "power."

However, major differences exist. On one hand, the intent of evangelical feminist exegesis is to provide alternative understandings of texts supportive of hierarchalism. In so doing, they have correctly understood "helper" in Gen 2 not as "under the authority of" or "secondary to," but as

---

Women in Ministry Today, 27.   George W. Knight III, "The Ordination of Women: NO," *Christianity Today* 25 (1981): 260-261, who sees 1 Cor 11:8-9 as Paul's "exegesis and application of Gen 2:21-23."

[22]Foh, *Women and the Word of God*, 69.

"complementary." Likewise, their view of the first sin being one of "power," in the sense of "trying to be like God," is textually sound. However, their postulation of Adam's naming the animals as indicative of man's incompleteness, while an intriguing view, does not emerge from adequate exegetical analysis. Similarly, their view of Adam's sin as essentially his not instructing Eve very well is based on an assumption, not on compelling exegetical analysis. In general, one gets the impression that some evangelical feminist exegesis of Gen 1-3 is basically an exercise in which feminist prejudices become evangelical feminist biblical conclusions, and not always truly objective exegesis. It is not surprising that evangelical feminists conclude that "he shall rule over you" is a post-Fall *descriptive* statement (giving the result of sin) stating the human dilemma that involves the unfortunate legacy of male dominance.

On the other hand, hierarchal complementarian exegesis is a direct response to evangelical feminism. Taking Adam's naming of the animals to indicate "authority over" them, and his naming of Eve as indicating "authority over," is simply an inference that does not reflect solid exegetical analysis. Also, that Eve's sin was that of "usurping male authority" is merely another inference from hierarchical prejudice. That "helper" in Gen 2 means that woman is subordinate to man will not withstand rigorous analysis. It is not surprising that complementarians conclude that "he shall rule over you" is *prescriptive* and that Gen 2-3 presents God's pre-Fall intent of male leadership and female submission.

The impasse requires a refocusing of the discussion. The question of woman's role in the Genesis narrative is a good one, and certainly a proper understanding of Gen 1-3 is vital to any responsible view of women. However, to identify the sin in the Garden as centering on the relationship of men and women skews the emphasis in the text on humankind's desire to displace God. To address Gen 1-3 in terms of the questions and prejudices generated by current controversy places restrictions on interpretation that hinder accurate understanding of the major focus of the text, which is to introduce God, sin, and redemption as essential to the larger context of Genesis. This developing theological thrust of Genesis should control any understanding of manhood and womanhood in Gen 1-3.[23] The roles of man, woman, and sin as prototypical at the beginning of Genesis must be related to the way all of this plays out in the developing narrative on through Gen 50:26.

4. A Responsible Understanding of Gen 1-3

Recently Marrs[24] has published a solid exegesis of Gen 1-3. His theological analysis addresses wider concerns in the text and brings them to bear on the topic of women in a scholarly and dispassionate way.

Working carefully with the literary structure of Genesis, especially the relationship between 1-11 and 12-50, Marrs views Gen 1 as setting the stage for Gen 2-11. The overview of the creation of the world in Gen 1 emphasizes God's role in creation and serves as a backdrop for four episodes: 1) Adam and Eve, 2) Cain and Abel, 3) Noah and the flood, and 4) the Tower of Babel.[25] Marrs notes,

> Scripture opens with a powerful affirmation of what it means to be human in a God-centered and God-ordered world. Humankind, consisting of male and female, reflect the very image of God. The sovereign Lord of the universe has entrusted to his sovereign subjects direct responsibility for the rest of creation. . . . Humankind as male and female finds its meaning, direction, and purpose only in relation to its benevolent and gracious creator (11-12).

It is frequently held that Gen 1 expresses an "order of creation" in which male superiority and female inferiority

---

[23]See Clark Pinnock's "Climbing out of a Swamp: The Evangelical Struggle to Understand the Creation Texts," *Interpretation* 43 (1989): 143-155, appeal to avoid prejudice in exegesis.

[24]Rick R. Marrs, "In the Beginning: Male and Female (Gen 1-3)," *Essays on Women in Earliest Christiantiy*, 2.1-36.

[25]See F. E. Deist, "Genesis 1:1-2:4a: World Picture and World View," *Scriptura* 22 (1987): 1-17, for discussion of the creation narrative in Gen 1 in its literary and cultural context.

were the will of God from the very beginning. In this regard, Marrs admits at the outset that there is an order *in* creation—not, however, a move from superiority to inferiority, but from incompleteness to completeness (19). This counters hierarchical assumptions of an "order of creation" involving superiority and inferiority in writers such as Stitzinger,[26] who admits that "there is nothing in the text of Gen 1 to suggest hierarchical relationship, but there is also nothing to deny it." On the other hand, Davidson[27] is on firmer ground in holding, "sexual differentiation is presented as a creation by God, and not part of the divine order itself." "Order of creation" involving male superiority and female sub-ordination should be viewed as the result of hierarchical prejudice.

Marrs, then, finds no stated or implied superiority or subordination in Gen 1 (8). This is in agreement with the Staggs,[28] who argue,

> In the creation narrative of Gen 1:26-30 there is no subordination, unless this be inferred from the listing of "male" before "female" in v. 27. In v. 26 the Hebrew term *'adham* is used generically, for male and female or "the human race.". . . Both are created together: "male and female he created them." Sexual distinction is here seen as a creation of God. This is of far-reaching implication. Gen 1:27, "he created *them*," excludes the idea that man originally was "androgynous," i.e., one self as both male and female, only later to be divided into separate sexes. . . . In this perspective, "man," i.e., the human being, was created heterosexual, male and female; and they were so created as to find fulfillment in relationship with each other.

---

[26]Michael F. Stitzinger, "Genesis 1-3 and the Male/Female Role Relationship," *Grace Theological Journal* 2 (1981): 26.

[27]Richard M. Davidson, "The Theology of Sexuality in the Beginning: Genesis 1-2," *Andrews University Seminary Studies* 26 (1988): 6-7.

[28]Evelyn and Frank Stagg, *Woman in the World of Jesus* (Philadelphia: Westminster, 1978): 19.

In this vein, Trible[29] makes four important observations regarding Gen 1:27, which reads, "So God created man in his own image, in the image of God he created him; male and female he created them" (NIV). First, she notes that the shift from the singular "him" to the plural "them" shows that "man" is "not one single creature who is both male and female but rather two creatures, one male and one female" (18). Second, the singular "man" shows that "male and female are not opposite but rather harmonious sexes" (18). Third, the parallelism between "man" and "male and female" shows that "sexual differentiation does not mean hierarchy but rather equality . . . . male and female are not superior and subordinate" (18). She notes further that 1:26 reads "Let us make man in our image," regarding both male and female, and "let *them* rule over" the earth, a terminology that continues in 1:28-29. Fourth, she says that one should be cautious "against assigning 'masculine' and 'feminine' attributes to the words *male* and *female* "regarding tasks involved in having dominion over the earth (19).[30]

Davidson[31] says that there is no hint of spiritual or functional superiority between male and female in Gen 1. Both share in dominion over the earth and in procreation, and both participate equally in the image of God. Even so, Stitzinger[32] argues that, "spiritual equality between man and woman does not prohibit a distinctiveness in role relationships." However he is forced to admit that, "feminists, by an argument from silence, may be correct in supporting complete positional equality." Still, he argues, Gen 2 makes clear that while male and female share equally in the "image of God," equality of roles is not of God.

---

[29]Phyllis Trible, *God and the Rhetoric of Sexuality* (Philadelphia: Fortress, 1978): 18-19. Cf. the critique of Trible by Ann Gardner, "Genesis 2:4b-3: A Mythological Paradigm of Sexual Equality or of the Religious History of Pre-Exilic Israel?" *Scottish Journal of Theology* 43 (1990): 1-18.

[30]See Bernhard W. Anderson, "' Subdue the Earth': What Does It Mean?" *Bible Review* 8 (1992): 4, 10.

[31]Davidson, *Andrews University Seminary Studies* (1988): 7.

[32]Stitzinger, *Grace Theological Journal* (1981): 26-27.

Marrs holds that Gen 2-3 focuses on humankind's role in God's creation. Specifically, these chapters treat man's, i.e., male and female, privileged status and role in creation and the disintegration of that life through disobedience (13-14). Noting hierarchical interpretations of Gen 2:21-25 (18-19), Marrs observes that the so-called "order of creation," i.e., man first and woman last, is often taken to mean that "first" connotes superiority while "last" denotes subordination. However, he counters that the actual "order of creation (man first, woman last) intends not a move from superiority to inferiority, but through *inclusio* (man/woman) a move from incompleteness to completeness" (19). Davidson[33] notes that Hebrew literature often makes use of an *inclusio* device in which the points of central concern occur at the beginning and end of the unit of text. This is the case in Gen 2. The creation of man at the beginning and woman at the end correspond to each other in importance. Only with the creation of woman does creation reach its climax. Thus, the "order of creation" in Gen 2 does not teach male superiority or female subordination.

Further, regarding the hierarchical view that woman is man's "helper" and therefore subordinate, Marrs observes that the Hebrew term for "helper" used here also occurs in the OT to refer to God as the helper of humankind. Even so, one should not take this to mean that God is subordinate to humans. Rather, the relationship is in focus. The Hebrew term "helper" does not specify rank or position. One should understand the specific meaning from the context. Whereas Stitzinger[34] holds, without stating precisely his reasons, that the context does not support equality of position, Davidson[35] holds correctly that Gen 2:18 and 20 clearly indicate equality of position. So, Marrs concludes, "Woman is created as a companion (neither subordinate nor superior) who alleviates man's isolation through identity" (20).[36]

---

[33]Davidson, *Andrews University Seminary Studies* (1988): 14.

[34]Stitzinger, *Grace Theological Journal* (1988): 31.

[35]Davidson, *Andrews University Seminary Studies* (1988): 15.

[36]See Michael L. Rosenzweig, "A Helper Equal to Him," *Judaism* 35 (1986): 277-280, who argues against the radical feminist

Also, Marrs concludes that the hierarchical view that man's naming of woman, like his naming of the animals, implies superiority, is without foundation.[37] He notes that this naming is spontaneous on man's part, that the designation "woman" is not really a name but a generic term, and that in naming "woman" he simultaneously names himself. Man's naming of woman connotes no power or authority over her, but is merely an exultant acknowledgement of God's having created a suitable partner for him (21). This "suitable partner" culminates in their union as "one flesh" (2:23-24), a designation not of differentiation, but mutuality.[38]

Marrs holds that the temptation story in Gen 3:1-7 highlights the inclination to become like God, but that the woman is intelligent, informed, and perceptive (24).[39] This precludes the notion that the woman is weak, feeble-minded, and gullible. Contrary to popular opinion, the text does not state that the man is absent when the serpent speaks with the woman. Actually, the serpent uses the plural form of address and the woman answers in the first person plural. V. 3:6b makes it clear that the man was "with her" at the time. At no place does the text state or imply that the woman was a "temptress" or that she "enticed" her husband to eat the forbidden fruit. The sin was not so much in eating the fruit as in deciding to eat the fruit.[40] In their choice, man and woman desire independence that enables them to decide for themselves, and in so doing become like God (26-27).

---

theory that the Hebrew term "equal to him" should rather be translated "greater than him," as well as against the common reading, "opposite to him."

[37]Stitzinger, *Grace Theological Journal* (1981): 32.

[38]See Lee McGlone, "Genesis 2:18-24; Ephesians 5:21-6:9," *Review and Expositor* 86 (1989): 243-247.

[39]See also George Coats, *Genesis* (Grand Rapids: Eerdmans, 1983): 54; and Claus Westermann, *Genesis* 1-11 (Minneapolis: Augsburg, 1984): 249.

[40]See Gerhard Von Rad, *Genesis* (trans. J. Marks; rev. ed.; Philadelphia: Westminister, 1972): 88.

This pattern occurs throughout the OT, beginning with Cain
assuming a prerogative not really his and killing his brother
(Gen 4).[41]

Admitting to God their choice, they, along with the
serpent, face swift judgment (3:14-19).[42] There exists no
little difficulty in understanding the judgment on the woman
in 3:16. One problem has to do with whether her
punishment is only pain in childbearing or pain in
childbearing and desire for her husband. Marrs notes three
interpretations. One view is that,

> "Her desire, whatever it may be, will not be her own. She
> cannot do what she wishes, for her husband rules over her like
> a despot and whatever she wishes is subject to his will."[43]

Marrs states that the view that woman usurped man's
authority has no solid textual basis behind it. Further,
man's failure to control his wife is not mentioned in his
punishment in 3:17-19 where it might be expected (31).

A second interpretation of 3:16b involves woman's
desire to dominate her husband and the relationship. Foh,[44]
assumes that God intended male headship from the very
beginning and that it was not the result of or punishment for
sin. Interestingly, instead of locating the meaning of the
Hebrew noun "desire" in the Hebrew verb *shaqa* (to desire,
excite), she locates its etymology in the Arabic *saqa* (to urge,

---

[41]See John J. Scullion, "Genesis 1-11: An Interpretation," *St.
Mark's Review* 122 (1985): 11-17; and Marsha M. Wilfong, "Genesis
2: 18-24," *Interpretation* 42 (1988): 58-63, esp. 61-62.

[42]See Jack P. Lewis, "The Woman's Seed (Gen 3:15)," *Journal of
the Evangelical Theological Society* 34 (1991): 299-319, who critiques
the view that this passage is to be interpreted as a messianic promise
rather than being part of the curse on the serpent.

[43]Edward J. Young, *Genesis* 3 (London: Banner of Truth, 1966):
127.

[44]See Susan Foh, *Women and the Word of God*, 69; and Richard
Hess, "The roles of the woman and the man in Genesis 3," *Themelios*
18 (1993): 15-19, esp. 17, where he prefers, "he *will* rule over you."

drive on, impel). So, woman's "desire" for her husband was not sexual desire, but the desire to possess and control him. However, two problems militate against Foh's view: 1) her presupposition of male headship prejudices her reading of the text, and 2) her attempt to locate the meaning of the Hebrew noun in the Arabic word for "to drive on, impel" rather than in the Hebrew verb for "to desire" is not at all convincing. Simply put, the text of Gen 3:16 does not say that woman's sin was in attempting to dominate the man.

Both of these alternatives presuppose a hierarchical reading of Gen 2 and a reading of the temptation scene for which there is no solid evidence (usurping man's authority).

A third alternative, and the one Marrs prefers (31-32), is that the woman's desire involves primarily her sexual desire for her husband. Marrs notes 1) Eve's derivation from Adam does not presume subordination,[45] 2) the Hebrew term "helpmate" does not imply subordination, 3) Adam's naming of Eve reflects recognition rather than dominion and subordination, and 4) 2:24, God created woman for companionship. There is no indication in 3:1-7 that the woman's temptation involved separation from the man. Her sin was not that of "usurping man's authority," but of exalting herself above God. This, I think, is correct.

Busenitz[46] observes that 1) in the context of Gen 3:14-19 each recipient of God's judgment receives one punishment, 2) in each judgment the nature of the punishment has no essential relationship to the nature of the sin committed, 3) the judgments on man and woman both revolve around propagation and seed, 4) 3:16 addresses the woman, 3:17-19 the man, and 5) the pronouncement occurs first in each punishment, followed by an explanatory

---

[45]Davidson, *Andrews University Seminary Studies* (1988): 16, argues that derivation does not imply subordination. Adam, for instance, was derived from the ground (v. 7), but one cannot conclude that the ground was his superior.

[46]Irvin A. Busenitz, "Woman's Desire for Man: Genesis 3:16 Reconsidered," *Grace Theological Journal* 7 (1986): 206-207.

statement. In actuality, Marrs notes, the pronouncement on the woman is the only pronouncement in this series that contains no curse (29). This being true, the context does not speak of the desire of the woman to dominate the man, but of the continuation of life in the face of death. This is the central point of 3:16a. This is the focal point of 3:17-19. There is then good reason to believe that this is the point in 3:16b. Marrs concludes,

> If v. 16b has any relation to v. 16a, we would expect the woman's desire to have some connection to the pain that now accompanies her giving birth. It seems plausible that given the extreme pain that will now attend childbirth, the woman's desire for intimacy would be diminished. V. 16b counters such as assumption. However, her desire will be met with rule (32).

So, "he shall rule over you"[47] came about, not because woman usurped the leadership role of the man, but because she exalted herself above God. Her sin had nothing to do with denying Adam a rightful role. The only role Eve usurped was God's—a usurpation characteristic of all acts of wrong by people of both sexes at all times. Woman, then, may desire to dominate man, but that is not a punishment pronounced by God upon woman. Self-exaltation naturally results in the desire to dominate. Any act of domination by a woman is an action that is the consequence of sin on her part, not the result of a judgmental "curse" in Gen 3:16.

Gen 1-2, then, teach that originally man and woman shared an equality in a pristine world designed by God. The Fall in Gen 3 shattered this equality and began a long history of gender conflict based upon male hierarchy. Patriarchy is an unfortunate result of the Fall, not something designed by God. A question arises, however, whether Jesus accepted hierarchalism or whether he attempted to restore the equality that existed before the Fall.

---

[47]Cf. John J. Schmitt, "Like Eve, Like Adam: *msl* in Gen 3:16," *Biblica* 72 (1991): 1-22 who prefers, "he will have such desire as you."

6

JESUS' VIEW OF WOMEN

1. *Jesus' View of Women in Evangelical Feminism*

Jesus did not teach explicitly on the subject of women, but his attitudes are detectable indirectly in his teaching and by noting differences with negative Jewish opinions. Jesus evidenced an open attitude toward women, even somewhat scandalous. Breaking with custom, Jesus allowed women disciples (Lk 8:1-3), but maintained unwavering purity in his relations with women. He had theological discussions with women (John 4:1-42). He helped sinful women and women in need without demeaning them (Lk 7:36-50; 13:10-17; Mk 5:25-34). He treated men and women alike regarding their faith and their foibles (Lk 7:1-17). Women are among those who took care of him (Matt 27:55), showed loving gestures (Matt 26:6-13), remained at the cross when others had fled (Lk 23:27-29), were first at the tomb (Matt 28:1-10), were first witnesses of the resurrection (Mk 16:11), and were among those foremost in proclaiming the Christ (Rom 16).[1]

Jesus broke down many of the culturally-imposed restrictions regarding contact between males and females and replaced hierarchalism with mutual acceptance.[2] He was a male, but had no patriarchal axe to grind or a "male ego" to defend.[3] "Without sentimentality, condescension, or

---

[1]Ruth A. Tucker and Walter Liefeld, *Daughters of the Church: Women and Ministry from New Testament Times to the Present* (Grand Rapids: Zondervan, 1987): 41-48.

[2]See McClelland, "The New Reality in Christ," *Gender Matters*, 62.

[3]Letha D. Scanzoni and Nancy A. Hardesty, *All We're Meant to Be* (3rd ed.; Grand Rapids: Eerdmans, 1992): 72.

undemanding indulgence, he accepted them as persons."[4]
He was a servant to both men and women and stressed
mutual respect and service in relationships. True, Jesus did
not include women among the twelve, but the logistics of
women being in that role were simply impractical and would
have scandalized and obscured Jesus' true mission.
Nevertheless, Jesus' openness to women, in spite of the
prevailing patriarchal culture of that day, was so powerful
that even thirty or so years after Jesus' death the Gospels
continue to reflect this attitude of reverse patriarchalism.[5]

2. Jesus' View of Women—A Complementarian View

Hierarchalists point out that Jesus did not speak to the
status of women in Judaism. Consequently, they conclude
that Jesus must have approved of the cultural status quo of
his time regarding hierarchalism.[6]

Borland,[7] who to his credit does not disparage
evangelical feminists as unregenerate as does Foh, argues
that Jesus did indeed place a high value on women in a
world that regarded women as second-class citizens. The
depersonalizing of women in that world-view, however,
was a deviation from God's original intent. For instance, in
quoting Gen 1:27 (Matt 19:4), Jesus viewed women as
created in the image of God just as men are. Jesus viewed
women as genuine persons, not simply as the objects of
male desire or as property (Matt 5:28). In his view of
divorce, Jesus advocated the equality of men and women
(Matt 5:32; 19:9). Jesus served the needs of men and

---

[4]Ibid., 75.

[5]Ibid., 61. C.F.D. Moule, *The Phenomenon of the New
Testament* (Naperville, IL: Allenson, 1967): 65, says that, in light of
first-century patriarchal culture, Jesus' behavior toward women is so
extraordinary as to be evidence of Scripture's supernatural authenticity.

[6]Stephen B. Clark, *Man and Woman in Christ* (Ann Arbor:
Servant, 1980): 251.

[7]James A. Borland, "Women in the Life and Teachings of Jesus,"
Recovering Biblical Manhood and Womanhood, 113-120. See also
Hurley, *Man and Woman in Biblical Perspective*, 82-114.

women alike, whether physical or spiritual. Jesus accorded women dignity by illustrations in his teaching (Matt 12:42), teaching women theological truths (Matt 24:41; Jn 20:17), and having women participate in his life and ministry (Jn 11:20; 12:2-8; Lk 8:3). Women were the initial witnesses to the resurrection (Matt 28:1-10). Further, women often labored with men in the early church (Acts 16:14-15; Rom 16).

However, women were not included among the twelve.[8] This could not be because Jesus was afraid of scandal, for he criticized Pharisees in public (Mk 1:21-27), ate with sinners (Matt 9:11) and boldly cleansed the temple (Jn 2:14-17). The only reason for selecting an all-male group of twelve was emphasis upon maintaining God-given role distinctions regarding leadership. As leaders (Acts 2:14; 5:12, 18, 40, 42; Gal 1:17) ruling over the "twelve tribes of Israel" (Lk 22:30) and having a special teaching ministry (Jn 14:26), their roles were different from the roles of the women who followed Christ or were served by him. In the search for a replacement in Acts 1:21, it is stipulated that he be a male. Further, in Acts 6 the church was asked to select seven qualified *men* as leaders. Therefore, while Jesus treated women as equal with men and maintained their dignity and worth, the pattern of male leadership in the early church continued the role distinction between men and women and a leadership role for men.[9]

3. *Summary and Critique*

Not unexpectedly, many similarities exist regarding the view of Jesus across the evangelical spectrum. Jesus did not address directly the status of women, but held a high view of women in a world that often viewed women as second-class. Quoting Gen 1:27, he held both man and woman were created in the image of God. Consequently, he helped both men and women on an equal basis, taught theological truths

---

[8]Borland, "Women in the Life and Teachings of Jesus," *Recovering Biblical Manhood and Womanhood*, 120-122.

[9]House, *The Role of Women in Ministry Today*, 74-75.

to both men and women, and included both men and women in his ministry. Women are portrayed as the initial witnesses to the resurrection and as having worked alongside men in the early church.

Also, not unexpectedly, there are major differences regarding Jesus' view of women. Evangelical feminists see him as differing with prevalent Jewish hierarchalism and replacing it with mutual respect and acceptance, whereas complementarians see him as approving of that hierarchalism. Whereas complementarians stress the absence of women from the twelve, evangelical feminists argue the logistical impracticality of their inclusion.

Interestingly, the impasse occurs basically regarding egalitarianism and hierarchalism—precisely the two prejudices that have generated polarity throughout the history of the women's issue. Certainly Jesus taught mutual respect of males and females and just as certainly he worked within the social structure of his day. However, it has not been demonstrated from biblical exegesis that Jesus maintained egalitarianism or hierarchalism—both of which must remain presuppositions to exegesis rather than conclusions.

This impasse also requires refocusing of the discussion. Certainly one's understanding of Jesus' view is central to a responsible Christian view of women. However, since Jesus did not address the topic specifically, one must respect that silence and exercise great care before attributing any particular view to him. Questions about the understanding of women by Jesus are proper; however, they are not best addressed by pressing modern agendas onto the text, but by permitting the Gospel narratives to inform the modern question. Serious evangelical scholarship is extant and forthcoming both in exegesis of the Gospels and in Christology. However, it is important to observe that: 1) rigorous exegetical scholarship must be used in learning from the narrative the historical understandings of the writer and the participants, and 2) insights into Jesus' view of women must of necessity be considered in terms of the wider context of Christology—both of which are major oversights in the current discussion of women among evangelicals. Even then, one must remember that an explicit doctrine of women does not occur in Scripture, nor does Jesus attempt to provide such a doctrine. What Jesus does do is provide clear insights into the ancient intent of God concerning the treatment of "people." A responsible quest for the "mind of Christ," then, is the primary task for the Christian community. One must not circumvent or manipulate this task in study of the "role" of women in the church or any other similar issue. As said above, "women in the church" is not at the heart of the Christian message. The central element in Christianity is the call of God in Christ. That provides the context for all other discussions.

In this connection, several observations are important regarding Jesus' view of women.[10] In his life and teachings, Jesus redefined "power." Rather than use power to control others, Jesus advocated using power to serve, forgive, and encourage others in a context of mutual deference (see Eph 4:15-16). Jesus insisted upon equity for both men and women regarding laws of marriage and divorce. This is exemplary of his understanding of power and is a direct application of that teaching to husband-wife relationships (see Matt 19:1-12; 5:31-32; Mk 10:1-12). In all four Gospels, Jesus refused to allow his male disciples to view women as sex objects. This made possible a mixed group of male and female followers to travel along with him. Later, Paul applies Jesus' view of power as service rather than control to the Corinthian situation. Paul states that the husband belongs to the wife in the very same way that the wife belongs to the husband (1 Cor 7:2-5). The same principle of mutuality holds true when he discusses divorce (7:2-13) and remarriage (7:14-16). Paul specifically applies Jesus' view of power in Eph 5:21, where mutual deference is characteristic of Christ's life and of the Christian life (see

---

[10]See further Gretchen G. Hull, *Equal to Serve: Women and Men in the Church and Home* (Old Tappan, NJ: F. H. Revell, 1987): 113-116; Mary J. Evans, *Woman in the Bible* (Downers Grove, IL: InterVarsity Press, 1983): 44-60; Scott Bartchy, "Jesus, Power, and Gender Roles," *TSF Bulletin* 7 (1984): 2-4.

also Phil 2:3-5; Rom 12:10). "Submit" in 5:21 continues as
the implied verb in v. 22, making the exhortation to mutual
deference applicable to Christian wives. Similarly, mutual
deference applies to Christian husbands in 5:25-33a, where
there are three exhortations for husbands to love their wives
in the same way Christ loved the church. Most would think
that power is "over" someone, but Paul's point is that
Christ's relationship to the church was *service*. This
comparison of a husband's love with Christ's sacrifice in
Eph 5 challenged radically the long tradition of male-
dominance in existence since Gen 3. It presented men with a
new basis for relating to their wives, and wives with a new
basis for relating to their husbands—voluntary mutual
deference. Nothing is said about decision-making roles, or
of unique division of gender roles—only that for Jesus the
pre-Fall ideal of human equality should be restored.

7

Gal 3:28—"Neither Male and Female"

There's a great text in Galatians,
   Once you trip on it, entails
Twenty-nine damnations,
   One sure, if another fails.

Robert Browning, *Soliloquy of the Spanish Cloister*

Snodgrass[1] calls Gal 3:28 "the most socially explosive statement in the New Testament," and with good reason.

1. *Gal 3:28—An Evangelical Feminist "Magna Carta"*

Jewett[2] terms Gal 3:28 the "Magna Carta of Humanity," and sees in Gal 3:28 a restoration of the original relationship of man and woman before the Fall (Gen 1:27). Many view it as "the necessary theological starting place for any discussion on the role of women in the church."[3] One should read restrictions placed on women elsewhere in the Bible in terms of Gal 3:28, and not vice-versa. Hence, some evangelicals dismiss 1 Cor 14:34-35 as a non-Pauline interpolation.[4] Others believe Paul's thought on the matter changed over time. Thus Paul's earlier letters are

---

[1]Klyne Snodgrass, "Galatians 3:28: Conundrum or Solution?" *Women, Authority & the Bible* (ed. A Mickelsen; Downers Grove, IL: InterVarsity Press, 1986): 161.

[2]Jewett, *Man as Male and Female*, 142.

[3]W. Ward Gasque, "Response," *Women, Authority & the Bible*, 189.

[4]Gordon D. Fee, *The First Epistle to the Corinthians* (Grand Rapids: Eerdmans, 1987): 699-708.

inconsistent in theory and practice with his later letters.[5]
Still others view Paul as more concerned with the success of
the mission than on radical social change, so he set out his
principle, but made accommodations to the social culture of
the day.[6] Gasque[7] concludes, "It is hermeneutically
illegitimate to set up as theologically normative passages
such as 1 Cor 14:34-35 and 1 Tim 2:11-12 where Paul is
dealing with concrete local situations."

Snodgrass[8] argues the impossibility of interpreting Gal
3:28 with reference only to salvation, unrelated to social
issues. Rather, Paul is focusing on the new social reality
created by baptism into Christ—namely, the practical
implications of the new social reality of interrelationships of
Jews and Gentiles, slaves and free persons, and men and
women. Although pressing the Jewish-Gentile relations, the
radical implications of the other two parallel pairs mentioned
in this text are clear. Snodgrass also argues Gal 3:28 to be at
the heart of Paul's theological concern and certainly not
peripheral. He rejects Jewett's view that Paul speaks
inconsistently. Rather, he says (180),

> I view 1 Corinthians 14:33b-36 and 1 Timothy 2:11-15 as
> statements necessitated by specific problems in Corinth and
> Ephesus, respectively, and as shaped by an ancient culture.
> These texts do not become less important than Galatians 3:28,
> but they are less direct in their application.

So in evangelical feminist circles Gal 3:28 is viewed as
having meaning beyond the topic of salvation, especially
with regard to new social interrelationships in Christian
thought.

---

[5]Richard N. Longenecker, *New Testament Social Ethics for Today*
(Grand Rapids: Eerdmans, 1984): 26, 68.

[6]See James G. Sigountos and Myron Shank, "Public Roles for
Women in the Pauline Church: A Reappraisal of the Evidence," *Journal
of the Evangelical Theological Society* 26 (1983): 293.

[7]Gasque, "Response," *Women, Authority & the Bible*, 189.

[8]Snodgrass, "Gal 3:28," *Women, Authority & the Bible*, 161-
188.

2. Galatians 3:28 in Complementarian Thought

Concerning Gal 3:28, Johnson,[9] minister at Believer's Chapel in Dallas, says, "the vigorous debate over sex roles has, in effect, lifted it from its exegetical under-pinnings and set it as a lonely text, a kind of proof-text, in the midst of swirling theological debate." Complementarians argue that here Paul is only addressing salvation[10] and that to go beyond this violates the text. They underscore that inerrancy precludes interpolation or any development in Paul's thinking that might result in textual inconsistency. House[11] says, "The Bible is inspired—infallible, entirely true and without error in original manuscripts. The women's issue touches the believability and applicability of portions of God's word." Hurley[12] says, "The authority of Scripture is the issue which is finally under debate." So, in stressing their theological presuppositions, complementarians view Gal 3:28 in terms of their "order of creation" argument. In harmonizing fashion, Gal. 3:28 is not understood in terms of Galatians, but is reinterpreted to fit their presuppositions.

Actually the history of Christian interpretation buttresses the basic complementarian argument on Gal 3:28 rather than appeal to the biblical text.[13] They stress that distinctions in role function do not indicate lesser value and that submission does not make inferiority necessary. Even so, complementarians have not responded convincingly to the argument that, "it is nonsense to insist on female subordination while simultaneously insisting that subordination does not imply inferiority."[14]

---

[9]S. Lewis Johnson, "Role Distinctions in the Church: Galatians 3:28," *Recovering Biblical Manhood and Womanhood*, 154.

[10]Hurley, *Man and Woman in Biblical Perspective*, 126.

[11]House, *The Role of Women in Ministry Today*, 106.

[12]Hurley, *Man and Woman in Biblical Perspective*, 204.

[13]Johnson, "Role Distinctions in the Church: Galatians 3:28," *Recovering Biblical Manhood and Womanhood*, 163-164. See also Knight, *The Role Relationship of Men and Women*, 5.

[14]Virginia Ramey Mollenkott, "Evangelicalism: A Feminist Perspective," *Union Seminary Quarterly Review* 32 (1977): 97.

3. *Summary and Critique*

Why would Paul make such a bold statement about "the oneness" of Jews and Gentiles, slaves and free, and (dare he add) male and female? At issue is whether Gal 3:28 treats only salvation or the broader topic of social relationships. To resolve this issue, we must understand how this text fits within Paul's developing argument in Galatians.

The epistle makes clear that the opponents think 1) Paul is not one of the original apostles but is dependent upon Jerusalem, and 2) Christians must become part of the historic "Israel of God," including "taking on the yoke of Torah" (5:1) and circumcision.[15] In Gal 1-2, Paul insists that his apostleship and message came from God, not from the Jerusalem church. Attempts by "false brethren" (2:4, 12) to alter that message are unacceptable. Christ must remain the defining point in life.

In 2:15-21, Paul raises the issue of "righteousness" in terms of Christ versus "law." This both concludes his point in chaps 1-2 and introduces the problem of legalism beginning in chap 3. Three elements are at work: 1) the pagan worldview from which the Galatian Christians had come, 2) the principal identifying marks of Judaism, and 3) Paul's view of Christ as the center of Christian identity.

The Galatian readers were formerly pagans. However, as new Christians, they had not concentrated upon Christ for their new identity, but had incorporated aspects of Jewish legalism. Paul notes that they had done well to abandon pagan elements of identity, but were wrong to substitute Jewish elements for those. Instead of being syncretistic, Paul argues that they should concentrate upon Christ for their new definition as Christians. This is the point in 3:1-5.

---

[15]See Luke Timothy Johnson, *The Writings of the New Testament: An Interpretation* (Philadelphia: Fortress, 1986): 302-14. Gal. 3:1-4:1 is properly viewed as a *probatio*, giving the central argument against the opponents. See Bernard H. Brinsmead, *Galatians—Dialogical Response to Opponents* (Chico, CA: Scholars Press, 1982): 52.

Paul begins chapter 3 by asserting that the Galatian Christians did not receive the Spirit through observing the "works of law" (3:2).[16] Rather, they received the Spirit through "hearing in faith" (3:5).[17] In 3:6-20, Paul supports this contention with appeals to Scripture. Paul's use of the OT may seem strange to modern readers not acquainted with ancient Jewish ways of argumentation. Certain arguments may not persuade modern readers unless they keep in mind Paul's emphasis on the centrality of Christ. Paul's arguments carried weight in his day, even though they may not necessarily be convincing by today's standards.

Paul constructs three arguments from Scripture.[18] First, in 3:6-9 Paul identifies Abraham as a man who was declared righteous through *faith* (Gen 15:6). He concludes that Christians (including former pagans) are likewise declared righteous through their own faith.

Second, in 3:10-14, Paul presents an elaborate argument based upon several OT texts. In typical Jewish fashion, he cites two texts that appear to contradict one another. Deut 27:26 puts a curse on one who does not keep the commandments of the Law. On the other hand, Hab 2:4 says that, "the righteous will live by faith." In 3:12 Paul restates this contradiction, saying that "the Law is not based on faith," but Lev 18:5 still says that life comes from obeying the decrees and laws. Paul appeals to Deut 21:23, which reads curiously, "anyone hung on a tree is under God's curse." In crucifixion Jesus was cursed, but instead of death, life was the result. Paul's point is that Jesus' death on the cross nullified Deut 27:26, leaving Hab 2:4 as still commanding attention. "The righteous will live by faith."

---

[16]Brinsmead, *Galatians*, 78-82, notes that 2:15-21 is a *propositio*, which sets the stage for chaps 3-4 by discussing "justification." 3:1-5, then, is an *interrogatio*, or main argument against the opponents. It is directly related to the *propositio* (2:15-21). The bulk of chaps 3-4 is the *probatio*, or central argument.

[17]"believe what you heard" NIV; "hearing with faith" RSV.

[18]See Johnson, *The Writings of the New Testament*, 310-12.

Third, in 3:15-20 Paul returns to the promise made to Abraham, the father of all who have been justified by faith. God made a promise to Abraham and his "offspring" (Gen 12:3-7; 17:7). Paul takes "offspring" not to mean "Abraham's descendants," but to mean Christ. Further, he extends the term to cover Christ's followers. Paul stresses that Christ continues the promise, not the Mosaic covenant. So, God's promise is still in effect (3:17).

These three arguments, then, raise a major question. If the Law was unable to fulfill the promise, how is one to view the Law? Well, the *intent* of the Law is not at all problematic, but the Law was incapable of leading to life (3:21). While the Law made clear morality and sin, it lacked power to transform. As such, the Law could not fulfill the promise (3:21-22; 3:23 simply restates the sense of v. 22). To provide an answer for the question of how one should view the Law, Paul uses the analogy of a "schoolmaster" (*paidagogos* Gk). Rather than referring merely to a "teacher" (*didaskalos* Gk), the Greek term *paidagogos* implies not only educational and instructional functions, but also discipline and supervision. So, the point of Paul's analogy is not that the Mosaic Law was a positive preparation for Christ, but rather that it was supervisory.[19] The point is that the coming of Christ and "sonship" displaces the reign of the Law and subordination.

Whereas the preceding discussion states negatively why the Law could not justify, 3:26-29 states positively what it means to live apart from legalism as a Christian. All who come into the new spiritual experience in Christ are "one in Christ," i.e., Christ-centered. Gal 3:26 states succinctly that the true "children of Abraham" are those who through Christ are "children of God." Verses 27-28, then, comment on and confirm v. 26. Baptism is a symbol of the unity of Christians with Christ. In this context, the first part of v. 28 states that social, cultural, and gender distinctions

---

[19]Richard N. Longenecker, *Galatians* (WBC 41; Dallas: Word, 1990): 146-48. See also F. F. Bruce, *Commentary on Galatians* (NIC; Grand Rapids: Eerdmans, 1982): 182.

do not affect unity with Christ. The second part of v. 28, "all one in Christ," states the central point of the discussion. Verse 29 is the conclusion, i.e., the relationship of all Christians to Abraham and God's promise in Gen 12:3-7 (17:7).

In 4:1-7, Paul compares slavery to old pagan ways with "sonship" in Christ, and in vv. 8-11 he evidences concern for the Galatians' reversion to old ways. The "fundamental principles" (*stoicheia* Gk; v. 9) of paganism have been replaced, not with Christ, but with external rites (v. 10). The term for mixing a little Christianity with a little of the past is "syncretism." Paul agonizes in v. 11 that he might have wasted his efforts. This frustration continues in 4:12-20 as Paul makes an unusually strong emotional plea for them to avoid syncretism. He follows this plea in 4:21-5:1 with an allegory in which Hagar represents return to slavery and Sarah represents freedom. Paul concludes this part of the epistle in 4:31-5:1 with an emphasis upon "freedom in Christ" and a stern warning against any return to old ways, which would be slavery.

Now, regarding this developing point in Galatians, it seems clear that 3:28 serves as a comment on 3:26, which emphasizes what it means to be "in Christ." The three groups in v. 28 underscore that social, cultural, and gender distinctions do not affect unity with Christ.

Many of the meanings attributed to this verse in current discussion do not seem appropriate to this context. A question does arise concerning the extent to which the evident meaning of v. 28 can be properly extended.

All three pairs in the verse signify an unequal relationship with potential for oppression. Each involves a stronger and weaker partner in terms of power, and there are distinctions within each pair that lead either to social or

religious consequences, or both.[20]   The question of
salvation for women and slaves seems not to have been an
issue. So, Paul's use of the slave-free and male-female
examples was to strengthen his arguments for Gentile
salvation. Christ is the defining point of life. All united in
Christ are of equal value. As part of a unified diversity,
unnecessary barriers and distinctions should give way to
reconciliation and mutual responsibility.

Complementarians, as mentioned above, stress that 3:28
treats only the matter of salvation. Evangelical feminists, on
the other hand, view this text as saying that in Christ all
distinctions between male and female are removed. While it
is theoretically possible to extend the text, there are problems
with both views above. For instance, while in Philemon
Paul stresses that both Philemon and Onesimus are "one in
Christ," the cultural categories of master and slave continue.
Obviously, "in Christ" did not do away with those cultural
categories. Similarly, male and female roles are viewed
differently in various places and times, but this should not
affect "oneness in Christ." "In Christ" does not mandate
doing away with cultural categories of gender.   This
precludes using Gal 3:28 as a "magna carta" of feminism.

At the same time, limiting Gal 3:28 to salvation does not
make necessary a hierarchical view of gender relationships.
That would be to impose a view that is not inherent within
the text and might, in fact, militate against Paul's emphasis
upon "oneness in Christ."

Even when gender distinctions remain, unity with
Christ can and must still play out in practical ways.

---

[20]See Jan Faver Hailey, "'Neither Male and Female' (Gal 3:28),"
Essays on Women in Earliest Christianity (ed. Carroll D. Osburn;
Joplin, MO: College Press, 1993): 1.130-66.

8

WOMEN IN APPOINTED
AND/OR ASSUMED ROLES

Women functioned in a variety of roles in the early church, including deacon, patron, and teacher. We will discuss different views as part of the exegetical process.

1. *Phoebe (Rom 16:1-2)* [1]

Rom 16:1 mentions a Christian lady named Phoebe who was a "deacon" who lived in the port town of Cenchrea near Corinth. The KJV translates "a servant of the church," as does NIV. However, RSV renders "a deaconess of the church," and NEB reads, "who holds office in the congregation." Fiorenza[2] even contends that Phoebe was "an official teacher and missionary in the church of Cenchrea." A question thus arises whether Paul refers to her as a designated "servant" or as an official "deaconess."

Now it is not uncommon for those who do not like to view Phoebe as a "church official" to argue that she could not have been a "deaconess" because the Greek language in NT times had only the masculine form [*diakonos*] of the word, but not the feminine form.[3] However, this argument illustrates a vital misunderstanding of the Greek language, for the masculine form of the noun refers both to males and

---

[1]This section summarizes the essay of James Walters, "'Phoebe' and Junia(s)—Rom 16:1-2, 7," *Essays on Women in Earliest Christianity*, 167-90.

[2]Elisabeth Schüssler Fiorenza, *In Memory of Her: A Feminist Theological Reconstruction of Christian Origins* (New York: Crossroad, 1983): 171.

[3]See F. Lagard Smith, *Men of Strength for Women of God* (Eugene, OR: Harvest House, 1989): 216.

females during the NT period.[4]   The feminine form
[*diakonissa*], referring to an official church position, dates
no earlier than the Council of Nicea in AD 325.

It is important to understand precisely the meaning of
the terms used here. One must distinguish clearly between
"female deacon," referring to the NT concept, and
"deaconess," referring to the later official position. The
earliest clear reference to deaconesses as church officials is
in the third-century *Didascalia Apostolorum* 16,[5] suggesting an Eastern innovation.[6] It is more than interesting
that no sources reflect an order of deaconesses even in the
West at this later period. Some see in Rom 16:1, however, a
"definite office"[7] like that which came later, but this is to
read later practice back into the first century. Although in
later practice the role of "deacon" became an official position
in the church, there is no indication in the NT itself that the
term "deacon" ever meant anything more than a "designated
servant"—whether male or female.[8]

---

[4]E.g., Clement of Alexandria, *Stromateis* 3.53.3. See further,
W.F. Arndt and F.W. Gingrich, *A Greek-English Lexicon of the New
Testament* (2nd ed. rev. Gingrich and F.W. Danker; Chicago: Univ. of
Chicago Press, 1979): 184.

[5]See A. Vööbus, *The Didascalia Apostolorum in Syriac*
(Louvain: CSCO, 1979): iv, 156-158.

[6]See Jean LaPorte, *The Role of Women in Early Christianity*
(Studies in Women and Religion, 7; New York: E. Mellen, 1982):
114.

[7]See among others, C. E. B. Cranfield, *The Epistle to the
Romans* (Edinburgh: T. & T. Clark, 1979): 718. There is no reason
to read "administration" into the term as does E. Best, *The Letter of
Paul to the Romans* (Cambridge: Cambridge Univ. Press, 1967): 174.

[8]See 1 Cor 3:5; 2 Cor 3:6; 6:4; 11:15, 23; Gal 2:17; Eph 3:7;
6:21; Col1:7, 23, 25; 1 Thess 3:2. In Rom 13:4, it is used of civil
magistrates. There is no evidence that "deacon" in the earliest churches
was an office at all. See J. Daniélou, *The Ministry of Women in the
Early Church* (tr. G. Simon; London: Faith, 1961): 7f; John N.
Collins, *Diakonia: Re-Interpreting the Ancient Sources* (Oxford:
Oxford Univ. Press, 1990): 235-244; and Aimé Martimort,
Deaconessses: An Historical Study (tr. K. Whitehead; San Francisco:
Ignatius, 1986): 18-20.

It appears, though, that Paul calls Phoebe a "deacon" not because she merely "serves" Christ, but because she performs a specific type of service. If he only wanted to call attention to her service, Paul could have used the verb "to serve," as in Rom 15:25 and 16:6, or the phrase "the service of the saints," as in 1 Cor 16:15. However, Paul wrote "being a deacon of the church in Cenchrea," which suggests a role of some responsibility.[9] If "deacons" in Phil 1:1 refers to a special designation within the Philippian congregation, one must understand Phoebe to be a "deacon of the church in Cenchrea" accordingly.

Some advocate that Phoebe indeed filled a special role as deacon, but that she would have served only women.[10] As Haldane put it, "As deacons were appointed to attend to the poor, so deaconesses were specially set apart in the churches in order to attend to the wants of their own sex."[11] Now the third-century *Didascalia Apostolorum* mentions official deaconesses who assisted in the baptisms of women and cared for sick women, but to understand Phoebe as a "deaconess" in terms of this later practice would be anachronistic. To suggest that Phoebe served only, or even primarily, women is to make a distinction that the biblical text does not make.

There are helpful hints in the text regarding her service as "deacon."[12] The Greek words "to serve" [*diakoneo*] and "service" [*diakonia*] often refer in the NT to serving meals or tending the poor. For instance, in Matt 8:15 after Jesus

---

[9] See among others, James Dunn, *Romans* (Dallas: Word, 1988): ii. 887.

[10] W. Sanday and A. C. Headlam, *The Epistle to the Romans* (Edinburgh: T. & T. Clark, 1895): 417.

[11] R. Haldane, *Exposition of the Epistle to the Romans* (London: Banner of Truth, 1963 reprint): 633.

[12] See Lawrence Hennessey, "*Diakonia and Diakonoi* in the Pre-Nicene Church," *Diakonia: Studies in Honor of Robert T. Meyer* (ed. T. Halton and J. P. Williman; Washington, D. C.; Catholic Univ. of America Press, 1986): 60-86, for a survey of usage from the classical period through the fourth-century church.

had reduced the fever of Peter's mother-in-law, "she *served* them." In Lk 8:3. Joanna and Susanna *"served"* Jesus, *i.e.*, "supported" him financially.   Some Grecian widows complained in Acts 6:1 of being neglected in the daily *"service"* of food.   2 Cor 8:4 describes the contribution of the saints to the poor in Jerusalem as *"service."* Rom 15:25 reads, "I am on my way to Jerusalem in the *service* of the saints there."   See also Lk 10:40; 12:37; Jn 12:2; and 2 Cor 9:1. With the Greco-Roman world of that period filled with so many needy people, there would have been great demand for people to devote time to helping the poor and sick.

Rom 16:2 mentions Phoebe as a "helper," (RSV), "good friend," (NEB), and "of good help to" (NIV). The Greek term used here [*prostatis*] is normally translated "patron." Many inscriptions from the era of the NT indicate that patronage was performed by women as well as men. One very important inscription dating from the mid-first century AD honors Junia Theodora, a neighbor of Phoebe in nearby Corinth.[13] Called a *"patron* of the greatest loyalty to the Lycian federation," she is commended specifically for extending hospitality in her own home to Lycian travelers as well as Lycians living in Corinth, supplying everything they needed.   That this patronage was much more than mere domestic service is clear from a statement in the inscription that she successfully arranged for Lycian authorities to meet with Corinthian leaders and dealt with ambassadors from Lycia at both the city and national level.

While the range of meanings in the term *prostatis* includes "ruling over" or "governing," the inscription mentions nothing about Junia Theodora holding civic office. Nothing is said about her work being under the direction or oversight of a man. Her considerable influence as "patron" apparently was due more to her wealth and social status. Marshall, professor at Aberdeen, has observed that

---

[13]D. Pallas, "Inscriptions lyciennes trouvées à Solômos près de Corinth, "*Bullletin de correspondence hellénique* 83 (1959): 496-508.

In Roman eyes, the influence and prestige of these wealthy women was not really based upon, or expressed by, the degree of actual political power vested in whatever civic offices they might hold. . . . The real leverage was of the kind exerted by Junia Theodora in Corinth.[14]

MacMullen's comment on the inscription is perceptive:

. . . what she was able to bring to bear, from (of course) a naturally favored social position, can have been nothing but a network of connections woven and made to work for the objects of her interest, in the way politicians of both sexes and every period in history have done since time began.[15]

Saller[16] has argued convincingly that patronage involves 1) an exchange of goods and services, 2) a personal relationship of some duration, and 3) an unequal status that makes patronage different from friendship between equals. The centurion in Lk 7:2-5 who built a Jewish synagogue is an example of such a "patron," although the term itself does not occur there.[17]

Although Rom 16:2 does not describe Phoebe's work as "patron" on behalf of Paul as fully as does the lengthy account in the inscription to Junia Theodora, there is no doubt that she acted as "patron" for Paul in accord with Saller's definition. There is nothing to support Fiorenza's[18] notion that Phoebe served as governing officer or president of the congregation, nor that she served as an official of any kind.

---

[14]A. J. Marshall, "Roman Women and the Provinces," *Ancient Society* 6 (1975): 125.

[15]Ramsay MacMullen, *Changes in the Roman Empire* (Princeton: Princeton Univ. Press, 1990): 168.

[16]Richard Saller, *Personal Patronage under the Early Empire* (Cambridge: Cambridge Univ. Press, 1982): 1.

[17]See J. H. Elliot, "Patronage and Clientism in Early Christian Society," *Forum* 3 (1987): 40.

[18]Fiorenza, *In Memory of Her*, 181.

A second-century reference to female "deacons" in Bithynia occurs in Pliny's letter to Trajan in AD 112.[19] To learn about Christian activities, Pliny tortured and questioned "two female slaves who were styled deacons" [*quae minisrae dicebantur*]. *Dicebantur* suggests that the term *ministrae* [servants] was used by these females to describe themselves. Since in the NT "deacon" does not serve to denote Christians in general, the term *ministrae* refers here to a function or role that was special among the Christians. Phoebe was a "deacon in the church at Cenchrea" in the sense of designated "servant," and as well she was a "patron" of Paul and many others. It is certain that, "Whatever the 'deacons' were at Philippi, that Phoebe was at Cenchrea."[20]

2. *Female Deacons* (1 Tim 3:11)[21]

In 1 Tim 3:11, Paul says, "Women likewise must be serious, not slanderers, but temperate, faithful in all things." Where ASV and NRSV read "women," RSV and NAB read "the women," and KJV NEB and NIV read "their wives." The RevEB reads, "the women in this office." Variation in translation reflects not textual difficulty, but contextual confusion over precisely what women are in mind. That the text refers to all Christian women[22] or to the wives of elders and deacons[23] is rarely held and improbable. However, is the focus on "wives of deacons" or "female deacons"?

---

[19]*Pliny* (LCL; Cambridge: Harvard Univ. Press, 1915): ii. 405. A. N. Sherwin-White, *The Letters of Pliny* (Oxford: Clarendon, 1966): 708, argues that the Latin *ministrae* translates the Greek *diakonos,* but cf. J. G. Davies, "Deacons, Deaconesses, and the Minor Orders of the Patristic Period," *Journal of Ecclesialstical History* 14 (1963): 2.

[20]C. H. Dodd, *The Letter of Paul to the Romans* (New York: Harper & Bros., 1932): 235.

[21]See Barry L. Blackburn, "The Identity of the 'Women' in 1 Tim 3:11," *Essays on Women in Earliest Christianity*, 303-311.

[22]See Davies, *Journal of Ecclesiastical History* (1963): 1f. But why would all female Christians suddenly be addressed within a unit addressed to deacons?

[23]Burton Coffman, *1 & 2 Thessalonians, 1 & 2 Timothy, Titus, & Philemon* (Austin, TX: Firm Foundation, 1978): 182.

Two arguments favoring "wives of deacons" are negative questions. First, some argue that if female deacons were meant, would not a more specific term have been used rather than the general term "women" [*gunaikas*]? Second, it is argued, if "women" refers to female deacons, why does the discussion revert to male deacons in v. 12?

The first argument has no basis in that the masculine form of "servant" [*diakonos*] was used of both men and women in NT times (see Rom 16:1). Roloff[24] observes that if deacons' wives are meant, v. 11 would surely be expected *after* the reference to marriage in v. 12 rather than here. Further, he asks, why would reference be made to deacons' wives, but no references at all made to elders' wives? If reference is to "female deacons," "women" [*gunaikas*] would be used to denote females of the category "deacons" under discussion in vv. 8ff.[25] If reference had been to "wives of deacons," "*their* wives" [*tas gunaikas auton*] would be expected, but "*their*" in KJV NEB NIV is not in the Greek text. Further, "*the* women" in RSV NAB is incorrect. There is no Greek article "the" in the Greek text. Ancient Greek manuscripts do not read "*their* wives" or "*the* women," but "women," a term understood in Greek as "women" of the category under discussion in the context.[26]

The resumption of male characteristics in v. 12 poses a special problem in the NIV. That version reads in v. 8, "Deacons are to be men . . .," v. 11, "their wives are to be women . . .," and v. 12, "a deacon must be the husband of one wife." Now this certainly sounds as though "deacon" is strictly a male role. However, we noted that v. 11 does not read, "their wives," but "women," and the NIV even has a footnote indicating that women could be meant. So v. 11 is really not the problem. "Are to be men" in v. 8 in the NIV is not in the Greek text either. The text only says, "Deacons

---

[24]J. Roloff, *Der erste Brief an Timotheus* (Zürich: Benziger, 1988): 165.

[25]See Kelly, *The Pastoral Epistles*, 83f.

[26]Gordon Fee, *1 and 2 Timothy, Titus* (San Francisco: Harper and Row, 1984): 51, is incorrect in viewing v. 11 as an "afterthought."

(must be [v. 2]) . . . ." This addition of "are to be men" has
no foundation. The only real problem here is that v. 12
might seem to indicate that only males can be deacons.

Presumably Paul was writing within and to an Ephesian
culture that was hierarchal. However, some women in the
Ephesian church had overstepped traditional roles and had
assumed more visible roles in church life (2:9-15). Others
were serving in honorable ways (5:9-13). So while all of
the eldership and much of the designated servantship was
male, some Ephesian women were involved significantly in
servant roles. Vv. 1-7 certainly discuss elders in terms of
maleness. In the same way, vv. 8-10 and 12 would also
give the impression that deaconship involved only males, but
v. 11 was inserted to include characteristics for the females
also serving in that particular capacity. In v. 13, he specifies
that all those who serve well "gain an excellent standing."

Five matters favor the reading "female deacons." 1)
"Likewise" relates v. 11 to vv. 8-10. "Likewise" v. 8 in turn
relates vv. 8ff to vv. 1-7. Each unit of text (elders, vv. 1-7;
deacons, vv. 8-10; females, v. 11) is dependent upon the
verb "it is necessary" [*dei*] in v. 2. So, three groups are in
mind, all related to the same verb in v. 2. 2) Note the
parallelism evident between the four items in v. 8 dealing
with males and the four in v. 11 treating females. Characteristics for male deacons are, "worthy of respect, sincere, not
indulging in much wine, and not pursuing dishonest gain."
Similarly female deacons are to be, "worthy of respect, not
malicious talkers, temperate, and trustworthy." 3) When the
noun "woman" occurs with no article (*the*) or pronoun, it
relates female(s) under consideration to the context.[27]
"Women" in v. 11 is used without an article or pronoun and
should be taken to refer to females of the category of
"deacons" being discussed in vv. 8-10. 4) In 5:9-13, older
widows who met certain requirements were designated
servants in the Ephesian church. 5) Phoebe was a "deacon"
in the church in Cenchrea.

---

[27]F. Blass and A. Debrunner, *A Greek Grammar of the New
Testament* (tr. R. Funk; Chicago: Univ. of Chicago Press, 1961): 134.

1 Tim 3:8-10, then, treats selected characteristics of male deacons and v. 11 treats similar characteristics of female deacons.[28]   Actually, the women in 1 Tim 3:11 are inserted into the discussion as an extension of the point in vv. 8-10, a supplementary note necessitated by the fact that there were some women in Ephesus also in that category. In this respect, v. 11 is not unlike 1 Cor 14:34-35, where the tongues speakers and prophets were the focus, but certain women were also creating disruption in the Corinthian worship and were included as an extension of the point in the context that worship should be for edification and not disorderly. As in 1 Cor 14:36, verse 12, then, resumes the discussion with a new sentence treating matters of marriage and family life. "Husband of one wife" simply reflects that most of the deacons in Ephesus were males, but in view of v. 11 "deacons" cannot be taken solely with regard to males.

It should be observed that "deacons," whether male or female, were not "officials" in the earlier churches. Viewing deacons as junior officials in the church came along later when churches adopted a Roman organizational model.

Bishop
Elders
Deacons
Members

However, deacons in the first instance were merely "servants" charged with taking care of matters of service too important to be left to chance. Rather than viewing "deacons" in 3:8, 11, as officers, it is best to view these men and women simply as "designated servants."

---

[28]With Carl Spain, *The Letters of Paul to Timothy and Titus* (Austin, Tx: R. B. Sweet, 1970): 66f; Michael Green, *Called to Serve* (Philedelphia: Westminister, 1964): 55; Fee, *1 and 2 Timothy, Titus,* 50f; Kelly, *The Pastoral Epistles,* 83f; E. Schweizer, *Church Order in the New Testament* (London: SCM, 1961): 86; et al.

3. *Prisca (Priscilla): Helper, Bishop, or Teacher?*

A few years ago, I examined Prisca as an example of the early Christian view of women.[29] Although never referred to by herself in the NT, Prisca and her husband Aquila are occasionally mentioned as outstanding workers in the early church. He was a Jewish tentmaker from Pontus who had moved to Rome, but was expelled along with other Jews by the Emperor Claudius. Moving to Corinth, Aquila and his wife allowed Paul to stay with them and to work in their shop during his initial work there. They then went with him to Ephesus where they remained while he went on to Antioch (Acts 18). Later they moved back to Rome (Rom 16:3), then returned to Asia Minor (2 Tim 4:19). While not much is known for certain about this couple, they (especially Prisca) have attracted considerable attention in recent Christian thought.[30]

Assessments of Prisca's role vary considerably. Traditionalists view her merely as a "helper" of Aquila, and presupposing women could not teach Scripture to men, her role was merely one of "encouragement."[31] On the other hand, feminists also read into Prisca their views, e.g., "Priscilla was one of the most prominent women in the early church, perhaps functioning much like a bishop."[32] These varying estimates require careful sifting of biblical data to ascertain precisely Prisca's contribution to our understanding of women in the early church.

---

[29]Priscilla, diminutive form of the name Prisca, occurs in Acts, whereas Paul prefers Prisca (NIV mistranslates "Priscilla" in Paul).

[30]Adolf von Harnack, "Probabilia über die Adresse und den Verfasser des Hebräerbriefs," *Zeitschrift für die neutestamentliche Wissenschaft* 1 (1900): 16-41, unconvincingly proposed Prisca and Aquila as the writers of Hebrews.

[31]House, *The Role of Women in Ministry Today*, 139.

[32]Denise Lardner Carmody, *Biblical Woman: Contemporary Reflections on Scriptural Texts* (New York: Crossroad, 1992): 121.

In recent scholarship, some stress that she was the prominent one, not Aquila.[33] Basing the argument on the fact that her name is mentioned before Aquila's in Acts 18:18, 26, Rom 16:3, and 2 Tim 4:19, it is common to turn to Acts 18:26, where it is argued that her teaching of an outstanding scholar such as Apollos warrants viewing her as an outstanding teacher of at least equal strength. Typical of this thinking is Fiorenza, for whom this one text provides a full-blown character sketch of Prisca's role in the early church. Fiorenza[34] holds that Prisca's name occurs before Aquila's in four out of six instances because her own outstanding missionary work is in focus rather than her role as a wife. Fiorenza[35] concludes that Prisca's teaching of Apollos reflects a powerful intellect eloquently convincing an extremely intelligent male of her point of view on a theological matter, which then becomes paradigmatic for Christian women.

However, it is fair to ask whether this characterization of Priscilla accurately reflects biblical data. Two notions underly the idea that she was the dominant of the two: 1) that her name precedes his in four NT texts, and 2) that she was of higher social standing. On the latter, speculation abounds. Ramsay suggests,[36] "Probably Prisca was of higher rank than her husband, for her name is that of a good old Roman family. . . . Aquila was a Jew, while Priscilla was not. . . . Aquila was probably a freedman." Now Prisca was a fairly common Latin name among Roman women, and that could indicate that she was a Roman.

---

[33]Note "Prisca the missionary, with her husband" in Adolf von Harnack, *The Mission and Expansion of Christianity in the First Three Centuries* (trans. J. Moffatt; 2nd ed.; London: Williams & Norgate, 1908): 1.79.

[34]Elisabeth Schüssler Fiorenza, "Women in the Pre-Pauline and Pauline Churches," *Union Seminary Quarterly Review* 33 (1978): 156.

[35]Fiorenza, *In Memory of Her: A Feminist Theological Reconstruction of Christian Origins* (New York: Crossroad, 1983): 179.

[36]William Ramsay, *St. Paul the Traveller and the Roman Citizen* (3rd ed.; London: Hodder & Stoughton, 1897): 268-269.

However, Aquila's name was also a Latin name, although he was a Jew (Acts 18:2). That both had Latin names might merely reflect the custom of Greeks and Jews taking Latin names while living in Rome. At any rate, there is nothing to confirm the view that she belonged to an old, noble Roman family and left to marry a lowly Jewish tentmaker.[37] Accordingly, we know nothing of her race or social standing, or whether either were former slaves.

The primacy of Prisca actually hinges on the sequence in which their names occur in the NT. In Acts, the major characters are Peter and Paul, with principal secondary characters being the twelve, Stephen, Philip, Barnabas, James, and Apollos.[38] It could be that Prisca and Aquila serve as minor characters to establish a connection with the broader historical context.[39] It is more likely that they serve to introduce Apollos, who, for the first time since chap 15, plays a role in the narrative not involving Paul.

In Acts 18:2, the first mention of this couple in the NT, there is a translation problem. The common reading (KJV, NIV, NASB, RSV, NRSV), "Aquila. . . who had recently come from Italy *with* his wife Priscilla," is not as good as, "Aquila. . . who had recently come from Italy *and* his wife Priscilla" (JerB, NEB). Her name occurs second in 1 Cor 16:19 as well.[40] Accordingly, it is only a guess that the

---

[37]E.g., Sanday and A. C. Headlam, *The Epistle to the Romans* (Edinburgh: T. & T. Clark, 1902): 418-420, who unsuccessfully attempt to link Prisca with the Acilian family in Rome and conclude that since "for a noble Roman lady to travel about with a Jewish husband engaged in mercantile or even artisan work is hardly probable," Prisca and Aquila were both likely "freed members of a great household."

[38]See Adolf von Harnack, *The Acts of Apostles* (trans. J. Wilkinson; London: Williams & Norgate, 1909): 119ff. On Apollos, see 1 Cor 1:12; 3:4-6, 22; 4:6; 16:12.

[39]Luke Timothy Johnson, *The Acts of the Apostles* (Collegeville, MN: Liturgical Press, 1992): 325.

[40]The later Byzantine manuscripts read Aquila first at Acts 18:26, but the older manuscripts read Priscilla first. Some Syriac and Coptic

order of their names signifies that Prisca was the dominant person of the two. Any notion constructed on the inference that she was the dominant personality is precarious indeed. The text mentions neither Aquila nor Prisca as the dominant person.

Acts 18:24-28 is the crucial text. Both those who view her as dominant and those who view her only as a "helper" to Aquila approach this text with presuppositions that enable them to arrive at their preferred conclusions. Witherington, professor at Ashland Theological Seminary in Ohio, says,[41] "her name is mentioned first, so that if anyone is indicated by Luke as the primary instructor, it is Priscilla," and further, "Apollos is not just any convert to the faith, but a man 'well versed in Scripture', and this presupposes that Luke wants his audience to see that . . . he would accept it from both a woman and a man."[42] However, this is to miss Luke's intention regarding Apollos and to read modern concern into the text. When the text says that Apollos was "a learned man" who "spoke with great fervor," that is not to stress that he was corrected by a female, but to emphasize that with this new information, he was able (v. 28) "vigorously" to refute "the Jews in public debate, proving from the Scriptures that Jesus was the Christ." This text is not so much about Prisca *teaching* as about Apollos *learning*!

---

copies at 18:21-22 insert, "and he left Aquila and Priscilla at Ephesus, and he travelled by sea."

[41] Ben Witherington III, *Women in the Earliest Churches* (Cambridge: Cambridge Univ. Press, 1988): 154.

[42] In a classic overstatement, Carmody, *Biblical Woman*, 122, says, "The authority Priscilla shows in dealing with Apollos suggests that she enjoyed high status in the Pauline community at Ephesus. Far from being a back-bencher, she took the lead and set a talented, most likely strong-willed man straight." Note also Simon Kistemaker, *Acts* (Grand Rapids: Baker, 1990): 668, that Apollos demonstrated remarkable restraint in consenting to come to the home of a tentmaker "and to receive instruction from a humble craftsman but also from a woman."

152   Carroll D. Osburn

Spencer, relying on the word-order theory, wants to
make the teaching of Apollos by Prisca in *public*. She says
the verb used here "connotes a public declaration and
exposition."[43] However, one must remember that Prisca
and Aquila "invited him *to their home* and explained to him
the way of God more accurately" (Acts 18:26). Note, "they"
invited and "they" explained in a private or semi-private
context. On the other hand, to suggest that Luke wants to
stress that she was not involved in any *public* teaching is to
read modern concerns back into the text.[44] The point is that
Apollos received instruction. He had been persuasive in
teaching that Jesus was the Messiah, but he knew only the
baptism of John. They were able to explain to him the
significance of Christian baptism. With better insight, he
was in position to become a powerful proclaimer to the Jews
(v. 28). Nothing in Acts 18:24-28 suggests that Prisca took
the lead or was the primary instructor.[45] The plural verb
(*they* instructed) leaves no room for House's view[46] that
Aquila taught Scripture and Prisca merely encouraged.
There is no reason to suppose that Luke intended this
account to mean that a woman can teach a man only with her
husband or that it must be in private.[47] There is no basis for
the view that a woman can instruct only other women.

---

[43]Spencer, *Beyond the Curse*, 107, however, seems oblivious to
the devastating critique of illegitimate root usage by James Barr, *The
Semantics of Biblical Language* (Oxford: Oxford Univ. Press, 1961),
and responsible word-study advocated by John F. A. Sawyer, *Semantics
in Biblical Research* (Studies in Biblical Theology, 24; Naperville, IL:
Allenson, 1972).

[44]It is curious that hierarchicalist Werner Neuer, *Man & Woman
in Christian Perspective* (trans. G. Wenham; Wheaton: Crossway,
1991): 110, 132, does not treat Prisca, but only mentions her in
passing as a special friend of Paul and that "with Aquila gave private
instruction in the Bible" to Apollos.

[45]Against Witherington, *Women in the Earliest Churches*, 154.

[46]House, *The Role of Women in Ministry Today*, 139.

[47]Ernst Haenchen, *The Acts of the Apostles* (Philadelphia:
Westminister, 1971): 539, correctly notes that ". . . shows that they
were so important to the history of the Christian mission that Luke
could not overlook them."

Throughout, Prisca and Aquila are portrayed as equals. Fiorenza[48] notes correctly that this "partnership-mission" appears to "have been the rule in the Christian missionary movement." Paul mentions that the "church met at their house" in 1 Cor 16:19 and Rom 16:5. In the absence of special church buildings in the early church, such house churches were common and posed no threat to society. They actually gave a sense of legitimacy to religious group meetings.[49] Nothing is known about the role of women in early Christian house churches, however, and any suggestion of Prisca's role in this regard is speculative, either that she presided at the meetings in her home or that she merely served as hostess. We only know that she was involved equally with Aquila in instructing Apollos.

What we need to avoid are extremes that read cultural preferences into the text. We need to refocus the question about Prisca and ask what, if anything, is paradigmatic about her for today's church. There is nothing to indicate that Luke intended Prisca to serve as a model either of a mere assistant to her husband or of a dominant female teacher. Actually, Prisca occurs in the NT as a highly-respected worker in the early church and competent in instruction. While women in the Greco-Roman world generally did not address public assemblies,[50] Prisca's sharing in the teaching of Apollos with her husband at their home would have been acceptable in that society.

---

[48]Elisabeth Schüssler Fiorenza, "Missionaries, Apostles, Co-workers: Romans 16 and the Reconstruction of Women's Early Christian History," *Word and World* 6 (1986): 431, also cities Clement of Alexandria, *Stromateis*, 3.6.53.3, that married women, as sisters, "might be co-missionaries in dealing with housewives."

[49]See David C. Verner, "The Household in the Hellenistic-Roman World," *The Household of God: The Social World of the Pastoral Epistles* (Chico: Scholars Press, 1983): 27-81; Abraham Malherbe, *Social Aspects of Early Christianity* (2nd ed,; Philadelphia: Fortress, 1983): 95-96.

[50]Sterling, "Women in the Hellenistic and Roman Worlds," *Essays on Women in Earliest Christianity*, 1.72.

4. *Summary*

Some women of special ability and prominence served financially and influentially as "patrons." In this service, they were not designated, but were more self-appointed, working in accord with their capabilities and ingenuity. On the other hand, specially-designated widows also served.[51] Other women in the NT served as "female deacons." Deacons, whether male or female, were not officers, but "designated servants." Any authority or power attached to the diaconate comes from tradition, not Scripture. No distinction was made between the service of female and male deacons in earliest Christianity. Around the second century, "widows" apparently merged with the "female deacons." Later, when only ordained males conducted worship,[52] "widows/female deacons" became "*official* deaconesses" and their role changed from that found in the earlier NT churches.[53] As far as teaching is concerned, it was acceptable for an informed woman to teach a man. While both Prisca and Aquila were involved in instructing Apollos and the teaching occurred in their home, nothing from this text mandates that a woman can teach only with her husband or that such teaching must be in private. While "teacher" is a designated role in the early church (1 Cor 12:27-31; Eph 4:11-13), Prisca seems to have assumed this role on this occasion without special appointment.

---

[51]See Jean Daniélou, *The Ministry of Women in the Early Church* (tr. G. Simon; London: Faith, 1961): 16-20.

[52]Yet there is no NT reference to a professional body of priests in the church. See J. Massyngberde Ford, "Biblical Material Relevant to the Ordination of Women," *Journal of Ecumenical Studies* 10 (1973): 685.

[53]Guy N. Woods, "*Adult Gospel Quarterly*, Gospel Advocate Series (Nashville: Gospel Advocate, Summer 1970): 19, observed correctly of 1 Tim. 3:11, "There is no support here, nor elsewhere in the scriptures, for the denominational practice of having *official* deaconesses in the church." Yet qualified women perform certain tasks and of them Woods writes, "it is not out of order to refer to women in this category as deaconesses. This is a scriptural term and denotes a scriptural work." However, his view of *official* male deacons has no support in Scripture either, only in tradition!

9

EPHESIANS 5:21-33
SUBJECTION, SUBMISSION, & HEADSHIP

Eph 5:21-33 has often been understood as necessitating male hierarchalism and female subjection. The text of vv. 22-24, for instance, reads:

> 21) Be subject to one another out of reverence for Christ. 22) Wives, be subject to your husbands, as to the Lord. 23) For the husband is the head of the wife as Christ is the head of the Church, his body, and is himself its Savior. 24) As the church is subject to Christ, so let wives also be subject in everything to their husbands. (RSV)

> 21) Submit to one another out of reverence for Christ. 22) Wives, submit to your husbands as to the Lord. 23) For the husband is the head of the wife as Christ is the head of the church, his body, of which he is the Savior. 24) Now as the church submits to Christ, so also wives should submit to their husbands in everything. (NIV)

Two terms are at issue here. *Hupotassomai* can mean "subject" or "submit," with either mandatory submission or voluntary deference in mind. *Kephale* can mean "head" or "source." Both terms have been the subject of considerable controversy, and each is related to the other in interpretation. Neller[1] has a useful discussion of these problems.

1. *Hupotassomai—Subjection, Submission, or Deference?*

First, in order to understand Eph 5:22-24, one must view it in its literary context. Actually 5:21 governs the

---

[1]Kenneth Neller, "'Submission' in Eph 5:21-33," *Essays on Women in the Church*, 1.243-60.

entire context of 5:22-6:9,[2] which is related to 5:15-21. Paul restates (see 4:1, 17-24) his appeal for Christian ethic in vv. 15-17 with a call to "take care how you walk." By way of example, he says in v. 18, "do not be drunk with wine," but "be filled in spirit." Five Greek participles follow, each specifying how Christian readers can avoid irresponsible living and be "spirit-filled" people. Three participles occur in v. 19: "*speaking to one another in psalms, hymns, and spiritual songs*," "*singing*," and "*making melody your hearts to the Lord*." The fourth occurs in v. 20, "*giving thanks always*." And the fifth is "*being subject to (submissive to / deferential to) one another*" (v. 21).

Now 5:21 reads in English Bibles,

Be subject to one another out of reverence for Christ. (RSV)

Submit to one another out of reverence for Christ. (NIV)

In reality, "Be subject" (RSV) and "Submit" (NIV) do not occur in the Greek text of v. 22. The verb in v. 22 must be supplied from v. 21, where Christians are to be "*hupotassomai* (submissive to / deferential to) one another." How one understands "submission" in v. 21 has much to do with how one understands all that follows in 5:22-6:9, where mutual submission is stressed among husbands and wives, parents and children, and masters and slaves.[3]

A. *The Evangelical Feminist View.*

Scanzoni and Hardesty[4] state that "*Both* husbands and wives are told to be submissive to one another in the realization that *all* Christians should be subject to one another

---

[2]See, for instance, J. P. Sampley, *And The Two Shall Become One Flesh: A Study of Traditions in Ephesians 5:21-33* (SNTSMS, 16; Cambridge: Cambridge Univ. Press, 1971): 10, 27, 117, and Markus Barth, *Ephesians* (Anchor Bible Commentary, 34: Garden City, NY: Doubleday, 1974): 609.

[3]See extended discussion in Barth, *Ephesians*, 603-758.

[4]Scanzoni and Hardesty, *All We're Meant To Be*, 148.

(Eph 5:21)." They continue, holding that Eph 5 presents a new "*way*" that husbands and wives are to relate.

> The headship / subjection pattern was transformed. Wives were to submit in a totally new way—as part of the mutual submission of *all* believers to one another. . . . From this, the husband takes his cue as to how he is to be the "head" of his wife—a way so startlingly different from older ideas of male headship that the first husbands who read this epistle must have been astonished (149).

At this point, the authors bring up the *kephale* (meaning "source") argument which we will discuss later, basically arguing that man is not the dominator of woman, but the "beginning," "origin," or "source" of woman.

More representative of evangelical feminist use of the biblical text here is Bilezikian.[5] To his credit, Bilezikian recognizes the relationship of 5:21 to vv. 18-20, correctly identifying the five participles in vv. 19-21 as illustrative of being "spirit-filled." He also correctly observes the relationship of 5:21 to vv. 22-33, stating,

> If verse 21 is separated from verse 22—as some versions do through faulty paragraphing (the NIV provides a prime example)—verse 22 becomes meaningless, since the sentence is devoid of a verb in the original text. . . . Verse 22 derives its verb from verse 21. (162).

Bilezikian views 5:21 as introducing the topic of "mutual submission," e.g., mutual relationships between husband and wife. This means that *hupotassomai* is understood to mean "mutual submission" of believers to one another in the church (5:18-20) and at home (5:22-23). The conclusion, then, is drawn in vv. 31-32 with the reference to Gen 2:24, that, "for this reason shall a man leave his father and mother and be joined to his wife, and the two shall become one." Throughout this text, he understands the subordination of oneself to the interests of the other as focal.

---

[5]Bilezikian, *Beyond Sex Roles*, 162-73.

Specifically, Bilezikian sees in 5:21-24 the expression of mutual submission for the wife. Some submission, he says, is manipulative and self-serving. Other submission is nothing more than inferiority and self-deprecation. Some submission is mere compliance that avoids conflict. Other submission is resentful resignation to the inevitable. However, when Paul says in v. 22 that submission is "as to the Lord," this does not mean that her husband now becomes for her "a lord."[6] "As to the Lord," he says, "means that a wife submits to her husband in the same kind of loving service that she renders to the Savior," . . . "not in servility but in servanthood" (166). A wife's "submission" is not based upon authoritarian obedience, but upon a loving response to Christ's love.

"For," in v. 23, introduces Paul's explanation of the statement in v. 22. The man is "head" (*kephale*) of the wife as Christ is "head" (*kephale*) of the church. Bilezikian holds that, "Both Christ and man are 'head' or 'source of life' to their respective brides, the church for One and the woman for the other" (166).

The admonition in v. 24 for the wife to be submissive to her husband (*hupotassomai*) is understood to mean that,

> the submission of the church to Christ and of the wife to the husband is something more demanding than and different from obedience to codes, or conformity to authority, or acceptance of rulership. It is the disposition of one's whole being for another's sake, the espousing of total servanthood in every dimension of shared lives, a life orientation of service joyfully assumed in response to love (167).

---

[6]Note Thomas Aquinas, *St. Paul's Epistle to the Ephesians* (trans. M. Lamb; Albany, NY: Magi, 1966): 2.216f., says, "Let women be subject to their husbands as to a lord," and further, ". . . *as to a lord* since the relation of a husband to his wife is, in a certain way, like that of a master to his servant." John Calvin, *Sermons on the Epistle to the Ephesians* (London: Banner of Truth, 1973): 572, says of wives that "it is also for their benefit to be under their husbands and to yield them obedience."

Bilezikian continues,

> The word *authority* is never used in the New Testament to describe any aspect of the husband / wife relationship (except in 1 Cor 7:4). Husbands are never instructed to exercise authority over their wives. Wives are never commanded to obey their husbands or to submit to the authority of their husbands, and no threat ever accompanies the injunction for wives to submit to their husbands. . . . Only a Christian woman can submit to her husband in servanthood "as to the Lord" (167).

After having asked wives to submit to their husbands, one might expect a section in which husbands are given instruction on the proper use of authority and on keeping their wives in subjection. However, that is precisely what is *not* done in the text. Instead, the opposite approach is taken—husbands are to have love-motivated self-surrender that is willing to subject itself even to death for the sake of their wives. This requirement is actually more stringent than the submission expected of wives.

In v. 25, husbands' love for wives is defined by the love exemplified by Christ on the cross. In the same way, husbands are to give themselves up for their wives. "It is not," Bilezikian says, "His power, His lordship, and His authority that are presented as traits to emulate, but His humility, His abnegation, and His servant-behavior" (169). This call finds practicality in v. 28 where husbands are to give their wives the same consideration that they would expect for themselves, treating them as their own persons. This is what is meant by "one flesh" of Gen 2:24. Reciprocity, according to Bilezikian, is the essential principle underlying the concept of "mutual submission."

So, in vv. 29-33, Paul drives home the point that Christian husbands should not take advantage of the submission of their wives as an occasion to assume authority over them. Instead, the proper Christian response for wifely submission is the reciprocal submission of husbands in which husbands love their wives as themselves.

B. *The Hierarchal Complementarian View.*

Perhaps the best hierarchal study of Eph 5:21-33 is that of Hurley,[7] who also holds that, "verse 21 is grammatically related to both the preceding and the following material. It is in fact a transitional verse" (140). He cites   1 Cor 11:1 as a parallel usage to Eph 5:21.

In 5:22-6:9, Hurley states, the emphasis is upon the submission of believers to one another, in each instance discussing the submissive partner first—wives are to submit, children and slaves are to obey. It follows that it would be improper to restrict the mutual submission to the wife / husband relationship alone.

While mutual submission would be meaningful for wife / husband and child / parent relationships, it is not seen as fitting the slave / master relationship. Hurley holds that, "The idea of mutual submission is, however, appropriate if it is addressed to the congregation at large, and exemplified in these three relations in which one member must yield to another" (140-41). So Hurley says v. 21 ought not be viewed as advocating submission of both partners in the wife / husband, child / parent, and slave / master relationships—just wives, children, and slaves (141).

The call for women in Ephesus to understand their relation to their husbands in terms of their relation to Christ means that as the church itself submits to Christ, so wives should submit themselves to their husbands in everything (Eph 5:22-24). But how does this take place?

According to Hurley, the Greek verb *hupotasso* means "sub-ordinate" and is best translated "to make subject" or "to submit oneself" or "to be obedient to." "Each of the forty New Testament uses of the verb," he says, "carried the overtone of authority and subjection or submission to it" (142). In this connection he cites the uses in Rom 13:1, 5; 1 Cor 14:32, 34; and 15:27.

---

[7]Hurley, *Man and Woman in Biblical Perspective*, 138-52.

Hurley does not agree that the use of *hupotassomai* in Eph 5:21 means a "mutual" submission, i.e., husbands and wives, parents and children, and slaves and masters to submit to the needs of one another. Although admitting this view to be attractive, Hurley nevertheless argues that in 5:21 it is only the subordinate who is asked to submit. While bending to meet the needs of a weaker partner is present throughout the discussion, Paul always uses a word other than *hupotassomai* to describe that action. Husbands, parents, and masters are never asked to "submit" to the subordinate.

So while husbands are to love their wives as themselves and expend every effort to build up their wives (Eph 5:22-24), the NT does not use "submit" (*hupotassomai*) to convey that idea. To conclude, Hurley views 5:21 as a general heading indicating that there will be certain instances in which believers must yield to the authority of others. He understands 5:22-6:9 as presenting three particular relations in which this is the case. "Mutual submission," then, has more to do with the various members of the congregation than with the two partners in each pair.

The hierarachal complementarian view is given by Knight, Professor of New Testament at Knox Theological Seminary. His view differs somewhat from that of Hurley.[8] Viewing 5:21 as a transition from vv. 18-20 to the following verses, Knight correctly sees *hupotassomai* in v. 21 as the fifth in a series of five participles in vv. 19-21 which conclude the point made in v. 18. He also is correct in noting that v. 22 must imply its verb from v. 21. He states that *hupotassomai* in v. 21 is in a form of the Greek verb that means, "what one does to oneself," a "voluntary yielding in love" (166). The motivation for submission is noted to be "reverence for Christ." He then views 5:21 not as a general statement of specifics for the wives, children, and servants, but as a general principle to be incorporated into all

---

[8]George Knight, "Husbands and Wives as Analogues of Christ and the Church: Ephesians 5:21-33 and Colossians 3:18-19," *Recovering Biblical Manhood and Womanhood*, 165-78.

relationships, whether wife or husband, parent or child, slave or master. This would, he says, be in line with Phil 2:3, "let each of you regard one another. . ." and 1 Pet 5:5, "clothe yourselves with humility toward one another" (167).

Knight takes the view that as 5:21 is a transition to the entirety of the section on household responsibilities, mutual submissiveness is the theme of the entire section. However, the mutual submission to which all are called in the section does not rule out the specific and different roles and relationships to which husbands and wives are called in the verses directed to them (168).

"Every passage that deals with the relationship of the wife to her husband," Knight says, "tells her to 'submit to' him, using this same verb (*hupotasso*): Eph 5:22; Col 3:18; 1 Pet 3:1; Tit 2:4" (168). He also notes that the NT never commands husbands to subordinate their wives, i.e., force them to submit (169). *Hupotassomai* means "submission in the sense of voluntary yielding in love" (168). Knight continues,

> Paul is not insisting that every relationship between a woman and a man is one of submission and headship, but that where leadership is an ingredient of the situation, as in marriage, the woman should submit to that leadership (headship) of the man (169).

In noting that Paul stresses that "the husband is the head of the wife *as* Christ is head of the church," Knight states that Christ is the head of the church as the authority over it and that is why the church submits to Christ. Thus Paul uses the term *kephale* (head) for the husband as he does for Christ because he is the one who has the authority and is the leader. In this connection, the extent of the wives' submission is all-encompassing. "Wives should submit themselves to their husbands *in everything*" (5:24). This should not be taken, Knight says, to mean that husbands can rule their wives insensitively (170).

2. *Kephale—Headship or Source?*

In Eph 5:23 Paul says that the husband is "head of the wife." Two views exist about the meaning of "head." 1) Some say that "head" in the NT does not refer to a leader or one in authority, but means "source" or "beginning."[9] This means that men / husbands are the "source" of women / wives, but have no authority over them. Eph 5:23, then, would refer to mutual dependence and unity. 2) Another view is that "head" refers to some type of leadership role and/ or authority.[10] This means that "head" rarely means "source" in Greek literature. So "head" must refer to some sort of leadership or authority over the wife by the husband.

A. *The Evangelical Feminist View.*

Representative of the evangelical feminist perspective on *kephale* (head) in Eph 5:23 and 1 Cor 11:3 is the study of the Mickelsens.[11] It is argued that the term *kephale* (head) in Greek does not have just the one meaning of "authority," but actually has other meanings. In the NT, "head" meaning "source of life" occurs in Col 2:19 (the Head, from whom the whole body, nourished and knit together through its joints and ligaments, grows), Eph 4:15 (we are to grow up

---

[9]This is the view of Berkeley and Alvera Mickelsen, "What Does *Kephale* Mean in the New Testament?" *Women, Authority & the Bible* (ed. A. Mickelsen; Downers Grove, IL: InterVarsity, 1986): 97-117; Bilezikain, *Beyond Sex Roles*, 215-52; Catherine Kroeger, "The Classical Concept of Head as 'Source'," *Equal to Serve: Women and Men in the Church and Home* (ed. G. Hull; Old Tappan, NJ: F. H. Revell, 1987): 267-83; and Gordon Fee, *The First Epistle to the Corinthians* (Grand Rapids: Eerdmans, 1987): 502f.

[10]This is the view of Wayne Grudem, "Does *Kephale* Mean 'Source' or 'Authority Over' in Greek Literature? A Survey of 2,336 Examples," *Trinity Journal* 6 (1985): 38-59; and J. A. Fitzmyer, "Another Look at *kephale* in 1 Corinthians 11:3," *New Testament Studies* 35 (1989): 503-11.

[11]Berkeley and Alvera Mickelsen, "What Does *Kephale* Mean in the New Testament?" *Women, Authority & the Bible*, 97-117. See also Philip Barton Payne, "Response," *Women, Authority & the Bible*, 118-32.

in every way to him who is the head, into Christ, from whom the whole body, joined and knit together by every joint). The meaning "top, crown, or extremity" occurs in Col 2:10, Eph 1:20-23. "Head" as "source, base derivation" occurs in 1 Cor 11:3 (the head of every man is Christ, and the man is head of woman, and God is head of Christ). The term means "originator or completer" in Col 1:18, Eph 5:23.

"Head" in Eph 5:23 is part of the "head / body" metaphor in Ephesians which stresses the unity of Christ and the church just as the head and body are dependent upon each other. The Mickelsens stress that "wives to your husbands" in v. 22 is dependent upon v. 21, "be submissive to one another," for its verb. This means for them that v. 22 refers to the same kind of submission demanded of all Christians in v. 21.

So, when Paul says that the husband is "head of the wife," this view understands him to be emphasizing the oneness of husband and wife. The Mickelsens note that there is no necessary hierarchy in Gen 2:24 (Eph 5:31-32), and that if hierarchy were intended Paul would probably have referred to Gen 3:16, "your desire shall be for your husband and he shall rule over you," instead of 2:24. Thus, for evangelical feminists "giving oneself sacrificially for the other" is an example of the submission taught in Eph 5:21.

B. *The Hierarchal Complementarian View.*

Representative of hierarchal complementarian thought is Grudem.[12] Grudem finds the suggestion that *kephale* means "source" to be surprisingly weak on two counts. First, arguments favoring "source" as the meaning depend upon two examples of *kephale* in ancient literature: Herodotus 4.91 (where *kephale* refers to the source of a river) and *Orphic Fragments* 21a (where Zeus is called "head" of all things). Both of these texts date more than four hundred

---

[12]Grudem, "Does *Kephale* Mean 'Source' or 'Authority Over' in Greek Literature? A Survey of 2,336 Examples," *Trinity Journal*, 38-59.

years before the time of the NT.   On the other hand, Grudem's search of 2,336 examples of *kephale* from a wide range of Greek literature produced no convincing examples in which *kephale* means "source."

Second, there is considerable evidence to support the claim that *kephale* can mean "authority over." This is the meaning found in the Greek lexicons, except in the classical lexicon of Liddell-Scott. In Grudem's search of 2,336 examples, forty-nine texts emerged where *kephale* had the meaning of "person of superior authority or rank, or 'ruler'," indicating this to be an accepted meaning for the term at the time of the NT. Grudem argues that the meaning "authority over" suits many NT contexts.

Cervin[13] responded to Grudem, arguing that "head" does not mean "authority" or "source" in Paul's epistles, but "preeminent." Grudem responds to Cervin by criticizing his avoidance of examples of *kephale* elsewhere in the NT, in the Septuagint (Greek translation of the OT), in Plutarch (ca. 50-120 AD.), and in the early church fathers, as well as his rejection of NT lexicons in favor of ancient lexicons using Greek literature far removed from the time of the NT. [14]

For Grudem, the meaning of *kephale* as "head" with the connotation of "authority over" is clear from such texts as 1 Cor 11:3, Eph 1:22, Eph 4:15, Eph 5:22-24, Col 1:18, Col 2:10, and 18-19 (434-35).

Grudem also responds to the Mickelsens' argument that "head" in the NT often meant "source," but never "head."[15] The translators of the Septuagint, they say, used *kephale* to

---

[13]Richard Cervin, "Does *Kephale* Mean 'Source' or 'Authority' in Greek Literature? A Rebuttal," *Trinity Journal* 10 (1989): 85-112.

[14]Wayne Grudem, "The Meaning of *Kephale* (Head): A Response to Recent Studies," *Recovering Biblical Manhood and Womanhood*, 425-68. Grudem also responds here to the aforementioned studies of Payne and Bilezikian and the commentary of Gordon Fee on 1 Cor.

[15]Berkeley and Alvera Mickelsen, "What Does *Kephale* Mean in the New Testament?" *Women, Authority & the Bible*, 97-117.

translate the Hebrew word *ro'sh* ("head") in only eight of the 180 instances in which *ro'sh* means "leader" or "authority over." They suggest, then, that *kephale* was not the term of preference for the meaning "head." Grudem responds that while it is true that *archon* was the principal Greek term used for "ruler" in Greek prior to the NT, still *kephale* was used to mean "ruler" or "authority" in a metaphorical sense of "head" on occasion. There are, he says, certainly no instances of *kephale* meaning "source" in the OT.

Grudem's critique of Kroeger[16] is essentially that her attempt to prove the meaning of *kephale* as "source" in classical Greek literature fails becauase her examples are drawn from literature *after* the time of the NT. Also, when Kroeger translates texts, she translates them with the meaning "source," thus reading her theory into the texts. The important thing to understand, he says, is not what *kephale* meant four centuries before or four centuries after the NT, but what Paul meant by it in his epistles.

Grudem concludes that the meaning "ruler, authority over" is found in more than forty ancient texts in both biblical and non-biblical literature, while the meaning "source" is practically non-existent during NT times.

3. *Discussion.*

So, does *kephale* mean "authority" or "source"? What is really meant by *hupotassomai* in terms of "submission"? In view of the tremendous arguments raging over these important terms, we must take a closer look at the use of both *hupotassomai* and *kephale*.

In the NT, when the verb *hupotasso* is used in the active voice, it means "to subject, subjugate," and God is always the subjugator, except in Phil 3:21 where Christ is the subjugator. When the active voice is used, there is always

---

[16]Catherine Clark Kroeger, "The Classical Concept of Head as 'Source'," *Equal to Serve: Women and Men in the Church and Home*, 267-83.

some problem between the subjugator and the subjugated. Nowhere in the NT is there basis for a human being to subjugate another human being.

The Greek middle voice is used when one does something to or for oneself. The middle form of *hupotasso* is *hupotassomai*. Now a problem exists in that the middle form *hupotassomai* (willing submissiveness) is also the same as the passive form (be in subjection). The difference can be seen in certain translations of the NT. For instance, "submit yourselves to every human authority" (middle, KJV; NIV) is a more accurate translation of 1 Pet 2:13 than "be subject to every human institution" (passive, RSV). Similarly, in Heb 12:9, "willing to submit ourselves to our spiritual Father" (middle, JerB) is more accurate than "be in subjection to the Father of spirits" (passive, KJV). Whether the term *hupotassomai* is middle (to or for oneself) or passive (something is done to the subject) depends upon the context.

In the NT, only God and Christ have the right to subjugate others, and they only do so when the others are antagonistic. When a person is called to submit, submission is always voluntary on the part of the person. The middle sense of *hupotassomai* meaning "voluntary submission" is found in several NT texts, e.g., Rom 13:1 ("Everyone must submit himself to the governing authorities"), 1 Cor 16:16 ("submit to such as these"), and Eph 5:21 ("Submit to one another out of reverence for Christ").

Once it is agreed that the Greek middle form should be translated "voluntary submission," the precise meaning of the term in Eph 5:21-24 hinges on how one understands the relationship of v. 22 to v. 21. As was said earlier, v. 22 gets its verb from v. 21. However, does the reference to "voluntary submission" in v. 21 affect only the wives, children, and slaves in vv. 22-6:9? Or is this "voluntary submission" intended for all?

Hurley,[17] you will remember, argued correctly that Eph 5:21 should be viewed both as the conclusion of 5:18-20 and as the introduction to 5:22-6:9. However, he held that the mutual submission involved does not extend to both pairs (wives / husbands; children / parents; slaves / masters), but was limited to wives, children, and slaves. On the other hand, Knight[18] argued that the mutual submission does extend to all pairs, not just wives, children, and slaves. However, he held that mutual submission does not do away with roles that were established in creation.

Bilezikian[19], you recall, held that 5:21 introduces the topic of mutual relationships between husband and wife under the rubric of "mutual submission." This means that *hupotassomai* is understood to mean "mutual submission" of believers to one another in the church (5:18-20) and at home (5:22-23). The conclusion, then, is drawn in vv. 31-32 with the reference to Gen 2:24, that, "for this reason shall a man leave his father and mother and be joined to his wife, and the two shall become one." Throughout, he understands the subordination of oneself to the interests of the other as focal.

It seems to me that the theme of Eph 5:15-6:9 is daily conduct of the Christian life. Paul specifically enjoins the readers in 5:15 to "take care how you walk, not as unwise but as wise." Rather than singing the songs of drunkenness (v. 18), Christians should sing decidedly Christian songs that underscore and encourage the Christian walk (v. 19), continue with a daily prayer life (v. 20), and show mutual deference ("voluntary submission") to one another (v. 21).

The appeal in v. 22, then, is for wives to demonstrate "voluntary submission / mutual deference" to their husbands. The way husbands show "voluntary submission / mutual deference" is by loving their wives. In a reciprocal relationship, a Christian couple can "walk wisely."

---

[17]Hurley, *Man and Woman in Biblical Perspective*, 140-44.

[18]Knight, "Husbands and Wives as Analogues of Christ and the Church," *Recovering Biblical Manhood and Womanhood*, 167.

[19]Bilezikian, *Beyond Sex Roles*, 163.

Similarly, the way children demonstrate "voluntary submission / mutual deference" to their parents is by obeying them. Parents demonstrate this attitude by helping their children to mature through responsible instruction and up-bringing. In this reciprocal relationship, Christian families can "walk wisely."

Too, the way Christian slaves demonstrate "voluntary submission / mutual deference" to their masters is through obedience and diligent work. The way masters demonstrate this "voluntary submission / mutual deference" is by avoiding threatening, domineering behavior. In this reciprocal relationship, Christians can "walk wisely" in the culture of slavery in operation at the time.

In this sense, "mutual submission" in v. 21 is urged of all Christians, not just wives, children, and slaves. This is certainly in line with the teaching throughout the NT that Christians are to "submit to one another"—Matt 20:26-28; Phil 2:3; 1 Pet 5:4-5. Neller[20] puts it this way,

> The primary focus of 'submit yourselves' must be on attitude. One can be forced to obey the government or a slave can be made to obey a master, but Christian submission is a voluntary surrender of one's own rights, a placing of oneself at the disposal of, or in the service of, someone else. Submission is a willing deference.

Barth[21] describes this voluntary submission as,

> a voluntary attitude of giving in, cooperating, assuming responsibility, and carrying a burden. . . . It is a demonstration of that 'total humility, gentleness, mutual bearing, love, unity, peace' which in 4:1-3 were described as the constitutive works not of miserable slaves and bootlickers but of the free children of God.

---

[20]Neller, "'Submission' in Eph 5:21-33," *Essays on Women in Earliest Christianity*, 1.249.

[21]Barth, *Ephesians*, 710.

Now such mutual respect would be admirable if it led to women and men putting themselves out to help one another. However, cultural roles continue. That pleases Knight[22] whose hierarchalism is evident when he says,

> it could be argued that the command given husbands to love their wives is but another way of calling them to mutual submission. But even if that were so, Paul still calls the husband "the head" of the wife and therefore the one to whom she should submit in everything (verses 22-24).

While exegesis suggests that *kephale* should be taken as "head," Knight nevertheless fails in his attempt to ground the cultural roles of women in NT times in the ancient intent of God.

On the other hand, any continuation of ancient cultural roles into today's world annoys Carmody,[23] who says,

> wives are to be subject to their husbands, but no parallel line immediately comes along to balance this admonition and bid husbands be subject to their wives. If wives should consider husbands like Christ, their Lord, and willingly submit to their husbands' wishes, why should husbands not consider their wives like Christ, and show a similar willingness to submit to their wives wishes? . . . I am afraid the author of Ephesians was all too human, all too little penetrated by the radical vision of the new life in Christ, and so could not see beyond the sexist assumptions of the day.

Carmody asks, "Why should the husband have all the priority in a marriage?" She answers, "The only reason seems to be the author's acceptance of the cultural standards of the day" (140). Carmody is miffed that Eph 5:21-33, "so shortchanges feminine human nature and so limits the potential of marriage that I cannot think it God's revelation." As a feminist, she concludes that "it just is not true that men

---

[22]Knight, "Husbands and Wives as Analogues of Christ and the Church," *Recovering Biblical Manhood and Womanhood*, 168.

[23]Denise Larder Carmody, *Biblical Woman: Contemporary Reflections on Scriptural Texts* (New York: Crossroad, 1992): 139-40.

by nature are the heads of women, the leaders in households, the superior in the marital relationship, the one who should receive subjection but not give it." This text only serves, according to Carmody, as a temptation for men,

> to become paternalistic, head patting, superior, condescending, and overbearing and for women to become wrongly docile, helpless, foolish, irresponsible, childish, and weak. Does God want weak, simpering women? Does God think men by nature nobly made to be heads? I cannot believe She does, because I know She sees more than I see, and what I see makes such a view laughable (142).

Here, the prejudices which control so much discussion on this volatile topic are easily seen.

This author concludes that in Eph 5:21-24 Paul calls for a mutual submission, a voluntary deference for all Christians, whatever their roles in life. It is vital to understand that neither Paul nor Jesus before him called for the radical overthrow of hierarchalism. Both had ideals along egalitarian lines, yet both worked within the cultural systems of the day—whether regarding slavery or gender roles—and taught Christians to "walk wisely" given certain cultural constraints. Paul's admonition for mutual submission is still valid for twenty-first century Christians.

10

1 CORINTHIANS 11:2-16
CULTURAL SENSITIVITY IN WORSHIP

One of the most important texts in the NT regarding women in early Christianity is 1 Cor 11:2-16. Here, Paul speaks positively of women in the Corinthian church praying and prophesying, but asks them to respect contemporary customs of appearance while doing so. Paul's discussion of reasons for this admonition raises several problems of interpretation.[1] Major questions include 1) whether a public or private assembly is in mind, 2) what is meant by "headship," and 3) why wearing the veil and having long hair is important for women.

1. *Public or Private Assembly?*

Much current discussion concerns the relationship between 1 Cor 11:2-16 and 1 Cor 14:34-36. In 11:2-16 Paul approves of women praying and prophesying. However, in 14:34-36, Paul appears to forbid women to speak in corporate worship. Does this mean that Paul contradicts himself?

Two views exist regarding the relationship of 1 Cor 11:2-16 to 14:34-36. 1) Since women pray and prophesy in 11:2-16 with Paul's approval, but are forbidden to speak in corporate worship in 14:34-36, some conclude that chap. 11 must refer to worship in a private setting. 2) Alternatively, if the section 11:2-14:40 treats problems in Corinthian worship, then women in 11:2-16 pray and prophesy in the public worship with Paul's approval, but are asked not to disregard widely-accepted cultural norms when doing so.

---

[1]See Mark Black, "1 Cor 11:2-16—A Re-investigation," *Essays on Women in Earliest Christianity*, 1.191-218.

That 11:2-16 refers to a private setting is a commonly-held view, but rarely defended with thoughtful argument. In Restoration thought, Lipscomb[2] maintains that a private setting is in view, but provides no argument, other than to mention that in the NT there are no examples of women speaking or leading prayer publicly. Ferguson[3] also views 11:2-16 as a private setting and suggests that Paul transitions to matters of public worship in v. 17. He posits without argument, "Praying and prophesying could be in a group or in 'public,' but not in an assembly of the church."

However, the view that 11:2-16 refers to a private setting is certainly not the principal view in Restoration thought. The more common view is that 11:2-16 refers to the public assembly. After careful exegesis of the text, McGarvey[4] concludes firmly that, "Paul is here discussing how men and women should be attired when they take a leading part in public worship." McGarvey argues 14:34-36 to be "the regular, formal meeting of the church" (143). He specifies that "the customs of the age made it a shameful thing for a woman to speak in public," but that the prophecy in Acts 2:17, "your sons and daughters shall prophesy," demands viewing 11:5 as an exception to the cultural norm. He continues,

> The powers of woman have become so developed, and her privileges so extended in gospel lands, that it is no longer shameful for her to speak in public. . . . The Christian conscience has therefore interpreted Paul's rule rightly when it applies it generally, but admits of exceptions, . . . those women who have a marked ability, either for exhortation or instruction, are permitted to speak in the churches.

---

[2]David Lipscomb, *A Commentary on the New Testament Epistles* (Nashville: Gospel Advocate, 1935): 2.163, who provides no arguments for the view.

[3]Everett Ferguson, *The Church of Christ: A Biblical Ecclesiology for Today* (Grand Rapids: Eerdmans, 1996): 342.

[4]J. W. McGarvey, *Thessalonians, Corinthians, Galatians, and Romans* (Cincinnati: Standard, 1916): 113.

Most Restoration writers, e.g., DeHoff[5] and Coffman,[6] understand 11:2-16 to refer to public worship. Certainly in the academic world, most scholars agree that 11:2-16 refers to women praying and prophesying in the public assembly. In fact, Fee[7] does more than most commentators when he includes, but dismisses, the private-setting view with merely a brief footnote.

Three reasons may be given as to why it is unlikely that 11:2-16 refers to a private setting.[8] 1) It is difficult to understand why Paul would make such a strong appeal for a wife to wear a head-covering in the presence of her husband in a private setting. 2) The argument that Paul approves a practice in 11, only to place restrictions on it a few chapters later has never convinced many. 3) 1 Cor 10:31-11:1 forms the conclusion of the section which began in 8:1, all of which treats eating (in a domestic setting) meat offered to idols.[9] This means that 11:2-16 forms the first part of the unit 11-14, which treats problems in Corinthian worship. In fact, the two matters of praying and prophesying in 11:2-16 are precisely the two matters which present so many problems in the worship at Corinth and which are in focus in chaps 12-14.

---

[5]George W. DeHoff, *Sermons on First Corinthians* (Murfreesboro, TN: Christian Press, 1947): 99, who notes, "There is no verse in the Bible which teaches that women must teach God's word *in private*. The 'in private' is added by false teachers."

[6]Burton Coffman, *1 and 2 Corinthians* (Austin, TX: Firm Foundation, 1977): 165, notes, "This writer admires and respects the immortal Lipscomb," but also detects in Lipscomb "a basic misunderstanding of this difficult passage."

[7]Gordon D. Fee, *The First Epistle to the Corinthians* (Grand Rapids: Eerdmans, 1987): 505, n. 54.

[8]See further Carroll Osburn, "1 Cor 11:2-16—Public or Private?" *Essays on Women in Earliest Christianity*, 2.307-16.

[9]Wendell Willis, *Idol Meat in Corinth* (SBLDS 68; Chico, CA: Scholars Press, 1985): 223-63.

Mitchell[10] correctly sees 11:2-14:40 as a section in which Paul urges unity instead of factionalism. From the very first hint of it in 1:10-17, Paul addresses factionalism as a basic problem in 1 Cor. It is not surprising that such factionalism would surface when persons assemble for worship who have little genuine concern for other Christians. Throughout 11:2-14:40, Paul continues to stress unity with the appeals to "building" and "body" imagery which he had used earlier in 1 Cor. Paul is not merely concerned with women in the church, but with the larger problem of proper and orderly conduct of Christian worship. The purpose of 11-14, then, is to persuade the Corinthians to be united rather than divided when they worship. As we look at Paul's arguments, we must remember that Paul is attempting to persuade women of ancient Corinth to wear head-coverings, not women of today. Consequently, his arguments may have made good sense to ancient readers, but may appear to be somewhat strained to modern readers.

2. What is meant by "headship"?

First, Paul states in v. 3, "I want you to realize that the head of every man is Christ, and the head of the woman is the man, and the head of Christ is God" [NIV]. Two points in the second pair are worthy of note: 1) "the" in front of "woman" is actually "a" in Greek, and 2) the Greek words "woman" and "man" also mean "wife" and "husband." Context determines which meaning is intended. So, v. 3 raises two important questions: 1) what is meant by "headship", and 2) are we dealing with male/ female relationships or husband/wife?

Now, turn to v. 2 in your Bible. It is important to observe that Paul begins by noting "tradition" [v. 2 RSV; Greek *paradosis*][11] and concludes with reference to

---

[10]Margaret M. Mitchell, *Paul and the Rhetoric of Reconciliation: An Exegetical Investigation of the Language and Composition of 1 Corinthians* (Louisville: Westminster/John Knox, 1993).

[11]KJV reads curiously, "ordinances," and NIV incorrectly reads, "teachings," giving the impression of Christian doctrine. The principal

"traditional practice; custom" in v. 16 [Gr. *synetheian*]. This indicates that the matter of women praying and prophesying in 11:2-16 reflects the customary practice of churches in Paul's day regarding women in congregational worship.[12]

In this connection, v. 3 addresses the relationships of men/husbands, women/wives, Christ, and God. This verse is often taken to imply a hierarchical "order of creation"— God, Christ, man, woman.[13] In this view, woman is to be in subjection to man just as Christ is in subjection to God.

However, this so-called "order of creation" argument has been challenged. Paul's argument hinges on a "word-play" with the Greek word "head" [*kephale*]. Also, the Mickelsens,[14] have claimed that "head" [Gr. *kephale*] in the NT never designates a leader or anyone with authority. Instead, "head" in the NT is taken to mean "source" or "beginning." This would mean that men/husbands are the "source" of women/ wives, but have no "authority" over them. They take 11:3 to mean that while Christ does have authority over the church, that authority is not actually in focus here. What is in focus, they say, is the unity of Christ and the church. Taking this view, Fee[15] states,

---

term for "teachings" in Greek is *didache*, whereas *paradosis* is the term for "tradition."

[12]Among others, Peter Cotterell and Max Turner, *Linguistics & Biblical Interpretation* (Downers Grover, IL: InterVarsity, 1989): 316.

[13]Against John Reuf, *Paul's First Letter to Corinth* (Philadelphia: Westminster, 1977): 108, who says, "Paul establishes here an order of precedence: God, Christ, man, woman," although he then comments, "What he seems to be mainly concerned with, however, is the difference in the outward appearance of men and women in the worshipping group."

[14]Berkeley and Alvera Mickelsen, "What does *kephale* mean in the New Testament?" *Women, Authority & the Bible* , 97-117. See also Bilezikian, "A Critical Examination of Wayne Grudem's Treatment of *Kephale* in Ancient Greek Texts," *Beyond Sex Roles*, 215-52; and Catherine Kroeger, "The Classical Concept of Head as 'Source'," *Equal to Serve: Women and Men in the Church and Home*, 267-83.

[15]Fee, *The First Epistle to the Corinthians*, 503-04.

> Paul's concern is not hierarchical (who has authority over whom), but relational (the unique relationships that are predicated on one's being the source of the other's existence). Indeed, he says nothing about the man's authority; his concern is with the woman being man's *glory*, the one without whom he is not complete (vv. 7c-9).

While Fee is incorrect in viewing "head" as "source," he has observed correctly that "head" here is relational, not hierarchical. So, what about this "source" argument?

The Greek word *kephale* [head] occurs in 11:2-16 nine times, four times referring to a physical "head," and five times with a metaphorical meaning. As Cotterell and Turner[16] observe, there are only two possible meanings for these five uses: the word means either "source" or it means "head." Since linguistic usage does not support *kephale* meaning "source," the meaning in 11:3 is "head." Since relationship is the focus of the text, we need to understand clearly what Paul had in mind when he wrote that "man is *head* of woman."

It is important to ask whether Paul has men/women in mind, or husbands/wives. As mentioned earlier, the same word is used in Greek [*gyne*] for both wife and woman, and the same word [*aner*] is used for both husband and man. While one might turn to 14:34-36 and observe that husband/wife is in focus in that text, it is important to look first within the immediate context of 11:2-16 for the intended meaning of these terms. Here Paul makes repeated reference to the creation narrative in Genesis, where "woman" was created *for* "man." This indicates that while it might not be wrong to read 11:3 with reference to husband/wife, Paul's reference in this text is probably to male/female relationships.[17]

---

[16]Cotterell & Turner, *Linguistics & Biblical Interpretation*, 317.

[17]Leon Morris, *1 Corinthians* (rev. ed.; Leicester: Inter-Varsity Press, 1985): 149-50.

Long ago, J. W. McGarvey and P. Y. Pendleton[18] noted perceptively that this text does not actually present the "order of creation," i.e., God, Christ, man, woman. They state,

> We would expect him to begin with God and descend by the regular steps, thus: God, Christ, man, woman. But the order is thus: Christ, man, man, woman, God, Christ. Subtle distinctions are to be made with caution, but it is not improbable that Paul's order in this case is determined by the delicate nature of the subject which he handles. Dominion is fruitful of tyranny, and so it is well, before giving man dominion, to remind him that he also is a servant. . . . the arrangement makes the headship of the man over the woman parallel to the headship of God over Christ, and suggests that there should be between husband and wife a unity of will and purpose similar to that which exists between the Father and the Son. . . . All Christian husbands and wives should mutually remember this parallel.

The actual order in the text is man—Christ, woman—man, Christ—God. Hierarchalists want to read this text only to conclude that in a hierarchical way, man is over woman. That, however, is not Paul's point—and is to *miss* Paul's point. The point is rather to be found in the three doublets which are used in v. 3 to make clear the proper relationship between males and females. The following illustrations of the relation of man to Christ and Christ to God involve a certain "unity of will and purpose." Paul's point is that man and woman should have a similar "unity of will and purpose."[19] How a woman conducts herself in worship reflects her view of male-female relationships and that is vital for the problem in the church at Corinth.

Paul is writing within and to a distinctly hierarchical cultural perspective. He is not concerned here, however,

---

[18]J. W. McGarvey and P. Y. Pendleton, *Thessalonians, Corinthians, Galatians and Romans* (Cincinnati: Standard, 1916): 109. See also Leon Morris, *The First Epistle of Paul to the Corinthians* (2nd ed.; Grand Rapids: Eerdmans, 1985): 150.

[19]See Reuf, *Paul's First Letter to Corinth*, in fn. 146.

with a hierarchical "order of creation," but with behavior
which shows blatant disrespect for cultural expectations.
Headship in this text does not connote hierarchalism or
authoritarianism, but a "head–body" metaphor which
focuses on the unity of will and purpose between man and
woman. This is Paul's meaning of "head" in this context.

As noted, this text actually begins the section 1 Cor 11-
14, which deals with relationships in the worship of the
Corinthian church. Emphasis, then, in this passage is upon
conduct in relationships. The problem is not one of Jewish
Christian women overstepping traditional boundaries in
Corinth. The problem is rather Gentile women and men in
the church who are either unaccustomed to traditions and
customs widely accepted in Christian worship, or perhaps
unsympathetic with such customs and traditions. This is
why Paul begins (v. 2) and concludes (v. 16) this
admonition regarding women and men in Christian churches
with appeals to contemporary custom and tradition.

3. *Why is wearing the veil important?*

Specific points in vv. 4-5 for the Corinthian situation
are: 1) any male who prays or prophesies in a culturally-
unacceptable appearance dishonors Christ,[20] and 2) any
woman who prays or prophesies in a culturally-unacceptable
appearance dishonors the males who are present.

It was acceptable for Roman and Greek women to go
unveiled in public.[21] However, in many places Jewish
women were veiled in public.[22] Jews thought it typical and
somewhat scandalous of Gentile women that they went
unveiled in public. In Roman custom a woman's veil would
be pulled up over her head during worship.[23] It is my

---

[20]See Morris, *1 Corinthians*, 150.

[21]See A. Oepke, *"apokalupto,"* *Theological Dictionary of the
New Testament*, 3.562.

[22]See Tertullian, *De corona*, 4, with reference to North Africa.

[23]R. MacMullen, "Woman in Public in the Roman Empire,"
Historia 29 (1980): 208-218.

understanding that this was common practice elsewhere in the Roman empire.[24] Oster[25] has argued well that some of the men in the congregation were wearing veils as well, a practice well-documented in the Greco-Roman world. He has assembled considerable evidence from archaeology, including ancient literature, inscriptions, and coins, to make his point.

Illustrative of this point, Athenaeus[26] says of men worshipping Hera,

> they wore bracelets on their arms, and when they celebrated the festival of Hera they marched with their long hair carefully combed down over the breast and shoulders. This custom is attested by the proverb, "Marching to the Heracum with braided hair." . . . And they, when they had combed their locks, would go to the precinct of Hera, swathed in beautiful clothing, with snowy tunics that swept to the floor.

He also says of the men of Colophon that they went,

> with their long locks decked with golden ornaments, as Xenophanes also says, . . . they used to walk to the place of assembly clad in robes all of purple, no fewer than a thousand in all, with proud mein, delighting in their beautiful locks.

---

[24]C. L. Thompson, "Hairstyles, Head-coverings, and St. Paul: Portraits from Roman Corinth," *Biblical Archaeologist* 51 (1988): 133.

[25]Richard Oster, "When Men Wore Veils to Worship: The Historical Context of 1 Corinthians 11.4," *NTS* 34 (1988): 481-505. He comments: "It is a pity that Prof. Gordon Fee has dismissed the possibility of a Roman context to 1 Cor 11.4 in his recent commentary . . . when he asserts, 'There is almost no evidence (paintings, reliefs, statuary, etc.) that men in any of the cultures (Greek, Roman, Jew) covered their heads'."

Antoinette Clark Wire, *The Corinthian Women Prophets* (Minneapolis: Fortress, 1990): 116-34, argues that the problem underlying 1 Cor is a major battle between the sexes and that the women were rebelling. She also holds that Paul is a misogynist. Neither contention is convincing.

[26]Athenaeus, *The Deipnosophists* (LCL; Cambridge: Harvard Univ. Press, 1955): 373.

Philostratus[27] comments on the festival of Dionysius, decrying their "dancing lascivious jigs" and dressing as "nymphs" (393). He decries their "soft dance and one of effeminate tendency" (395), saying,

> What do you mean by your saffron robes and your purple and scarlet raiment? Surely the Acharnians never dressed themselves up in this way. . . . You are softer than the women of Xerxes' day. . . . Now no one bears a helmet, but disguised as female harlequins, to use the phrase of Euripides, they shine in shame alone.

Clement of Alexandria[28] also rails against the effeminacy evident in much art of the period. Against this background, then, the problem in 11:4-7 surely involves both the veiling of the men and the unveiling of the women.

For a woman to take an active part in the public worship by praying or prophesying poses no problem for Paul. However, for her to do so unveiled would be inappropriate and would dishonor the males as much as having her own head shaved would dishonor her, for this would create the impression that she was sexually immoral. For a woman to remove her head-covering in public and expose her hair would be to signify that she was sexually promiscuous.[29] If shaving her head would be embarrassing for a woman, Paul argues that praying in public unveiled certainly should be considered equally embarrassing.[30]

In fact, Paul says in v. 6, if a woman does not wear a head-covering in worship, she might as well go on and

---

[27]Philostratus, *Life of Apollonius of Tyana* (LCL: Cambridge: Harvard Univ. Press, 1969): 393-97. See also Philostratus, *Imagines* (LCL; London: W. Heinemann, 1931): 11-13.

[28]Clement of Alexandria, *Exhortation to the Greeks* (LCL; Cambridge: Harvard Univ. Press, 1953): 139. See also, Plutarch, *Lives* (LCL; Cambridge: Harvard Univ. Press, 1959): 43.

[29]Lucian, *Dialogues of the Courtesans*, 5.13. See also Oepke, "*katakalupto*," *TDNT* 3.562-63.

[30]Reuf, *Paul's First Letter to Corinth*, 109, calls this "rhetorical overstatement."

shave her head because she is already disregarding an accepted cultural norm by not wearing the veil in worship. Although this is a classic overstatement, Paul implies that for a woman to have a shaved head would be to signify that she had been publicly disgraced because of something that she had done, or that she was flaunting her independence and refusing to be respectful to her husband or to males in general. Paul goes on to say that if it is disgraceful for a woman in Corinth to have her head shaved, she should wear a head-covering and show some respect. On the other hand, Paul says in v. 7 that a man ought not wear a head-covering because he is "the image and glory of God."[31] Man was created "for God," not vice-versa. A man should appear in a manner that reflects well on God and His intent for creation.

Now the phrase that man is the "image and glory of God" is very important to Paul's argument. The Greek word translated "glory" [*doxa*] also has other meanings, e.g., "splendor, radiance, fame,"[32] and "expectation."[33] NRSV translates 11:7, "image and *reflection* of God." This translation is based upon the connotation of "glory" [*doxa*] as "reputation, popular estimate."[34] By their conduct, individuals reflect upon those with whom they have a relationship. In Corinthian society, a Christian man's conduct would reflect on people's view of God. Similarly, a Christian woman's conduct would create a perception of her relationship with males and her view of the distinction of the

---

[31]Jerome Murphy-O'Connor, "Sex and Logic in 1 Corinthians 11:2-16," *Catholic Biblical Quarterly* 42 (1980): 482-500, sees here a reference to long hair and possible homosexuality, but alternatively Fee, *1 Corinthians*, 150, thinks a head-covering is Paul's concern.

[32]W. Bauer, *A Greek-English Lexicon of the New Testament and Other Early Christian Literature* (trans. W. F. Arndt and F. W. Gingrich; 2nd ed. rev. F. W. Gingrich and F. W. Danker; Chicago: Univ. of Chicago Press, 1979): 204.

[33]H. G. Liddell and R. Scott, *A Greek-English Lexicon* (9th ed. rev. H. S. Jones and R. McKenzie; Oxford: Clarendon Press, 1973): p. 444.

[34]For this use see Polybius *Histories* 15.22.3; 35.4.8; Diodorus Siculus, *History* 15.61.5; Appian, *Roman History* 2.9.

sexes. Public prayer by an unveiled woman or a veiled man would demonstrate a flagrant abuse of custom and be taken as flouting accepted norms of behavior—it would show blatant disrespect and be disruptive.

Referring in 11:8-9 to the Genesis account of creation, Paul gives two reasons for his appeal to culturally-acceptable behavior in worship. First, he says, woman was created from man (Gen 2:21ff). Second, woman was created for man (Gen 2:18). As v. 7b puts it, "Woman is the glory of man." This means that vv. 8-9 are analogous to v. 7a. That is to say, just as a man's behavior reflects upon God, so woman's behavior reflects upon man. His argument is that man and woman were originally intended to be in relationship. Any behavior which would militate against that relationship would be improper, and in Corinth that meant that women should wear veils when at worship, as this was culturally-expected.

In the preceding verses, Paul has argued that it is a cultural expectation that women should wear veils in worship and that men should not. In v. 10, Paul adds a further cultural argument that women should wear the head-covering "on account of the angels." Now this point, which is intended to conclude the argument in v. 7, may seem rather strange to modern readers. What would angels have to do with this situation?[35] Certainly Paul was thinking here of some danger women might face from angels, and *vice versa*. These two facets of this problem are important to discuss.

First, Paul may have in mind the prominent Jewish story of male angels being seduced by the beauty of women. Some take Paul's reference to be to "fallen angels" of 1 Enoch 6-11. This classic text mentions the "Watchers" (10:7; 9), "fallen angels" who left heaven, came to earth,

---

[35]We will not even attempt to survey the large number of conjectures which have been made about this text. In a book written over a century ago, Arthur P. Stanley, *The Epistles of Paul to the Corinthians* (London: J. Murray, 1876): 186, listed many.

saw women, lusted for them, and had sex with them. These evil angels taught women various charms and to use enchantments (7:1), bracelets, ornaments, costly stones, coloring tinctures, and beautifying eyelids (8:1-2). They committed fornication (8:2; 9:8), and made women pregnant (7:2). For this they were condemned to eternal punishment (10:11-16). Although there is no reference in the OT to such "fallen angels," I Enoch 6-11 was taken later by many to refer to Gen 6:1-4, where the "sons of God" had sexual relations with the "daughters of men."[36] The Greek translation of the OT, the Septuagint, took "sons of God" in Gen 6 as "fallen angels." The book of *Jubilees*, which was a rewriting of Genesis, alludes to 1 Enoch and this sin of the "fallen angels" with women.[37] In this view, Paul's stipulation would be that women should wear veils for their own protection from the prying eyes and lustful advances of evil angels.

Second, others see here a reference to "good angels," who would have an interest in Christian worship.[38] It has been argued by Fitzmyer and Hooker, for instance, that

---

[36]In Carroll D. Osburn, "Discourse Analysis and Jewish Apocalyptic in the Epistle of Jude," in *Linguistics and New Testament Interpretation: Essays on Discourse Analysis* (ed. D. A. Black; Nashville: Broadman, 1992): 296-97, I discuss the "fallen angels" legend in Jewish and early Christian perspective. U. Cassuto, *Biblical and Oriental Studies* (Jerusalem: Magnes, 1973): 17-28, argues well that fallen angels are not found in Gen 6, but that the idea arose at a later period. Certainly, by the time of 1 Enoch 6-16 and 86-88 the idea of fallen angels had achieved rather developed form. In the authoritative Jewish writings of the period, great stress is placed upon the fact that nowhere in Scripture is one to find reference to intercourse between angels and women. "Sons of God" in Gen 6 was taken to refer to "distinguished men" in Sifre Numbers 86 and Bemidhbar Rabbah 27:2-5. Jude 6 makes no reference to Gen 6:1-4 but to contemporary Jewish legend as found in 1 Enoch.

[37]See Everett Ferguson, *Demonology of the Early Christian World* (Lewiston, NY: E. Mellen, 1984): 69-104.

[38]Morris, *1 Corinthians*, 152-53;

angels were thought to be present at Christian worship.[39] If Paul considers angels to be present in Corinthian worship,[40] then he suggests either that women should not lead them into temptation or that women should wear a veil in shame before them. Héring[41] writes,

> it was in the cult, notably when inspiration was being spoken of, that contact was made with the supernatural world and the angels. 'Before the angels (*'elohim*) I will sing thy praise,' says the Psalmist in Psalm 137.1 (138.1)—with no intention of referring to a canticle sung after death.

It is clear that Paul's argument is based upon later Jewish intertestamental understandings of angels and not upon the OT text per se. Paul says, women need "authority" on their head when praying publicly. Morna Hooker[42] concludes correctly,[43]

> Far from being a symbol of the woman's subjection to man, therefore, her head-covering is what Paul calls it—authority: in prayer and prophecy, she, like the man, is under the authority of God.

In v. 11, then, Paul brings his argument in this section to a head, saying, "However, woman is not without man nor

---

[39]J. A. Fitzmyer, "A Feature of Qumran Angelology and the Angels of 1 Cor. xi.10," *New Testament Studies* 4 (1957): 48-58; and Morna D. Hooker, "Authority on her head," *New Testament Studies* 10 (1963-64): 410-16.

[40]Psa 138:1 in the Septuagint [137:1] reads, "I will sing praise to you before angels." English, however, renders the Hebrew text , "I will sing your praise before the gods." In the third century, Origen, *De oratione*, 31, says that angels surround Christian assemblies.

[41]Jean Héring, *The First Epistle of Saint Paul to the Corinthians* (trans. A. W. Heathcote and P. J. Allcock; London: Epworth, 1962): 107.

[42]Morna Hooker, "Authority on Her Head: An Examination of 1 Cor xi.10," *New Testament Studies* 10 (1963-64): 416.

[43]Against Martin Dibelius, *Die Geisterwelt im Glauben des Paulus* (Göttingen: Vandenhoeck & Ruprecht, 1909): 223ff., who suggests that the "veil" was to give power against invisible enemies.

is man without woman in the Lord." This is not an afterthought. It is the climax of Paul's argument that began in v. 2. From the beginning, he says in v. 12, the relationship between man and woman is set by woman being "out of the man" and man coming "through the woman"— in other words, the interdependence of the sexes is in focus. Héring[44] observes well the importance of male-female relationships in the church when he holds that, "only by referring everything to God can we fall into the line of the specifically Christian code of ethics." And Goudge[45] notes correctly that "man and woman are mutually dependent. Christianity does nothing," he says, "to make either self-sufficient." Robertson and Plummer[46] remark, "In the Christian sphere each is dependent upon the other, and both are dependent upon God (viii.6; Rom. xi.36); . . . Each sex is incomplete without the other." Paul's summation of his point in 11:2ff is put succinctly by Morris,[47]

> Paul makes it clear that what he has been saying is not meant as an undue subordination of women. There is a partnership between the sexes and *in the Lord* neither exists without the other (NEB, 'in Christ's fellowship woman is as essential to man as man to woman'). The man must not exaggerate the significance of his having been created first. There is fundamental equality.

In v. 13, Paul asks the readers to decide for themselves what is "fitting" in this regard. In vv. 14-15, he asks if long-standing custom does not have women wearing long hair and men short hair. If so, does not nature itself suggest that if she honors the cultural norm of long hair, she should also honor the custom of wearing a special covering in the assembly?

---

[44]Héring, *First Epistle of St. Paul to the Corinthians*, 109.

[45]H. L. Goudge, *The First Epistle to the Corinthians* (5th ed.; London: Methuen, 1926): 96-97.

[46]Archibald Robertson and Alfred Plummer, *The First Epistle of St. Paul to the Corinthians* (ICC; Edinburgh: T. & T. Clark, 1914): 234.

[47]Morris, *1 Corinthians*, 153.

In v. 16, Paul appeals to widely-practiced custom in the early church. That women should wear veils and men should not is a Christian "custom" which reflects a respectful relationship between women and men in the church.

4. *Conclusion.*

The ancient Joel prophecy (Acts 2:17), reads, "Your sons and your daughters shall prophesy." According to 11:2-16, women in the Corinthian church are praying and prophesying in the public worship. In 14:34-36, certain women are also speaking in the public worship in an instructional setting, but doing so in a disruptive way. The commonality shared by 11:2-16 and 14:34-36 is not "women speaking in public," but women showing disrespect for others, for decorum, and for propriety—and thus contributing to chaos, disruption, and disunity in the congregation. Both women and men in 11:2-16 are flouting commonly-accepted cultural norms and showing disrespect for one another. They are told that they should pray and prophesy in public worship in a way that would not dishonor others. Even so, Barclay[48] was correct in noting that, "it is quite unfair to wrest a local ruling from the circumstances in which it was given, and to make it a universal principle."

---

[48]William Barclay, *Letters to the Seven Churches* (London: SCM, 1957): 75.

11

1 CORINTHIANS 14:34-36
DISRUPTIVE CORINTHIAN WIVES

In 1 Cor 14:34-35,[1] Paul admonishes certain wives in the Corinthian church to be silent in the assembly. It is not surprising that this has served as a principal text concerning women in the church since the first century. Though only two verses, they have had, and still have, great influence in Christian churches. However, in recent times, changing views of women in the western world have altered long-standing cultural norms with the result that this text has become a virtual battleground.

For instance, David Lipscomb,[2] when asked to explain 1 Cor 14:34-35, commented,

> I cannot write it in simpler words, plainer, or put in a connection that would make it easier to be understood. "Let your women keep silence in the churches: for it is not permitted them to speak, but to be in subjection, as the law also says." . . . I do not know how to add a word that can make it clearer, more direct, or more forcible. One who can explain that away can explain away anything I can write.

However, as Sire[3] correctly observes, "the simplest error of reading is the failure to consider the immediate context of the verse or passage in question." Lipscomb's simplistic

---

[1]This section is an abbreviated summary of my "The Interpretation of 1 Cor 14:34-35," *Essays on Women in Earliest Christianity*, 219-242.

[2]M. C. Kurfees, ed., *Questions Answered by Lipscomb and Sewell* (Nashville: McQuiddy, 1921): 729.

[3]James W. Sire, *Scripture Twisting* (Downers Grove, IL: Inter Varsity Press, 1980): 52.

observation does not take into account the context of Paul's statement. Actually, careful exegesis of the text must be the determining factor. Exegesis is not "explaining away the text." Exegesis is simply following the normal rules of interpretation. Considerable clarification of these verses in their context is required if appropriate use is to be made of this admonition in current practice.

1. *1 Cor 14:34-35 in the Manuscript Tradition*

The place to begin is with the ancient biblical manuscripts. In most Greek manuscripts and the early translations into other languages, vv. 34-35 occur between v. 33 and v. 36. In a handful of Latin manuscripts, vv. 34-35 do occur following v. 40. For this reason, some argue that verses 34-35 are not original with Paul, but added into the text at a later period by another writer.[4] Fee,[5] for instance, argues that vv. 34-35 do not fit the flow of the argument and, as an absolute rule for "all churches," stands in conflict with 11:2-16. It was, he says, inserted into the text at the end of the first century by a later scribe.

Three observations are useful. 1) Never was v. 33b included with vv. 34-35 after v. 40.[6] 2) Never was v. 36 included with vv. 34-35 after v. 40.[7] 3) Vv. 34-35 occur after v. 40 only in limited circles in the Latin tradition.[8] As 1 Cor had been in circulation for decades, it is difficult to explain why no copies exist of an original short text if the words were added. All it would take would be one lone

---

[4]Only vv. 34-35: H. Lietzmann, *An die Korinther I/II* (Tübingen: Mohr, 1931): 75; Jerome Murphy-O'Conner, "Interpolations in 1 Corinthians," *Catholic Biblical Quarterly* 48 (1986): 90-92; and with caution, C. K. Barrett, *The First Epistle to the Corinthians* (London: A. & C. Black, 1971): 330-332.

[5]Fee, *The First Epistle to the Corinthians* 699-702.

[6]Cf. John Reuf, *Paul's First Letter to Corinth* (Philadelphia: Westminster, 1977): 154-155.

[7]Cf. Hans Conzelmann, *1 Corinthians* (trans. J. Leitch; Philadelphia: Fortress, 1975: 246).

[8]See Wire, *The Corinthian Women Prophets,* 149-152; 283-285.

scribe, making what was thought to be an improvement by moving vv. 34-35 to after v. 40, whose text was copied by a few scribes elsewhere. Therefore, there is no reason to view vv. 34-35 as a later interpolation, especially if the text can be demonstrated to make sense in its context.

It is likely that vv. 34-35 were thought unsuitable to a context dealing with "prophecy" (vv. 29-33, 37) and that vv. 33b and 36-37 naturally belonged together. Thus vv. 34-35 were transposed to after v. 40 by a few scribes, where it could conceivably make sense as an application of v. 40. Fee is correct in asserting that the flow of thought in the passage is important to the resolution of the problem. And the text does make sense if vv. 34-35 are removed from the context. However, manuscript evidence certainly favors leaving vv. 34-35 after v. 33 and taking it as an integral part of the letter.[9] But if vv. 34-35 do occur after v. 33, how does the text fit the context? And how does that view cohere with 11:2-16, where women do pray and prophesy?

2. A Corinthian Quotation that Paul Refutes?

Others argue that vv. 34-35 represent a quotation from the letter which Paul is answering (see 7:1) and that it does not express Paul's view, but the thinking of the *men* whom Paul chides in v. 36.[10] This view argues that, due to competition for ministries, arrogant males had devised a plan to eliminate women from competition.[11] The argument suggests 1) that the Greek word ἤ (translated "or") at the beginning of v. 36 should instead be translated "What!" and 2) the shift from the third-person pronoun ("they," females in vv. 34-35) to the second-person, the masculine pronoun

---

[9]See Bruce Metzger, *A Textual Commentary on the Greek New Testament* (corr. ed.; New York: United Bible Society, 1975): 565.

[10]See Katherine Bushnell, *God's Word to Women* (Oakland, CA: K. Bushnell, 1930): para. 189-215; Neal Flanagan and Edwina Snyder, "Did Paul Put Down Women in First Corinthians 14:34-36?" *Foundations* 24 (1981): 216-220.

[11]Gilbert Bilezikian, *Beyond Sex Roles* (2nd ed.; Grand Rapids: Baker, 1985): 146-147.

monous (you only),[12] means that, following this supposed "citation" of the Corinthian males, Paul responds, "What! Did the word of God originate with you *men* only?" However there is nothing awkward about the generic masculine *monous* (you only) in v. 36 referring to the entire congregation.[13] Further, the little Greek word ἤ (or), a disjunctive particle, does not necessarily contradict and dismiss a preceding clause, but often introduces a direct question or statement actually in support of that clause.[14] Liefeld[15] observes correctly that "what Paul negates by his use of the adversative Greek particle ἤ (or) is *not* the *command* in verses 34-35 but the assumed *disobedience* of it." Bilezikian is simply wrong. Vv. 34-35 are not a Corinthian quotation Paul refutes, but Paul's own statement. Vv. 36-40 are the conclusion of Paul's argument to the entire congregation, not only in terms of the immediate context of 14:26-35, but of the entire section on "orderliness in worship" beginning in 11:2.

3. *1 Cor 14:34-35 in its Context*

A. *The Larger Context.*

Paul's remarks about wives in vv. 34-35 are part of the larger context of chaps 11-14. Following his plea in chapters 1-4 for a strong christological basis for resolving conflict among the Corinthian Christians, Paul addresses

---

[12]David Odell-Scott, "Let the Women Speak in Church. An Egalitarian Interpretation of 1 Cor 14:33b-36," *Biblical Theology Bulletin* 13 (1983): 90-93; Bilezikian, *Beyond Sex Roles,* 286-288.

[13]See Charles Talbert, "Paul's Understanding of the Holy Spirit: The Evidence of 1 Corinthians 12-14," in *Perspectives on the New Testament* (ed. C. Talbert; Macon, GA: Mercer, 1985): 106.

[14]D. A. Carson, "'Silent in the Churches': On the Role of Women in 1 Cor 14:33b-36." *Recovering Biblical Manhood & Womanhood: A Response to Evangelical Feminism,* 149-151, denounces Bilezikian's, *Beyond Sex Roles,* 286-288, forced misunderstanding of ἤ.

[15]Walter Liefeld, "Women, Submission, and Ministry in 1 Corinthians," *Women, Authority and the Bible,* 149.

interpersonal problems and marital propriety in chaps 5-7 and the implications of eating food offered to idols in chaps 8:1-11:1. 1 Cor 11:2–14:40, then, addresses matters of corporate worship. Chapter 11 treats women's "covering" for worship (vv. 2-16) and abuses at the Lord's Supper (vv. 17-34). Chapters 12-14 are devoted to abuses of "spiritual manifestations," especially "tongues" and "prophecy."

Continuing his argument that tongues are minimally useful and certainly not the ultimate expression of Christian spirituality, Paul stresses prophecy as more desirable in chapter 14. In 14:16, Paul points out that if a stranger[16] enters the place where Christian worship is being conducted and hears a "spiritual" prayer (i.e. in a tongue), he will not understand what is happening. The prayer may have been a good one, he says in v. 17, but the stranger will have no clear insight into the Christian experience. So in v. 19, Paul appeals not to the experiential, but to the cognitive.

In v. 21, Paul paraphrases Isa 28:11-12, not treating its historical meaning[17] but setting out the idea of "not listening to tongues." Paul then notes in v. 22 that tongues are a sign not to the believers, but to the unbelievers, and just the reverse that prophecy is not for the unbelievers, but for the believers. Now, this might seem to contradict what has just been said in vv. 16-20 and what will be said in vv. 23-25. In fact, this leads Phillips to conclude that "we have here either a slip of the pen on the part of Paul, or, more probably, a copyist's error."[18] However, v. 22 makes good sense if it is not understood as the proper way to use tongues and prophecy, but *unfortunately how the Corinthians have come to use them!*[19] V. 22 is not an agenda to follow, but a

---

[16]The "stranger" here is not a Christian who does not speak in tongues, but (in view of 14:23-25) a non-Christian.

[17]John Bright, *The Kingdom of God* (New York: Abingdon, 1953): 84, notes "If they will not hear the lesson spelled out in plain Hebrew, then God will be forced to teach it to them in Assyrian!"

[18]J. B. Phillips' translation, note on 1 Cor 14:22.

[19]See Charles Isbell, "Glossolalia and Propheteialalia: A Study of 1 Corinthians 14," *Wesleyan Theological Journal* 10 (1975): 18; and

statement of surprise on Paul's part that this is what they are actually doing. If this is true, then vv. 23-25 set out the proper use of prophecy on the stranger (which is cognitive) rather than tongues (not cognitive, v. 14). The Corinthians are simply using the wrong things on the wrong people.

B. *The Immediate Context.*

Similarly, while many view the list of things done in worship in v. 26 as setting out a proper agenda for Christian worship, v. 26 is rather to be viewed as indicating Paul's frustration with what the Corinthians are actually doing in worship. The Greek sentence opens with a question, "How stands the case, brothers?"[20] In this context of misuse and abuse of tongues and prophecy in the assembly, Paul says that each[21] has a psalm, a teaching, a revelation, a tongue, or an interpretation. While these should be for edification,[22] the following discussion specifies how these Corinthian Christians are not conducting worship for edification. Although proper for Christian worship, the matters in v. 26 are being abused by the Corinthians. Pandemonium is the problem and v. 26, "All things must be for edification!" is the point of the overall context in chapter 14 and the "guiding rule" for the three following topics (tongues, prophecy, wives), *each of which involves verbal misconduct.*

Bruce C. Johanson, "Tongues, a Sign for Unbelievers?" *New Testament Studies* 25 (1979): 180-203.

[20]G. G. Findlay, *St. Paul's First Epistle to the Corinthians* (Expositors Greek NT; London: Hodder & Stoughton, 1917): 911.

[21]Bilezikian, *Beyond Sex Roles*, 146, erroneously concludes that Paul wants each member to come prepared to make some presentation for the edification of the group. However, Leon Morris, *1 Corinthians* (2nd ed.; Grand Rapids: InterVarsity Press, 1985): 194, correctly observes that we need not press "each" to mean that every member was expected to participate. Jean Héring, *The First Epistle of Saint Paul to the Corinthians* (trans. A. Heathcote & P. Allcock; London: Epworth, 1962): 154, notes that "there is hardly any need to stress the point that all 'inspired' movements have encountered similar difficulties."

[22]Reuf, *Paul's First Letter to Corinth*, 153.

Regarding tongues,[23] "only one may speak at a time!" Several speaking in tongues at the same time would create confusion. No more than two or three at the most should speak in any one assembly. If there is no interpreter, those speaking in tongues should be silent in the assembly. The Greek *sigato* here means, "Be silent!" Otherwise there is disorder and lack of cognition. There is no excuse for appealing to some "irresistible impulse" to speak in a tongue as basis for continuing to speak. So, it is with this problem of disorderliness in worship that Paul is concerned in his demand for the "tongue-speakers" to *defer* to the assembly, respecting decorum and edification.

In v. 29, Paul limits prophecy[24] to two or three at the most in any one assembly, one at a time, while others discern. If another wants to prophesy, the first prophet must "Be Silent!" (*sigato* as in v. 28). "The spirits of prophets are subject to prophets" (v. 32) is an axiom, i.e., a prophet can choose not to speak. Unlike tongue-speaking, prophecy is viewed by Paul as a a cognitive matter. However, as with speaking in tongues, Paul rebukes the verbal chaos generated by too many people prophesying at once. Pandemonium is intolerable. Orderliness, with an emphasis upon edification, is vital (v. 26). That is why Paul says that one prophet must *defer* to the next. There is no reason to give in to "irresistible impulse" to prophesy. Self-control is urged. Paul says that this is the case "in all the churches."

Now the statement, "as in all the churches of the saints," is taken with vv. 34-35 in many modern editions and translations, but it appears with v. 33a in many others. It is difficult to understand the objection[25] that "as in all the churches of the saints," does not make good sense if taken with v. 33. The problem in chapters 12-14 is verbal

---

[23]See Siegfried Schatzmann, *A Pauline Theology of Charismata* (Peabody, MA: Hendricksen, 1989): 42-43.

[24]See David Aune, *Prophecy in Early Christianity and the Ancient Mediterranean World* (Grand Rapids: Eerdmans, 1983).

[25]Among others, Carson, "Silent in the Churches," *Recovering Biblical Manhood and Womanhood*, 140-41.

misconduct by tongue-speakers and prophets. It is widely held that vv. 26-32, appealing for the cessation of the verbal misconduct of these two groups, ends appropriately with 33a, "God is not the author of confusion but of peace." This thought is directly related to "all things must be done for edification" v. 26. In light of this, an appeal is made in v. 33b for those involved to conduct themselves with customary Christian mutual deference.[26] V. 33 should read, "For God is not a God of disorder, but of peace, as in all the congregations of the saints," as in King James Version and Phillips' translation.

C. vv. *34-35*

However, a third item involved in the admonition to orderliness and edification from v. 26 begins in v. 34 simply admonishing *gunaikes* (wives/women?) to "silence" in the assembly. We must remember that females are not the only ones on whom this silence is imposed, but that *sigato* was also used for disruptive tongue-speakers and prophets in vv. 27-33 .

Now just what sort of "speaking" these females were doing is variously understood. While some suggest speaking of any sort in worship,[27] chattering,[28] "sacred cries" common to women in pagan worship, [29] or teaching

---

[26]With Barrett, *First Epistle to the Corinthians*, 329; F. F. Bruce, *1 and 2 Corinthians* (Grand Rapids: Eerdmans, 1971): 136; and William Barclay, *The Letters to the Corinthians* (2nd ed.; Philadelphia: Westminster, 1956): 149. This concluding appeal to common practice is similar to 11:16, where "if anyone is disposed to be contentious, we have no other practice, nor do the churches of God" closes the section of 11:2-16.

[27]F. W. Grosheide, *The First Epistle of Paul to the Corinthians* (Grand Rapids: Eerdmans, 1953): 343.

[28]James Moffatt, *The First Epistle of Paul to the Corinthians* (London: Hodder and Stoughton, 1938): 232.

[29]Richard and Catherine Kroeger, *Women Elders . . . Saints or Sinners?* (New York: Council on Women and the Church of the United Presbyterian Church in the U.S.A., 1981): 13.

men,[30] most view "speaking" to be limited by the context. Thus, some see speaking in tongues being prohibited,[31] while others think women judging the prophecies mentioned in vv. 29-33[32] is meant. As we shall see, the context warrants neither.

Now synagogues did not forbid women to speak in public in principle, but did so in practice. In the Greco-Roman world at this time, women speaking in public was done, but frowned upon. Plutarch, *Conjugal Precepts* 31, says, "Not only the arm but the voice of a modest woman ought to be kept from the public, and she should feel shame at being heard, as at being stripped." In the next paragraph, Plutarch continues, "She should speak either to, or through, her husband." In accord with ancient custom, then, is Paul stating a general rule of silence for all women in worship?

It is taken for granted by Paul in 1 Cor 11 that women prayed and prophesied in the early church, thus presenting an apparent contradiction with the prohibition in 14:34-35. Some are willing to accept a contradiction.[33] Others think that 1 Cor 11 and 14 belong to two separate Pauline letters.[34] Neither of these two views is commendable. Still others argue that 11:2-16 involves only praying or prophesying at home or in small groups of females, thus leaving 14:34-35 an absolute rule for public assemblies.[35]

---

[30]Neuer, *Man & Woman in Christian Perspective*, 117, based upon 1 Tim 2:11-14!

[31]Frederick D. Bruner, *A Theology of the Holy Spirit* (Grand Rapids: Eerdmans, 1970): 301.

[32]Margaret Thrall, *The First and Second Letters of Paul to the Corinthians* (Cambridge: Cambridge Univ. Press, 1965): 102; and Hurley, *Man and Woman in Biblical Perspective*, 193.

[33]J. W. MacGorman, *The Gifts of the Spirit: An Exposition of 1 Corinthians 12-14* (Nashville: Broadman, 1974): 113.

[34]W. Schmithals, *Gnosticism in Corinth* (Nashville: Abingdon, 1971): 90-96.

[35]Philip Bachmann, *Der erste Brief des Paulus an die Korinther* (3rd ed.; Leipzig: A. Deichert, 1921): 345-62; and Adolf Schlatter, *Paulus der Bote Jesu* (Stuttgart: Calwer, 1969): 390.

However, this view overlooks the unmistakable connection of vv. 2 and 17 with vv. 17-34, which obviously treats worship, as does the whole of 11:17-14:40. In 11:2-16, Paul addresses both men and women and nowhere suggests that his concern is with informal gatherings or private practice. If vv. 34-35 are intended as a universal rule for all women in all churches, it is difficult to understand the purpose of such a universal rule in the present context treating disorder in the Corinthian worship and in direct contradiction with 1 Cor 11:2-16.[36]

The admonition in 14:34-35 must be seen as directed to a particular problem in Corinth and *the only information provided by the text is that the women involved should ask questions of their husbands at home if they wish to learn* (v. 35). It is difficult to see the general verb *lalein* (to speak) as limited here specifically to either "tongues" or prophecy," since the context makes clear that these particular women are involved in some form of seriously disruptive speech.[37]

The present infinitive *lalein* (to be speaking), which occurs twice in vv. 34-35, provides the crucial insight into the "speaking" which so annoys Paul. The verb *laleo* (I speak) always takes its precise meaning from the context. In v. 28, it refers to "silent meditation." In vv. 23 and 27, it refers to "speaking in tongues." In v. 19 it refers to "cognitive prayer." But in vv. 34-35, there is no clear contextual indication of what is meant, but there is a significant grammatical indication. In Greek, when one wishes to use an imperative (Do this!), subjunctive (You should do this), or infinitive (to do this), one uses the past

---

[36]C. C. Ryrie, *The Place of Women in the Church* (New York: Macmillan, 1958): 76, suggests that 14:33-35 presents the general rule and 11:2-16 is a Corinthian exception, but fails to explain why Paul does not condemn a woman praying or prophesying as long as she is properly veiled. The praying and prophesying of women in 11:2-16 is not presented as a concession.

[37]See Barrett, *First Epistle to the Corinthians*, 332; William Baird, *The Corinthian Church—A Biblical Approach to Urban Culture* (Nashville: Abingdon, 1964): 127.

tense of the verb to do that, but with no reference to past action. This curious use of the past tense is just the Greek way to say that. However, when one wishes to denote continuing action in an imperative (Continue doing this!), subjunctive (You should continue doing this), or infinitive (continuing to do this), one uses a present form of the verb. This use of the present tense specifies ongoingness. In grammatical terms, the aorist (past) infinitive refers to the action without indicating anything about its continuance or repetition; the present infinitive, on the other hand, specifically refers to the action as continuing or being repeated in some way.[38] Grammarians recognize this fact.[39] Here, the two present infinitives make it clear that it is the "ongoingness" of the "speaking" that is in focus. Apparently they were doing more than merely "chatting,"[40] for Paul's admonition in v. 35 concerns their interest in *learning*. Paul does not prohibit the normal pursuit of learning by women in the assembly, including asking appropriate questions. Rather, *lalein* should be taken here to mean that they were "piping up," giving in to "irresistible impulses" to ask question after question, creating chaos in the assembly by interfering with communication.[41] In this respect, these women are creating the same sort of disruption in the assembly as that by the tongue-speakers and prophets.

Is this disruptive speech, though, by wives or women in general? To whom are these women to submit themselves? Arguing that all females are to be subject to males, *Lenski*[42]

---

[38]F. Blass and A. Debrunner, *A Greek Grammar of the New Testament* (trans. & ed. R. Funk; Chicago: Univ. of Chicago Press, 1961): 174.

[39]A. T. Robertson, *A Grammar of the Greek New Testament in the Light of Historical Research* (Nashville: Broadman, 1934): 890.

[40]Cf. J. Howard, "Neither Male nor Female: An Examination of the Status of Women in the New Testament," *EvQ* 55 (1983): 31-42.

[41]With Bruce, *1 and 2 Corinthians*, 135.

[42]R. C. H. Lenski, *The Interpretation of St. Paul's First and Second Epistle to the Corinthians* (Colombus, OH: Wartburg, 1946): 615-16; and W. H. Mare, *1 Corinthians* (Grand Rapids: Zondervan, 1976): 276.

says that since the OT Law subjects woman to man by the creation both before and after the fall, Paul means that "what is recorded concerning woman in Genesis is not a temporary arrangement but a permanent one that endures as such for the Christian church." On the other hand, most view *gunaikes* in this context to refer not to all women, but to certain Corinthian wives.[43] This latter view is preferred, since in the text the demand for silence is tied directly to the request for the *particular wives involved to direct their questions to their husbands outside the assembly.*

What, then, is meant by "silence"? Of course, those erroneously reading "women" rather than "wives" argue total "silence."[44] However, Liefeld argues correctly that since the verb *sigao* is used in vv. 28 and 30 with regard to tongue-speakers and prophets, its meaning in v. 34 is not a universal silence, but one dictated by circumstances.[45] As with the tongue-speakers and prophets, where self-control and *deference* is the emphasis, so in vv. 34-35 an appeal is made to Corinthian wives to "pipe down" and, in accord with v. 26, let everything be done for edification.

But what about Paul's appeal to "the law"? The view that "law" refers to Paul's own ruling in v. 29,[46] broken by these wives "taking the lead," is unacceptable because "law" is capable of a better understanding in this context. Further, nothing supports the idea that these wives were "taking the

---

[43]See William Orr and James Walther, *1 Corinthians* (Garden City, NY: Doubleday), 312; and J. Massingbyrde Ford, "Biblical Material Relevant to the Ordination of Women," *Journal of Ecumenical Studies* 10 (1973): 681.

[44]Neuer, *Man & Woman in Christian Perspective*, 117; LaGard Smith, *Men of Strength for Women of God* (Eugene, OR: Harvest House, 1989): 250-53; David Lipscomb, *First Corinthians* (ed. J. Shepherd; Nashville: Gospel Advocate, 1935): 216.

[45]Liefeld, "Women, Submission, and Ministry in 1 Cor," *Women, Authority and the Bible*, 150.

[46]Ralph Martin, *The Spirit and the Congregation: Studies in 1 Corinthians 12-15* (Grand Rapids: Eerdmans, 1984): 87.

lead." Some view the entire OT as the focus of the appeal,[47] but many tend to see a particular text in view, such as Gen 3:16[48] or Gen 2:21-24.[49] Yet if appeal is made to the OT, it is curious that no such text is quoted and that no argumentation is presented.[50] On the other hand, some take "the law" here to refer to "female silence," either in Rabbinic tradition of women's silence in worship[51] or Greco-Roman disdain of women speaking publicly.[52] However, taking "the law" here to refer to women's silence is grammatically incorrect, for "as the law says" is related not to *lalein* (speaking), but to *"being in submission"*! The text does not say that women are "not to speak as the Law says" but "to be in submission as the Law says."

So, what is meant by "submission, as the law says"? Note that Paul does not say "be in submission *to your own husbands*," but "submit yourselves." The reason for the admonition to silence is caused by disorder in family relations. Women are not being commanded to "submit" to their husbands in this text, but to orderliness in public worship, to silence and respect when another is speaking.[53]

The verb *hupotasso* (submit) "does not immediately carry with it the thought of obedience."[54] When it occurs in the NT in the active voice (the person referred to is doing the

---

[47]C. Hodge, *First Epistle to the Corinthians* (Grand Rapids: Eerdmans, 1953): 305.

[48]See Barrett, *First Epistle to the Corinthians*, 330; Lipscomb, *First Corinthians*, 216.

[49]See Bruce, *1 and 2 Corinthians*, 136; and Knight, *Role Relationship of Men and Women*, 25.

[50] In fact, this is one of Fee's, *First Epistle to the Corinthians*, 707, arguments for the inauthenticity of the passage. See 9:8 and 14:21.

[51]Jewett, *Man as Male and Female*, 114. Note Josephus, *Against Apion* 24.

[52]Liefeld, "Women, Submission and Ministry in 1 Cor," *Women, Authority & the Bible*, 149.

[53]Witherington, *Women in the Earliest Churches*, 102-03.

[54]Gerhard Delling, *"hupotasso,"* TDNT 8.41-42.

action), it always has God or Christ as subject and the meaning is forceful subjugation with resistance (e.g., 15:27-28). Never in the NT does this verb suggest one human being forcefully subjugating another for any reason. The middle (to do something for one's self) and passive (something is done to one) forms of the verb are identical.[55] Only the context can determine whether the meaning is middle or passive.[56] The middle form of this verb denotes "readiness to renounce one's own will for the sake of others, i.e., *agape* [love], and to give precedence to others."[57] It always involves willing submission, as in 1 Cor 16:16, "submit yourselves to one another." In 14:32, voluntary submission is obviously meant regarding a prophet willingly controlling the prophetic spirit. The entire context of chapters 11-14 evidences Paul's strong appeal for voluntary submission in the Corinthian congregation. This is specifically the point in 14:26-40. "Submit yourselves" in v. 34 should be taken to refer to the same sort of *deferential* behavior to the congregation demanded of the clamorous tongue-speakers and prophets, here rebuked for emphasizing personal freedom at the expense of Christian mutuality.

The two questions in v. 36,[58] then, are a direct confrontation, not with Corinthian wives, but with the congregation as a whole: "Did the word of God originate with you? Or are you the only people it has reached?" Fee[59] is wrong in suggesting that v. 36 makes no sense following v. 35. Vv. 34-35 are similar to the previous regulations of

---

[55]The middle form of this verb is described in A.T. Robertson, *A Grammar of the Greek New Testament in the Light of Historical Research* (Nashville: Broadman, 1934): 807, 809. J. H. Thayer, *A Greek-English Lexicon of the New Testament* (4th ed.; Edinburgh: T. & T. Clark, 1901): 645, lists 14:34 as an example of the middle.

[56]E.g., 1 Pet 2:13, "submit yourselves [middle] to every human authority" in KJV NIV NEB NASB is preferable to "be subject" [passive] in RSV.

[57]Delling, TDNT 8.45.

[58]NIV curiously omits the conjunction ἤ that relates v. 36 to vv. 34-35.

[59]Fee, *First Epistle to the Corinthians*, 710.

tongue-speakers and prophets in that three vital elements occur in each: 1) a third person imperative instruction, 2) an explanatory sentence, and 3) an example in conditional form telling what to do in a given case.[60] Words recur: "speak" vv. 27, 28, 29, 34, 35; "submission" vv. 32, 34; "learn" vv. 31, 35; and "be silent" vv. 28, 30, 34. From v. 36, it appears that the disruptive behavior Paul disdains in vv. 34-35 is related closely to v. 33: 1) God is not a God of disorder, and 2) this is true in all the churches of the saints. Vv. 34-35, then, add yet another significant dimension to regulation of verbal misconduct to those of tongue-speaking and prophecy. The Corinthians have no right to verbal misconduct either by tongue-speakers or prophets, *or* by certain questioning wives.

Vv. 37-40 are the conclusion, not only to this sub-section of 26-36, but the entire unit of chapters 11-14, all of which treats matters pertinent to Corinthian public worship. Here, Paul sums up that various spiritual manifestations are to be encouraged, but it is mandatory that orderliness be maintained in the proceedings and that an environment conducive to learning be maintained. So, vv. 37-38 appeal to all involved in disruptive speaking to recognize Paul's directive as "from the Lord," i.e., authoritative. Then in v. 39, Paul summarizes his extended discussion from chap. 12, emphasizing the priority of the former. There is no mention of the silence of women. We may infer from this that the mention of women in vv. 27-36 was not major to his discussion, but he attended to it significantly since it involved a similarly serious disruption of decorum. V. 40, then, summarizes not vv. 26-33,[61] but the entirety of the unit beginning in 11:2 which treats conduct in Corinthian worship. Everything should be done decently (12:33f) and orderly (33a). This certainly accords with Paul's theme in 1 Cor that unity and respect for others is greater than any uncontrolled expression of personal rights.

---

[60]Gerhard Dautzenburg, *Urchristliche Prophetie: Ihre Erfor-schung, ihre Voraussetzung im Judentum und ihre Struktur im ersten Korintherbrief* (Stuttgart: Kohlhammer, 1975): 254-55.

[61]Cf. Fee, *First Epistle to the Corinthians*, 713.

4. *Conclusion*

There is no reason to believe that vv. 34-35 are a Corinthian quotation Paul refutes in v. 36. There is no convincing evidence that the admonition in vv. 34-35 is an interpolation from a later period. There is no evidence that Paul contradicts what he had taught earlier in 11:2-16, that 11 represents a reluctant concession, or that he changed his mind between chapter 11 and 14. Two different matters are involved: the praying and prophesying by the women in chap. 11 in the assembly differs markedly from some wives continually "piping up" in the assembly in chap. 14. The insubordination which these wives had in common with that of the tongue-speakers and prophets caused Paul to include this firm directive at this point in the text.

Since 1 Cor 14:34-35 cannot be excluded on text-critical grounds, one must conclude that, "14:33b-36 are in their right place and quite authentic."[62] Paul is dealing with a particular problem in Corinth. The problem is not one of disdain for creation order or family order, but one of church order. Far from being intolerant, Paul neither teaches nor suggests in this text anything regarding hierarchalism or female subjection. Smith[63] wrongly concludes, "The real issue is the extent to which a woman may *participate* in the work and worship of the church." He simply has not understood what is being dealt with in the context. The real issue is not the *extent* to which a woman may participate in the work and worship of the church, but the *manner*. Paul's corrective does not ban women from speaking in worship,[64]

---

[62]Héring, *First Epistle of Saint Paul to the Corinthians*, 155. See also now Curt Niccum, "The Voice of the Manuscripts on the Silence of Women: The External Evidence for 1 Cor 14:34-5," *New Testament Studies* 43 (1997): 242-255.

[63]Smith, *Men of Strength for Women of God*, 250, appropriately subtitles his discussion of 14:34-35, "Grasping at Straws."

[64]Grosheide, *First Epistle to the Corinthians*, 343, has missed the point of the text in arguing that "everybody will agree that it is unbecoming for a woman to speak in a public meeting of the church."

but stops the disruptive verbal misconduct of certain wives who are giving free rein to "irresistible impulses" to "pipe up" at will with questions in the assembly by redirecting these questions to another setting where they can have access to information without causing verbal chaos.

This text remains authoritative regarding the point it was intended to make originally. Referring, as it does, to a very specific problem of unacceptably disruptive questions by these women, 1 Cor 14:34-35 teaches that these particular wives, like the uncontrolled tongue-speakers and prophets at Corinth, must *defer* to the assembly by voluntarily yielding to orderliness.[65] Specifically, if a woman (or man) speaks in a disruptive manner while someone else is speaking, this text authorizes the congregation to call that person out of order and to ask her (him) to be quiet. The general principle that is to be applied to contemporary church life is that decorum is mandatory for all in the public assembly without regard to gender.

As a footnote to this study, I might add that the text says nothing about women singing, praying, making announcements, reading Scripture, witnessing, reporting, asking questions, teaching, performing drama in a Christian assembly—whether standing or sitting, whether in front or not—as long as they do so in an orderly and non-disruptive manner. Even a decidedly literal interpretation of this verse need not forbid women from serving as ushers, serving communion, taking up the offering, passing out bulletins and orders of worship, or any such capacity of service. "Sit down and shut up!" is not a biblical mandate for Christian women. 1 Cor 14:34-36 may be considered a biblical mandate against disruptive behavior in any form in any Christian assembly.

Neither in this nor in any other biblical text is there a prohibition against women speaking in public, *on the ground that it is public.*

[65]Bruce, *1 and 2 Corinthians*, 137, "Much of the teaching in this chapter is relevant only to such exceptional circumstances as prevailed in the church of Corinth."

12

1 TIMOTHY 2:9-15
CONCERNING WOMEN TEACHING

1 Tim 2:9-15, with its admonition for women not to teach but to be silent, has figured prominently in the discussion of women in the church.[1]

1. *1 Tim 2:9-15 in Recent Discussion.*

In current evangelical literature, 1 Tim 2:9-15 remains a most important text, and understandings of that passage vary considerably. Books on 1 Tim 2:9-15 have been written by Catherine and Richard Kroeger[2] and by Köstenberger, Schreiner, and Baldwin.[3] Although the former base their work upon egalitarianism and the latter upon hierarchalism, the two volumes share certain strengths and weaknesses. Both attempt to engage biblical texts and both make an effort to assess the literary and historical background of the texts. Certainly, that much is appreciable.

---

[1]A. T. Hanson, *The Pastoral Epistles* (Grand Rapids: Eerdmans, 1982): 42, typical of much critical scholarship, incorrectly views these epistles as "made up of a miscellaneous collection of material. They have no unifying theme; there is no development of thought." However, I am inclined to agree with Peter G. Bush, "A Note on the Structure of 1 Timothy," *New Testament Studies* 36 (1990): 152-156, that there is structure to 1 Timothy and that it is a letter to a particular situation in the early church, not a manual on church order to a general audience.

[2]Richard and Catherine Clark Kroeger, *I Suffer Not a Woman: Rethinking 1 Timothy 2:11-15 in light of Ancient Evidence* (Grand Rapids: Baker, 1992).

[3]Andreas Köstenberger, Thomas Schreiner, and H. Scott Baldwin, ed., *Women in the Church: A Fresh Analysis of 1 Timothy 2:9-15* (Grand Rapids: Baker, 1995): 334.

However, as was discussed on pp. 97-102, there is a tremendous difference between "presuppositions" and "prejudices." We noted earlier that presuppositions are necessary starting points which an interpreter takes when beginning an investigation.[4] This means that both egalitarianism and hierarchalism have legitimate claim as starting points. Prejudices, however, are personal factors that affect the judgment of an interpreter and make objectivity difficult. It is unfortunate that the prejudices of the Kroegers and of Köstenberger, Schreiner, and Baldwin lead to manipulation and distortion of data to an extent that neither of these works on the text of 1 Tim 2:11-12 are commendable. We turn our attention first to the work of the Kroegers.

A. *The Kroegers' Work on 1 Tim 2:9-15*

Catherine Clark Kroeger, whose work was discussed earlier on pp 57-60 and repeated here for convenience, is exemplary of evangelical feminists who maintain the importance of the Bible in discussion of women in the church. However, the application of rigorous literary and historical controls in her use of the biblical text is unsatisfactory. For instance, in 1 Tim 2:12 the verb *authenteo* (which occurs only here in the NT) means "have authority, domineer"[5] and "to control, to domineer,"[6] yet is translated "usurp authority" (KJV), "have authority over" (NIV, NRSV), and "domineer" (NEB). Attempting to locate an alternative rendering, Kroeger suggested that *authenteo* in 1 Tim 2:12 is actually an erotic term referring to ancient female teachers in 5th century BC Athens who offered sex to

---

[4]Graham M. Stanton, "Presuppositions in New Testament Criticism," *New Testament Interpretation: Essays in Principles and Methods* (ed. H. Marshall; Grand Rapids: Eerdmans, 1977): 60.

[5]Walter Bauer, *A Greek- English Lexicon of the New Testament and Other Early Christian Literature* (trans. W. F. Arndt and F. W. Gingrich; 2nd ed. rev. Gingrich and F. W. Danker; Chicago: Univ. of Chicago Press, 1979): 121.

[6]Johannes P. Louw and E. A. Nida, *Greek-English Lexicon of the New Testament Based on Semantic Domains* (New York: United Bible Societies, 1988): 1.474.

their students after class.[7]   Kroeger says that it is that practice that is being forbidden by this text. Needless to say, this rather peculiar proposal was quickly countered by an avalanche of criticism from the scholarly world.[8] The classical texts that Kroeger cites do not support her view of a sexual connotation to the verb *authenteo*!

It is not at all surprising, then, that in a recent study of this text a different view is presented.[9] The Kroegers' new view is that the verse only prohibits women from teaching the gnostic heresies that women were created before men, that women were the source of all wisdom, and that bearing children was dishonorable. The Kroegers' treatment of this text purports to be an attempt to observe high standards of scholarship, including both philological and historical elements. They view the passage as refuting a specific heresy at a specific time and place, and thus should not be taken as a universal restriction on women in the church. However, in support of their current translation, that woman is not to "represent herself as originator of man" (103), the Kroegers fail both philologically and historically.

The Kroegers seem oblivious to proper word-study methodology.[10] In arguing that *authenteo* should be trans-

---

[7]Catherine Clark Kroeger, "Ancient Heresies and a Strange Greek Verb," *The Reformed Journal* 29 (1979): 12-15, a view popularized uncritically by such writers as Kari Torjesen Malcolm, *Women at the Crossroads* (Downers Grove, IL: InterVarsity Press, 1982): 78-80, and though not accepted, is mentioned as "an interesting idea" by Spencer, *Beyond the Curse*, 87, n. 15.

[8]See, for example, A. J. Panning, "ΑΥΘΕΝΤΕΙΝ—A Word Study," *Wisconsin Lutheran Quarterly* 78 (1981): 185-191; and Carroll D. Osburn, "ΑΥΘΕΝΤΕΩ (1 Timothy 2:12)," *Restoration Quarterly* 25 (1982): 1-12.

[9]Richard Clark Kroeger and Catherine Clark Kroeger, *I Suffer Not a Woman: Rethinking 1 Timothy 2:11-15 in Light of Ancient Evidence* (Grand Rapids: Baker, 1992).

[10]See James Barr, *The Semantics of Biblical Language* (Oxford: Oxford Univ. Press, 1961); and John F. A. Sawyer, *Semantics in Biblical Research* (Studies in Biblical Theology, 24; Naperville, IL: Alec Allenson, 1972).

lated "represent oneself as originator of," they ignore the fact that this verb is rendered "domineer" in NT times. They appeal to outdated sixteenth-century Greek lexicons for a meaning that they then project back into Greek texts of the fourth and fifth centuries AD.[11] While they cite much secondary literature, they repeatedly misunderstand the sources they cite,[12] and selectively omit recent literature that opposes their view.[13] They continue to repeat the misinformation that *authenteo* means "to murder" in ancient Greek. Now this meaning does occur for the noun form, but not for the verb form until the tenth century AD. While leaving the impression of engaging in scholarly investigation of the term (36-37, 84-102), in reality the Kroegers are merely scavenging the philological arena for an alternative to the traditional reading of the text. Wolters concludes,[14]

> . . . the Kroegers have conspicuously failed to make their case. No doubt the book will have considerable influence in the evangelical world, but it is very doubtful whether any serious commentary on 1 Timothy will ever adopt its basic thesis. . . its argumentation is a travesty of sound scholarship.

---

[11]See the extensive and scathing review of Albert Wolters in *Calvin Theological Journal* 28 (1993): 208-213. In addition, the Kroegers' interpretation takes the *oude* (negative) in v. 12 as a hendiadys (expression of an idea with two independent words connected by *and* [e.g., nice and warm] rather than a word and modifier [nicely warm]), making *authenteo* here function as an infinitive of indirect discourse. This vital grammatical point, however, is not supported with grammatical analysis, but simply with a reference to Philip Barton Payne (pp. 83-84), and this in spite of a negative response to Payne's view that they were aware of and quoted on p. 21.

[12]The Latin quote from Guillaume Budé on p. 102 (230, n. 27) is completely misunderstood, as is their mistranslation of a German citation on p. 101.

[13]L. E. Wilshire, "The TLG Computer and Further References to Αὐθεντέω in 1 Timothy 2:12," *New Testament Studies* 34 (1988): 120-134.

[14]Wolters, *Calvin Theological Journal* (1993): 213.

Historically, the Kroegers fail miserably.[15] No Gnostic sect such as they postulate ever existed in first-century Ephesus, or anywhere else. Their supposed Gnostic sect, which is the historical key to their view of 1 Tim 2:12, is merely constructed of various features of pagan religion in Ephesus and Asia Minor, and from considerably later Gnostic texts. In simply "proof-texting" ancient sources, the Kroegers evidence uncritical methodology and their treatment of secondary sources is certainly careless.   For instance, in their effort to locate sexual issues "under every stone" in Ephesus, they appeal to Vermaseren[16] to set the problem in 1 Timothy in a context of supposed widespread influence of the cult of Cybele in Ephesus. The Kroegers mention over "seventy inscriptions" honoring Cybele, yet only twenty exist and most of those are from a much later period—those that do exist were found at one small shrine. This does not constitute proof of "widespread influence." Careless historical work abounds in the Kroegers' work. Further, failure to treat extensive ancient sources that do refer to the late-first century church in Ephesus (the Fourth Gospel, Polycarp, Ignatius, Papias—none of which evidences the kind of Gnostic sect at Ephesus the Kroegers suggest) damages their case beyond repair.[17] Oster says,[18]

> . . . irrespective of one's sympathy for the pain and frustration of women who have been oppressed by "the traditions of men," . . . this publication does not present a cogent and defensible way to circumvent or neutralize 1 Tim 2:11-15. A judicious use of historical and archaeological data may someday help the Christian community to see 1 Tim 2:11-15 in a better way, but if and when that is accomplished, it will have to be done using better evidence and superior research methods to those found in this work.

---

[15]This historical critique follows the insightful, negative review by Richard Oster in *Biblical Archaeologist* 56 (1993): 225-227.

[16]M. J. Vermaseren, *Corpus Cultus Cybelae Attisdique* (Leiden: Brill, 1987): 1.184-203.

[17]See Thomas A. Robinson, *Orthodoxy and Heresy in Western Asia Minor in the First Christian Century* (Ph.D. dissertation at McMaster Univ., 1985, esp. chapter 2 on Ephesus).

[18]Oster, *Biblical Arachaeologist* (1993): 227.

The Kroegers' work evidences the strong influence of their feminist prejudices and, even though it cites much ancient data, its methodological failures and manipulation of data render it unusable.

B. *Köstenberger, Schreiner, and Baldwin on 1 Tim 2:9-15*

As was mentioned briefly on p. 83, a volume of essays was edited by Köstenberger, Schreiner, and Baldwin in 1995. In their work, preliminary essays addressing Ephesus in the first century and the literary genre of 1 Timothy are followed by major chapters on a word-study of the Greek term *authenteo* in 1 Tim 2:12 and on the sentence structure of that verse. Concluding the book are chapters on the interpretation of and hermeneutics involved in 1 Tim 2:9-15, and on the relationship of this text with Gal 3:28.

Certainly these are the principal matters involved in the study of this text, and at first reading one encounters in Köstenberger, Schreiner, and Baldwin what might appear to be *the* definitive volume on 1 Tim 2:9-15. The material is organized and presented in scholarly fashion, and is filled with references to ancient texts and involved argumentation. A responsible methodology is set out for word study that is now widely accepted among NT scholars.

However, significant problems in the volume leave it unconvincing. Major problems exist with their presentation of word study, grammar, and interpretation of this troublesome text. In fact, there are major problems with each of the seven chapters in the book, but for our present purposes the chapters by the three editors are deserving of closer examination because those surface the main issues of interpretation. We will undertake a detailed analysis of the arguments presented by Baldwin, Köstenberger, and Schriener, and will follow the critique of Giles concerning chaps 1,2,6,7, and Appendix I.[19]

---

[19]Kevin Giles, "A Critique of the 'Novel' Contemporary Interpretation of 1 Timothy 2:9-15 Given in the Book, *Women in the Church*," *Evangelical Quarterly* 72 (2000): 151-67, 195-215.

1. *Baldwin's Attempt at Word-study*[20]

Scott Baldwin, lecturer in NT at Singapore Bible College, presents a word-study of *authenteo* ("have authority" RSV; "domineer" NEB). The term occurs only in 1 Tim 2:12 in the NT. In order to get a view of its use elsewhere, he presents usages of the term in Greek literature. He groups the usages into categories which, at first glance, give the appearance of convincing data from ancient usage that the term must have a hierarchal meaning in 1 Tim 2:12.

However, there are three fatal errors in Baldwin's presentation of the data: 1) he makes distinctions of word meanings in English that do not hold up in Greek, 2) his groupings of ancient citations are not actually representative of Greek usage, but are contrived to prove his hierarchical prejudices, and 3) in some instances his argument is made upon mistranslations of Greek.

a. *Distinctions in English.* Baldwin mentions various word studies of *authenteo* over the past two decades, but he favors the meaning "to have authority over"[21] and rejects "to domineer." Baldwin dismisses "domineer" as even a possible meaning of *authenteo* in 1 Tim 2:12 by positing that the meaning "domineer" actually occurs only once in all Greek literature.[22] Now the way Baldwin has translated the texts and formed his groups might give this impression, but this is simply not true.

First, Baldwin presents categories of meaning for *authenteo* that are divided into twelve groups (78-79). His various groups are formed for argumentative reasons and do not accurately describe word usage. Too, not all the texts illustrate the meaning which Baldwin suggests.

---

[20]H. Scott Baldwin, "A Difficult Word: *authenteo* in 1 Timothy 2:12," *Women in the Church: A Fresh Analysis of 1 Timothy 2:9-15*, 65-80.

[21]With G. W. Knight III, "*Authenteo* in Reference to Women in 1 Timothy 2.12," *New Testament Studies* 30 (1984): 143-57.

[22]Baldwin, "A Difficult Word," *Women in the Church*, 75.

There are several problems with Baldwin's groups. For instance, he makes a distinction between the English terms "dominate" and "domineer." "Dominate" would forbid a woman "having authority over." "Domineer" would permit a woman to teach a man as along as she is not overbearing. He says (73, n.19),

> The distinction between domineer and dominate becomes an important one in the exegesis of 1 Timothy 2. Therefore, the two terms should not be taken as interchangeable. *The Compact Oxford Dictionary of the English Language* (Oxford: Oxford Univ. Press, 1971), ad loc., gives the meaning of "to dominate," a transitive verb, as "to bear rule over, to have a commanding influence on, to master." By connotation this is a negative term in some instances when used as a description of human relationships, but not necessarily so. In contrast, "domineer" is defined as an intransitive verb meaning "to rule or govern arbitrarily or despotically. . . . to exercise authority in an overbearing manner." Therefore, dominate and domineer are not synonyms unless it is shown that the domination is considered improper.

What he is trying to establish regarding the transitive and intransitive uses of the verb,[23] is that *authenteo* does not have a negative connotation, (to domineer), but rather a neutral meaning (have authority over). One must keep in mind that Baldwin is arguing that if *authenteo* means "have authority over," then in 1 Tim 2:12 Paul limits women's authority categorically. If, however, the term means "to domineer," Paul only prohibits these specific women from teaching men in a domineering manner.

Baldwin's argument on the English distinction between "dominate" as transitive and "domineer" as intransitive simply does not hold true in English, much less in Greek. Actually the terms are synonyms in standard English, "dominate" is just used more frequently than "domineer."[24]

---

[23]A transitive verb is one which takes a direct object; an intransitive verb does not take a direct object.

[24]*Webster's Dictionary of English Usage* (Springfield, MA: Mirriam-Webster, 1989): 360.

"Domineer" is used now mostly as a participle, *domineering*. "Dominate," can refer either to a position of being dominant or to the fact of being dominant.[25] *The Illustrated Reverse Dictionary*[26] also states that "dominate" simply means "to domineer." Baldwin's English argument has no basis.

Greek grammarians are aware that there is no distinction between transitive and intransitive uses of a verb in Greek. Smyth[27] says that the distinction between transitive and intransitive verbs is purely a grammatical convenience. Jannaris[28] notes, "In many cases, a Greek verb is used now in a transitive and now in an intransitive sense." Blass and Debrunner[29] confirm this understanding, stating that,

---

[25]*Dictionary of Modern American Usage* (B. A. Gauer, ed.; Oxford: Oxford Univ. Press, 1998): 220.

[26]*The Illustrated Reverse Dictionary* (Pleasantville, NY: Reader's Digest, 1990): 157. See also *Oxford English Dictionary* (2nd ed.; ed. J. A. Simpson and E. S. C. Weiner; Oxford: Clarendon Press, 1989): 4.947-948.

[27]Herbert W. Smyth, *Greek Grammar* (Cambridge: Harvard University Press, 1959): 389. He also notes on p. 355, # 1561, that in Greek, "the same verb may be used transitively or intransitively, often with little difference of signification." See also H. P. V. Nunn, *A Short Syntax of New Testament Greek* (Cambridge: Cambridge Univ. Press, 1945): 6, also notes, "Many transitive verbs may also be used intransitively."

[28]Antonius N. Jannaris, *An Historical Greek Grammar Chiefly of the Attic Dialect* (London: Macmillan, 1897): 328-29. H. E. Dana and J. R. Mantey, *A Manual Grammar of the Greek New Testament* (New York: 154), state that it "is not to be construed . . . that the verb is fixed as transitive or intransitive by its root meaning." W. W. Goodwin and C. B. Gulick, *Greek Grammar* (Dallas: Gin, 1930): 223, note, "The object denoted by the accusative may be the external object of the action of a transitive verb, or the internal (cognate) object which is often implied in the meaning of even an intransitive verb."

[29]F. Blass and A. Debrunner, *A Greek Grammar of the New Testament and Other Early Christian Literature* (trans. & rev. R. Funk; Chicago: Univ. of Chicago Press, 1961): 82, who note that the action of certain verbs, originally conceived absolutely, can be placed in relation to an object. See A. T. Robertson, *A Grammar of the Greek New Testament in the Light of Historical Research* (Nashville:

"Transitive use of original intransitives was always possible in Greek." What this means is that *authenteo* did not originally take a direct object, but on some occasions it does. So Paul could very well have written *authenteo* in this verse with the meaning, "woman is not to domineer (over) a man."

Only context can determine whether "dominate" means "to hold supremacy or mastery over by reason of superior power or authority," or whether it means "to hold in subjection through force."[30] Baldwin's suggestion that "dominate" is transitive and means "to exercise control" (neutral meaning), while "domineer" is intransitive and means "overbearing, bossy" (negative meaning), does not reflect either standard English or Greek usage. In fact, this argument clouds the issue and should be abandoned.

b. *Categories of Usage.* In an appendix,[31] Baldwin presents all known occurrences of the verb *authenteo* in Greek literature. He attempts to categorize these usages by dividing them into twelve groups (73). The result of Baldwin's numerous categories is his conclusion that:

> to domineer / play the tyrant," is substantiated by only a single case. . . . This is the sole unambiguous instance I have found where *authenteo* is plainly intended to convey the negative meaning of "tyrannize. (75)

Baldwin concludes that "play the tyrant" (domineer) is not supported by the context.

Broadman, 1934): 472, who says with regard to the freedom of the Greek verb, "The same verb may be used now transitively, now intransitively." See also Eduard Schwyzer, *Griechische Grammatik* (2nd ed.; Munich: C. H. Beck, 1959): 2.71-72.

[30]See *Webster's Third New International Dictionary of the English Language* (ed. P. B. Gove; Springfield, MA: Mirriam-Webster, 1993): 671-72.

[31]H. Scott Baldwin, "*Authenteo* in Ancient Greek Literature," *Women in the Church*, Appendix 2, pp. 269-305, based upon 1) *Greek Documentary CD-ROM (#6)*, and *Thesaurus Linguae Graecae CD-ROM #D*.

This abandonment of "domineer" as even a possible meaning is striking. While Baldwin included "domineer" as one of his twelve groups (78), he extends the meaning of "domineer" to "tyranny, to play the tyrant" (79) and then concludes hastily that "tyranny" is not consistent with the context of 1 Tim 2. So he dismisses the meaning "to domineer" from any further consideration. Significantly it is excluded from his list of possible meanings of *authenteo*. This sort of manipulation of data is intolerable.

    c. *Mistranslation of Greek Citations.* The single text in which Baldwin finds *authenteo* meaning "to domineer," or as he puts it, "to tyrannize," is found in the fourth-century church father John Chrysostom,[32]

> see how in nature also it hath been ordered, that the one should love, the other obey. For when the governing party loves the governed, then everything stands fast. Love from the governed is not so requisite, as from the governing to the governed; for from the other obedience is due. For that the woman hath beauty, and the man desire, shows nothing else than that for the sake of love it hath been made so. Do not therefore, because thy wife is subject to thee, *act the despot* [*authenteo*].

Baldwin notes, "In this unique usage Chrysostom has apparently transformed 'exercise sole authority' into 'play the tyrant'" (75). He extends Parker's translation "despot" to mean "tyranny." He then posits that "tyranny" is not supported by the context of 1 Tim 2:12. Thus Chrysostom's example is of no use. This permits Baldwin to dismiss the entire category of "domineer." While Baldwin makes much of the English translation here, the context is clear even to a casual reader that Chrysostom forbids husbands from being "domineering, overbearing, controlling, lording it over."[33]

---

[32]John Chrysostom, *In Epistulam ad Colossenses* (Homily 10.1) in J.-P. Migne, *Patrologia Graece* 62.299-392. See the English translation in John Parker, *The Homilies of S. John Chrysostom* (Oxford: J. H. Parker, 1879): 309

[33]G. W. H. Lampe, *A Patristic Greek Lexicon* (Oxford: Clarendon Press, 1961): 262, translates Chrysostom's text here as,

Baldwin's maneuvering simply avoids the possibility that
Chrysostom actually says, "Do not therefore . . . act
domineeringly toward her."

Another text also uses *authenteo* in the sense of "to lord
it over." In the third-century, Hippolytus[34] describes the
chaos at the end of the world, as Roberts[35] translates:

> Wherefore all shall walk after their own will. And the children
> will lay hands on their parents. The wife will give up her
> husband to death, and the husband will bring his own wife to
> judgment like a criminal. Masters will *lord it over their
> servants* savagely, and servants will assume an unruly
> demeanour toward their masters.

Baldwin disagrees with Robert's translation of *authenteo* as
"*lord it over* their servants," so he provides his own
translation, "*have legal authority over* their servants." He
cites two examples from the seventh-century *Chronicon
Paschale*[36] of the meaning "have legal authority over." The
first text, *Chronicon Paschale* 619.9, reads, "In this year the
Justinianic Codex was completed and it was ordered that it
be authoritative (authenteisthai) from the 16th day before
Kalends of April [17 March] of the current tax period 7."
Similarly *Chronicon Paschale* 634.1 reads, "It was ordered
that, the previous edition being made void, it should *be valid
(authenteisthai)* from the 4th day before Kalends of January
[29 Dec.], in indication 13." Regarding Hippolytus' citation,
Baldwin admits, "The case cannot be decided with
certainty," but he still bases "have legal authority over" on
the two instances from *Chronicon Paschale*.

"play the despot, act arbitrarily," as a meaning under "assume authority,
act on one's own authority."

[34]Hippolytus, *On the End of the World* 7 in *Hippolyt's kleinere
exegetische und homiletische Schriften* (GCS 1.2; ed. H. Achelis;
Leipzig: J. C. Hinrich's, 1897): 289-309.

[35]Alexander Roberts and James Donaldson, ed., *Ante-Nicene
Fathers* (Grand Rapids: Eerdmans, 1957 reprint of 1885-96 ed.): 5.243.

[36]*Chronicon Paschale* (ed. Dindorf; Bonn: Weber, 1832).

There is a significant problem with this maneuver. Baldwin avoids context in determining the meaning of words. *Chronicon Paschale* is concerned with the enforcement of decrees. Hippolytus is concerned with the very different topic of conduct at the end of the world.

Take a closer look at Hippolytus' citation. Is he not concerned about people treating one another in overbearing, insolent, high-handed ways? Note the beginning of the text: "all shall walk *after their own will*." The context is one in which children are insolent to parents, wives determine the fate of their husbands, husbands dominate their wives in court, inhuman masters *domineer over* their slaves, and slaves assume an unruly attitude toward their masters. The context is precisely one of domineering control over others—and the relationship of masters to slaves is described perfectly here by *authenteo*, "domineer, lord it over."

To conclude, Baldwin's dismissal of "domineer" for *authenteo* is wrong. Both Hippolytus and Chrysostom should be credited with the use of *authenteo* meaning "to domineer." This should be placed under the general meaning of "to dominate." By distorting and manipulating data, Baldwin wrongly dismisses "domineer" as even a possible meaning in 2:12.

2. *Köstenberger's Attempt at Sentence Structure*[37]

The sentence structure of 1 Tim 2:12 has been variously understood. Two major ways to read the text are:

1. I do not permit a woman to teach nor to have authority over a man

2. I do not permit a woman to teach a man in a domineering manner

---

[37]Andreas J. Köstenberger, "A Complex Sentence Structure in 1 Timothy 2:12," *Women in the Church: A Fresh Analysis of 1 Timothy 2:9-15*, 81-103.

In the first, the Greek *oude* (nor) prohibits two closely related, yet distinct, items (not to teach nor to exercise authority over).[38] In the second, *oude* (not) connects two infinitives as a single idea (not to teach domineeringly).[39] Andreas Köstenberger, professor of NT at Southeastern Seminary in Wake Forest, NC, prefers the former.

As basis for his view, he presents instances of *oude* (not) joining verbs, both in the NT and in extra-biblical Greek. He mentions Acts 16:21 as the only text in the NT in which the exact grammatical construction as 1 Tim 2:12 occurs. However, he notes fifty-two similar passages.

a. *Patterns of Usage.* Köstenberger contends that there are only two patterns of usage in these fifty-two examples:[40]

• Pattern # 1: two activities or concepts are viewed positively in and of themselves, but their exercise is prohibited or their existence denied due to circumstances or conditions made clear in the context (see Matt 7:6).

• Pattern # 2: two activities or concepts are viewed negatively and consequently they are prohibited or their existence is denied or they are to be avoided (see Lk 3:14).

Köstenberger's view of Greek usage is controlled by his notion that when two activities or concepts are prohibited, all that matters is whether they are viewed positively or negatively. While these two patterns of usage do occur in texts cited by Köstenberger (85-88), he has omitted another very significant pattern.

---

[38]See Douglas J. Moo, "What Does It Mean Not to Teach or Have Authority Over Men?" *Recovering Biblical Manhood and Womanhood*, 179-193.

[39]Preferred by Philip Barton Payne, "*oude* in 1 Timothy 2:12," in a paper read at the 1986 annual meeting of the Evangelical Theological Society, p. 10.

[40]Köstenberger, "A Complex Sentence Structure in 1 Timothy 2:12," *Women in the Church: A Fresh Analysis of 1 Timothy 2:9-15*, 85.

b. *Hendiadys.* In fact, the usage he omits is precisely the one that militates against his thesis. This third pattern is called "hendiadys"—"the coordination of two ideas, one of which is dependent upon the other."[41] Hendiadys means that one term is general, while another term comments in some specific way upon it. For example,

Acts 4:18 — Jewish leaders tell Peter and John "not to speak or teach at all in the name of Jesus." "Speak" is generic. "Or to teach at all in the name of Jesus" gives the specific prohibition, specifying what speaking is prohibited. Not *all* speaking is prohibited; only speaking in the name of Jesus. Here one phrase comments on the other.

Gal 1:16-17 — Paul says that after his conversion, "I did not consult any man, nor did I go up to Jerusalem to see those who were apostles before me." "I did not consult any man," is followed by the note that specifically he did not consult "those who were apostles before" him. The hendiadys here underscores Paul's point that his theology was not dependent upon human sources in Jerusalem, but upon God.

1 Tim 1:3-4 — Paul urges Timothy to stay in Ephesus in order to command certain people "not to teach error any longer, nor to devote themselves to myths and endless genealogies." The general statement, "not to teach error any longer," is followed by a second statement that qualifies and makes specific what he said generally in the first statement.

Acts 16:21 — The one text Köstenberger cites as exactly parallel to 1 Tim 2:12 has exactly this same usage. In Acts 16:21, certain Philippians complain of Paul and his group that, "They teach customs which it is not lawful for us to accept nor to practice being Romans." "Accept" is a general term made specific by the following statement that Romans cannot practice such things.

---

[41]Blass and Debrunner, *A Greek Grammar of the NT*, 228 [§ 442.16]

It is the view of several commentators that 1 Tim 2:12 involves hendiadys, and Payne presents the translation, "I do not permit a woman to teach in a domineering manner."[42] Köstenberger briefly critiques Payne (82-84), criticizing him for beginning with the assumption that *authenteo* means "domineer" and for making a circular argument. However, this is an instance of "the pot calling the kettle black," for Köstenberger himself begins by assuming that *authenteo* cannot mean "domineer" and then proceeds to make a classic circular argument in that regard. This omission of hendiadys from consideration in 1 Tim 2:12 is unconscionable.

Köstenberger makes the same mistake in his examples from ancient Greek writers in that he does not consider the important category of hendiadys (91-102). For example, Polybius, a second-century BC writer, says in his *History* 2.56.10 that,

> a historical author should not try to thrill his readers by exaggerated pictures, nor should he, like a tragic poet, try to imagine the probable utterances of his characters or reckon up all the consequences probably incidental to the occurrences with which he deals, but simply record what really happened.

Köstenberger sees this only as an example of two items viewed negatively and therefore inherently prohibited. However, here the first prohibition, that a historical writer "should not elaborate," is followed by two specific examples of not putting words in the mouths of his characters or making up hypothetical incidents regarding the story. This usage occurs in several of Köstenberger's examples.

Thus he concludes that *didaskein* (to teach) is always used positively in the NT and if a negative connotation had been intended in 1 Tim 2:12, the term *heterodidaskalein* (false teacher) would have been used, as in 1 Tim 1:3.[43]

---

[42]Philip Barton Payne, "*oude* in 1 Timothy 2:12," paper read at the 1986 annual meeting of the Evangelical Theological Society, p. 10.

[43]*Didaskein* is the principal word in the NT for "to teach," while *heterodidaskalein*, "to teach otherwise," occurs only in 1 Tim 1:3 and

However, Köstenberger's view that only two categories of usage are important for 1 Tim 2:12 is simply wrong. By omitting the important category of "hendiadys," restricting categories and manipulating data, Köstenberger presents a mass of material that gives only apparent support to his thesis. By distorting and manipulating data, Köstenberger wrongly dismisses "teaching domineeringly" as even a possible meaning in 2:12.

3. Schreiner's Interpretation of 1 Tim 2:9-15[44]

Thomas Schreiner, professor at Bethel Theological Seminary, writes on "Dialogue with Scholarship." His analysis of 1 Tim 2:9-15 concludes that women,

> should learn submissively and silently, and not engage in teaching or the exercise of authority. Women are prohibited from teaching or exercising authority because of the creation order.

Schreiner claims to have changed from a less to a more restrictive view of women due to intensive study. However, a careful reading reveals that he has merely changed presuppositions, which in turn have become his prejudices.

6:3. Actually, Köstenberger's argument does not hold in Matt 15:9, where Jesus chides those who "teach (*didaskein*) for doctrines the commandments of men,", nor in Tit 1:11, where the malicious intruders "teach (*didaskein*) things they ought not," nor at Rev 2:20, where John rails against Jezebel the prophetess who "by her teaching (*didaskein*) misleads my servants into sexual immorality and the eating of idol food." According to Köstenberger, all such texts should have been written *heterodidaskalein*. *Didaskalein* can have either a positive or negative connotation, depending upon the context.

[44]Thomas R. Schreiner, "An Interpretation of 1 Timothy 2:9-15: A Dialogue with Scholarship," *Women in the Church: A Fresh Analysis of 1 Timothy 2:9-15*, 105-154. Along this line, see M. D. Roberts, "Woman Shall Be Saved: A Closer Look at 1 Timothy 2:15," *TSF BULLETIN* 5 (1981): 5; and R. W. Pierce, "Evangelicals and Gender Roles in the 1990's—1 Tim 2:8-15: A Test Case," *Journal of the Evangelical Theological Society* 36 (1993): 347-48, 353.

a. *Critique of Views.* To his credit, Schreiner notes that 1 Tim is addressed to a specific situation and that it should be understood in terms of the circumstances that occasioned it (counter false teaching; 1:3-11, 18-20; 4:1-10; 5:11-15; 6:3-10, 20-21). He correctly views "Therefore" (KJV; "then" NIV, RSV) in 2:1 as relating the following section to the false teaching introduced in 1:3-11. A question exists, though, as to whether Paul's admonitions in 2:9-15 are aimed at that particular audience or whether they are timeless. On this point Schreiner concludes, "Paul may have responded to these specific problems with a general principle that is universally applicable" (109).

Schreiner finds the Kroegers'[45] argument (that the prohibition of women teaching men is due to the heresy in 1 Tim being an amalgamation of Jewish-gnosticism and the local Artemis cult) to be filled with methodological errors. [46] He finds Gritz'[47] argument (that the restriction on women teaching is due to the infiltration into the church of some from the Artemis cult) unconvincing due to failure to establish convincingly from solid data that the Artemis cult did in fact influence 1 Timothy. He finds Towner's[48] argument (that the Ephesian Christians believed that the resurrection had already occurred and that a spiritual resurrection with Christ was behind their food prohibitions, view of marriage, and emancipation of women to be a "promising" view [112]).

---

[45]Richard Clark Kroeger and Catherine Clark Kroeger, *I Suffer Not a Woman: Rethinking 1 Timothy 2:11-15 in Light of Ancient Evidence* (Grand Rapids: Baker, 1992).

[46]See critiques in Albert Wolters, "Review: *I Suffer Not a Woman*," *Calvin Theological Journal* 28 (1993): 208-13; and Richard Oster, *Biblical Archaeologist* 56 (1993): 225-27.

[47]Sharon H. Gritz, *Paul, Women Teachers, and the Mother Goddess at Ephesus: A Study of 1 Timothy 2:9-15 in Light of the Religious and Cultural Milieu of the First Century* (New York: University Press of America, 1991).

[48]Philip Towner, *The Goal of Our Instruction* (JSNTSup 34; Sheffield: Sheffield Academic Press, 1989):21-45.

b. *Schreiner's Examination of the Text.* Schreiner views 2:1-7 as stating God's desire for all to be saved, and sees "Therefore" in v. 8 (absent in NIV) beginning a new section closely connected with 2:1-7. He takes the call for men to pray "in every place" (everywhere, NIV) to refer to house churches. Consequently, 2:9-15 deals with public assemblies. Thus he understands vv. 11-12 to prohibit women from teaching or exercising authority over men in those assemblies. (112-114). In this connection, Schreiner views the relation between v. 8 and vv. 9-15 as follows,

> In verse 8 Paul considers the problem men have when gathered for public worship (anger and disputing in prayer), while in verses 9-15 two issues that have cropped up with the women in public gatherings (adornment and teaching men) are addressed. One should not conclude from the call to men to pray and women to adorn themselves properly that only men should pray in worship or that they should take the spiritual leadership in worship. First Corinthians 11:5 clarifies that women are allowed to participate by praying in public meetings (114).

While some[49] have argued that this reference is to husbands and wives, Schreiner concludes with most commentators that such a reference is improbable here. The instructions, he says, "are given instead regarding proper behavior for men and women in public meetings of the church" (117).

Most understand that the reference in 1 Tim 2:9 for women to "dress modestly, with decency and propriety" (NIV) refers to respectable behavior. Most hold that women's adornment in vv. 9-10 must be applied in the same way as prohibitions against women teaching in vv. 11-12.[50]

---

[49]Schreiner illustrates with Gordon Hugenberger, "Women in Church Office: Hermeneutics or Exegesis? A Survey of Approaches to 1 Tim 2:8-15," *Journal of the Evangelical Theological Society* 35 (1992): 341, 60; and Gritz, *Mother Goddess*, 125, 131, 133, 135-36, 140.

[50]See, among others, Gordon Fee, "Reflections on Church Order in the Pastoral Epistles," *Journal of the Evangelical Theological Society* 28 (1985): 150.

Similarly, most view wearing proper clothing as being closely linked to submission to husbands in Paul's day.[51] Scholer[52] says that hierarchalists have been inconsistent in enforcing the prohibition against teaching (vv. 11-12) while ignoring prohibitions against adornment (vv. 9-10).

Responding to this charge, Schreiner holds that the warning is against extravagant preoccupation with one's appearance, and suggests that the prohibition includes "seductive and enticing clothing" (119). However, he side-steps Scholer's argument that suitable clothing is linked with submission to one's husband with the passing comment that the ancient texts Scholer used to make this argument do not deal with submission but with unchastity (120). Aware that he is on thin ice here, Schreiner says that even if Scholer is correct that adornment is related to submission, the wearing of a golden wedding band, for instance, is different in our culture and would now be accepted. His way of avoiding the dilemma presented by Scholer and others is to say that neither v. 11 or v. 12 should be interpreted literally, but that the principles should be applied today. The question becomes, then, what are those principles?

The prejudice that drives his interpretation of vv. 11-12 is stated by Schreiner in his first paragraph, "we believe that it is a mistake for women to take on a pastoral role" (105). He disagrees with Keener,[53] who says that a woman can teach if she has good information. Schreiner says, "Two

---

[51]David Scholer, "1 Timothy 2:9-15 & the Place of Women in the Church's Ministry," in *Women, Authority & the Bible* (ed. Alvera Mickelsen; Downers Grove: InterVarsity, 1986): 200-202. See also his "Women's Adornment: Some Historical and Hermeneutical Observations on the New Testament Passages," *Daughters of Sarah* 6 (1980): 3-6, as well as Gordon Fee, *Gospel and Spirit: Issues in New Testament Hermeneutics* (Peabody, MA: Hendrickson, 1991): 57-58, and Craig Keener, *Paul, Women & Wives* (Peabody, MA: Hendrickson, 1992): 103-07.

[52]Scholer, "1 Tim 2:9-15," *Women, Authority & the Bible*, 193-219.

[53]Keener, *Paul, Women & Wives*, 107-08.

things are forbidden for a woman: teaching and exercising authority" (127). It is not unimportant that his argument is based upon the seriously flawed arguments of Baldwin and Köstenberger.

Interestingly, he allows, "We should not rule out the possibility that the context will incline us toward the meaning 'domineer' or 'play the tyrant' rather than 'exercise authority'," but "we shall see shortly that the definition 'exercise authority' is constrained by the context" (133). There is a major problem at this point, however, for nowhere in his following explanation is 'domineer' shown to be "constrained by the context." At this critical point where strong evidence is demanded, Schreiner has only his prejudice to show.

Fee,[54] among others, has argued that the reference to Adam and Eve in v. 13 does not refer to an "order of creation." Schreiner counters that an "order of creation" is very much in view (134-40). At issue is whether the connective "for" [Greek, *gar*] relates vv. 13-14 to vv. 11-12 as giving the reason or examples.

A succinct discussion of vv. 13 and 14 from a non-hierarchal point of view is that of Ben Witherington, professor at Ashland Theological Seminary.[55] Witherington makes three arguments. 1) The Greek term *gar* is not used here in an illative sense [for, because], giving the reason for the prohibition, but simply introducing an example [for example].[56] 2) Vv. 13-14 are a short exposition on Gen 2:7ff and 3:1ff, texts commonly used by Jewish expositors to teach women a lesson. 3) V. 15 concludes the admonition, stating that women in Ephesus are not to be like Eve in

---

[54]Fee, *Gospel and Spirit*, 61-62.

[55]Ben Witherington, *Women in the Earliest Churches* (SNTSMS, 59; Cambridge: Cambridge Univ. Press, 1988): 122-24.

[56]A. T. Robertson, *A Grammar of the Greek New Testament in the Light of Historical Research* (Nashville: Broadman, 1934): 1190, says that in Greek, *gar* "does not always give a reason. It may be merely explanatory."

being deceived, but are to go about life, not attempting to domineer over men or disseminate incorrect teaching, but by being married, having children, and raising them in responsible ways.[57]   There is, Scholer argues,[58] no evidence that these allusions to Genesis give vv. 11-12 universal significance.

Schreiner counters that *gar* most often states the reason for a command.[59]   He reads v. 13 in a "Can't you read plain English?" mode, claiming that he has "a higher view of biblical authority than these scholars" (137). However, he avoids the importance of context in deciding the significance to attach to a Greek connection.

Certainly *gar* can introduce an example and can be translated, "for example," as Witherington suggests. V. 13 can be taken to comment on "not domineering" in v. 12, simply stating that woman was created second for the purpose of being a meaningful complement. These Ephesian women, given their attitudes and actions, would not be fitting into their intended role, and should attempt to be "daughters of Eve" rather than arrogant and disruptive.

Similarly, the reference in v. 14 to Eve's deception and sin is drawn from Jewish adaptation of Gen 3. As Scholer puts it, "Women who were falling prey to the false teachers in Ephesus were being deceived and were transgressing as Eve did."[60] In Gen 3:1-7, the man and woman sin together, the serpent addresses the woman with the plural, "you," and v. 6 says the man was present with the woman.[61] Even so,

---

[57]See traditional Jewish exegesis of Gen 2-3 in 2 Enoch 31:6; 4 Maccabees 18:6-8; Babylonian Targum Yebamoth 103b, and Philo, *Questions on Genesis* 1.33.46.

[58]Scholer, "1 Tim 2:9-15," *Women, Authority & the Bible*, 208.

[59]Following Douglas Moo, "The Interpretation of 1 Timothy 2:11-15: A Rejoinder," *Trinity Journal* 2 (1981): 198-222, esp. 202-03.

[60]Scholer, "1 Tim 2:9-15," *Women, Authority & the Bible*, 211.

[61]RSV is not alone in omitting without justification the statement in v. 6 that, "he was with her at the time." NRSV corrects this unfortunate omission.

3:13 says that she ate the fruit first and took the blame.[62]
From this, Jewish tradition emphasized Eve's culpability.
For instance, Sirach 25:24, states, "From a woman sin had
its beginning, and because of her we all die" (RSV
Apocrypha). In Rom 5:12-14 and 1 Cor 15:21-22, Paul
attributes sin to Adam, not Eve. So v. 14 should be understood as an example from traditional Jewish interpretation
that selectively uses data from Gen 3 to suit the argument
that women with erroneous information should not teach.

Schreiner admits that v. 14 is difficult for hierarchalists
because to take it literally would mean that women are by
nature intellectually inferior and susceptible to deception
(141).[63] He attempts to avoid this difficulty by stressing
that the text does not say that these women are teaching a
wrong message (141). They are, he argues weakly, simply
teaching men. Although Schreiner makes an attempt to deny
misogyny (145-46), he concludes, "Women are prohibited
from teaching not only because of the order of creation but
also because they are less likely to preserve the apostolic
tradition."

However, this overlooks the obvious statement in 1 Tim
4:1-4 that the teaching involved deceiving spirits, teachings
of demons, abstinence from marriage and certain foods—
things certainly typical of various cults and religions of the
day (Cybele) and in philosophical discussions (Pythagoreans
and Stoics). Fee[64] and Witherington[65] are on more solid
ground in viewing the women in 2:11-15 as being involved
in the teaching of aberrant material.

---

[62]Philo, *Allegory on the Law* 3.61, expresses this point.

[63]With Douglas Moo, "Interpretation," *Trinity Journal*, 204.
Even James Hurley, *Man and Woman in Biblical Perspective* (Grand
Rapids: Zondervan, 1981): is forced to admit that it is, "very unlikely
that Paul meant to say . . . that all women are too gullible to teach."
See on this point, Towner, *The Goal of Our Instruction*, 217.

[64]Fee, *Gospel and Spirit*, 55.

[65]Witherington, *Women in the Earliest Churches*, 118.

Finally, Scholer[66] observes that v. 15 serves as the climax of the entire unit of text that begins at v. 9. This verse provides the positive conclusion to the negative statements in vv. 11-14. Although various suggestions have been made as to the interpretation of "being saved through childbirth," it is clear that in this context the writer is stressing that women find their place among the "saved" through traditional maternal and domestic roles clearly understood as proper for women in Paul's day.[67] This is especially important in view of the fact that the opponents were forbidding even to marry (4:3). In fact, throughout 1 Tim there is a strong emphasis upon proper domestic life.

Schreiner counters that the reference to childbearing is "appropriate because it represents the fulfillment of the woman's domestic role as a mother in distinction from the man" (151). "This rounds out the passage," he says, "because a woman should not violate her role by teaching or exercising authority over a man; instead she should take her proper role as a mother of children" (151). Schreiner has ended where he started, with his prejudice.

4. *Giles' Critique of Köstenberger, Schreiner and Baldwin*

Kevin Giles, an Anglican rector in Australia, has written a penetrating critique of the book edited by Köstenberger, Schreiner and Baldwin.[68] He begins by observing that the task of the book is to demonstrate that sound exegesis yields

---

[66]Scholer, "1 Tim 2:9-15," *Women, Authority & the Bible*, 196. See also Keener, *Paul, Women & Wives*, 118. Some hierarchalists do not even address v. 15, e.g., George Knight, *The New Testament Teaching*, and Susan Foh, *Women and the Word of God* (Grand Rapids: Baker, 1980): 128.

[67]See Sarah Pomeroy, *Goddesses, Whores, Wives and Slaves: Women in Classical Antiquity* (New York: Schocken, 1975), for the cultural context.

[68]Kevin Giles, "A Critique of the 'Novel' Contemporary Interpretation of 1 Timothy 2:9-15 Given in the Book,*Women in the Church Evangelical Quarterly* 72 (2000):151-67, 195-215.

the same meaning of 1 Tim 2:9-15 that all commentators have given until recent times, a view they call the "historic" position. Giles responds that what they claim to be the "historic" position is in fact quite novel. Instead, Giles claims, the writers, "are themselves practicioners of a 'progressive hermeneutic', 'Cartesians', who read the Bible in the light of their present situation—the very things they accuse their evangelical opponents of doing" (152). Giles observes,

> They are presenting evidence for what is already believed to be true. . . . (They are) full of generalisations, special pleading and highly emotive language. The editors in fact depict themselves as a faithful minority who are suffering and misunderstood for their obedience to the inspired Scriptures (152).

Giles' critique of the chapters by Yarbrough and Brown, as well as the appendix by Doriani, are important to note just here. In chap 6, Robert Yarbrough, a New Testament professor at Covenant Theological Seminary, discusses the hermeneutics of 1 Tim 2:9-15.[69] Yarbrough states that, "moving from the original message of the text in its historical setting to today, from 'signification' to 'significance', is complicated."[70] Giles agrees, on matters such as foot washing, hair styles, slavery and women in the church, but rejects Yarbrough's fundamentalist approach of holding that what the text says must always apply "one for one in every place for all time" (156). Yarbrough expresses three major problems with scholarship on 1 Tim 2:9-15: 1) too many Christians have been seduced by modern Western culture regarding women and are guilty of the 'Cartesian error' of giving new meanings to texts to make them fit their own cultural perspective, and 2) they have greatly overstated Gal 3:28, and 3) they have over-played the relationship between slavery and women in the church.

---

[69]Robert W. Yarbrough, "The Hermeneutics of 1 Timothy 2:9-15," *Women in the Church: A Fresh Analysis of 1 Timothy 2:9-15*, 155-96.

[70]Yarbrough, "Hermeneutics of 1 Timothy 2:9-15," *Women in the Church: A Fresh Analysis of 1 Timothy 2:9-15*, 157.

However, Giles notes, it is Yarbrough and his fellow essayists who are the real Cartesians with novel ideas. The important text of Gal 3:28 is not discussed by Yarbrough at all, causing Giles to conclude that Yarbrough's "emotive rhetoric implies that honestly dealing with the text is too difficult" for him. And Yarbrough simply denies, against current scholarship, that the NT endorses slavery.[71]

According to Giles, Brown's chapter on Gal 3:28 "is the most emotive and unscholarly in the book" (158).[72] Brown dismisses all who read 1 Tim 2:12, 1 Cor 14:34 and related texts other than he does as "an entire civilisation which has increasingly strayed from God's order of creation"[73] (158). Any attempt to deal with Gal 3:28 exegetically is lacking in Brown's chapter.

The most fascinating chapter, Giles notes, is the one by Daniel Doriani, who sets out to prove that the understanding of 1 Tim 2:9-15 as understood by Köstenberger, Schreiner and Baldwin is the view that has been held throughout the history of the church until the recent feminist controversy, when the text was given a novel interpretation.[74] "This chapter," Giles observes, "is absolutely foundational to the whole case put in this book," i.e., that their view is the "historic" interpretation of 1 Tim 2:9-15. It is here that Giles makes his strongest observation that these writers are the ones who are putting forth "a quite novel and ahistorical interpretation" (159). They have, he says, creatively reinterpreted the text,

---

[71]See among others, Willard M. Swartley, *Slavery, Sabbath, War & Women: Case Issues in Biblical Interpretation* (Scottdale, PA: Herald Press, 1983), and J. A. Harrill, *The Manumission of Slaves in Early Christianity* (Tübingen: J. C. B. Mohr, 1995).

[72]Harold Brown, "The New Testament Against Itself: 1 Timothy 2:9-15 and the 'Breakthrough' of Galatians 3:28," *Women in the Church: A Fresh Analysis of 1 Timothy 2:9-15*, 197-208.

[73]Op cit., 198.

[74]See Daniel Doriani, "A History of the Interpretation of 1 Timothy 2," *Women in the Church: A Fresh Analysis of 1 Timothy 2:9-15*, 213-67.

to make it 'fit' the changed context. They then claim
mischievously, or because they are blinded by dogma, that
what they are teaching is the 'historic' interpretation of the
passage in dispute (159).

Giles argues that the *actual* "historic view" is quite other
than that argued by Köstenberger, Schreiner and Baldwin
(160-64). For instance, over the centuries most writers have
argued that in 1 Tim 2:11 Paul demands total silence by
women in church. Giles notes Tertullian, Origen, Cyprian,
Cyril of Jerusalem, Chrysostom, Jerome and Aquinas.
Luther and Calvin argued from this text that women are to
keep silent in worship, but can sing hymns. Calvin allowed
them to lead prayer; Luther did not. And the general view of
this verse has been that women are to be subordinate to men
in all things in all situations.

Until recent times, Giles states, commentators agree that
"Paul forbids women in general from doing two things,
teaching in church and having authority over men" (160).
Chrysostom, he notes, is adamant that women are not even
to speak in church, let alone teach, and that all women in
every area of life are to be subject to men. This view holds
the field down through John Knox and the Puritans and on
into the modern era.

As far as v. 13 is concerned, Giles says the principal
interpretation is that "because woman was created second
she is to take second place to man; she is an inferior being"
(161). From the time of Chrysostom, it is held that "God
made man first to show male 'superiority'." Giles notes the
question of Aquinas, "does the fact that man was created
first, woman second, imply that she is a deficient or
defective male?" Aquinas answers, "Yes!" Giles cites
Douglas' conclusion that both Luther and Calvin were
"deeply influenced by the tradition which sees men as more
fully made in the image of God than women."[75]

---

[75]Jane Dempsey Douglas, "The Image of God in Women as Seen
in Luther and Calvin," in *The Image of God: Gender Models in Judeo
Christian Tradition* (Minneapolis: Fortress, 1991): 260.

V. 14 has historically been taken to mean that "Eve is to be blamed for all evil and death and that she and all her sex are more prone to sin and error than men" (162). Irenaeus says, "Having become disobedient, she (Eve) was made the cause of death, both to herself and the whole human race" (162). Tertullian wrote of women, "Do you not know that each of you is Eve? . . . You are the devil's gateway, you are the first deserter of divine law" (162). This view is held by most writers, including Chrysostom, Luther and Calvin.

Then the dominant view of v. 15 throughout Christian history has been that "here Paul is teaching that womens' special domain is to bear children" (163). Giles illustrates with Chrysostom's statement, "Be not cast down because your sex has incurred blame, . . . the whole sex shall be saved, notwithstanding, by childbearing" (163).

So this extreme view is actually the dominant view of 1 Tim 2:9-15 in Christian literature.

On the other hand, Giles notes that these so-called complementarians are the ones who have given a novel interpretation of this text. For instance, where the dominant historic view takes v. 11 to refer to the submission of all women to all men, Köstenberger, Schreiner and Baldwin insist that Paul is not demanding the submission of all women to all men, but only in the domain of the home and the church.

Also, Köstenberger, Schreiner and Baldwin hold that two things are forbidden in v. 12, women teaching in church or exercising authority in the church or the home. Giles notes, however, that,

> Schreiner admits that Paul's use of the verb *epitrepo* in the present, active indicative form, could mean that Paul is saying, 'I am not permitting women to teach or exercise authority *at this time*.' On its own the verse does not indicate this is a 'universal principle.' What proves that the double 'command is universal and for all time', he says, is verse 13 (125-27).

Now vv. 13 and 14 are viewed by Köstenberger, Schreiner and Baldwin as reasons for curtailing activity by women in the church. The Greek *gar* introducing the verses is understood to be causal in force. This means that they are forced to view v. 13 as reflecting an order of creation. Doriani puts it this way, "For complementarians, the phrase, 'Adam was formed or created first,'" refers beyond chronology to God's sovereign decree that made males the spiritual heads of God's kingdom, churches and homes."[76] Schreiner tries to argue that v. 13 does "not imply women are inferior to men" (135). However, this shift toward creation order and away from the historical view is in fact a *reinterpretation* of 1 Timothy 2:13 by complementarians, according to Giles (165). This is admitted by Doriani regarding v. 14.[77] It is more than interesting that Schreiner simply admits, "women are less prone to see the importance of doctrinal formulations, especially when it comes to the issue of identifying heresy and making a stand for the truth."[78] So, like it or not, Köstenberger, Schreiner and Baldwin begin to fall in line with the actual historic view in v. 14.

Then Schreiner views v. 15 as saying that Christian women "will be saved by adhering to their ordained role."[79] In comparing Schreiner's view to the actual historical view, however, Giles notes three things that stand out: 1) Blatant misogynist language is missing in Köstenberger, Schreiner and Baldwin, and women are not blamed for sin and death, resulting in a more positive view of women than that of the actual historical view. 2) Köstenberger, Schreiner and Baldwin actually contradict the historic interpretation of 1 Tim 2 by denying that God made women inferior to men and by insisting that the restrictions on women apply only in the church and the home. 3) Köstenberger, Schreiner and Baldwin ignore the historic view that places women in a

---

[76]Doriani, "A History of the Interpretation of 1 Timothy 2," *Women in the Church: A Fresh Analysis of 1 Timothy 2:9-15*, 262.

[77]Op cit., 258.

[78]Schreiner, "An Interpretation of 1 Timothy 2:9-15," *Women in the Church: A Fresh Analysis of 1 Timothy 2:9-15*, 144-45.

[79]Op cit., 151.

secondary place because woman was created second. Instead, Giles argues, they ground the differing 'roles' of men and women on a transcultural, permanently binding, constitutive order of creation.

In view of these observations, Giles concludes that the work of Köstenberger, Schreiner and Baldwin is not at all the actual "historic" view of 1 Tim 2:9-15, but a distinctively new interpretation (166-67). They actually, he says,

> embrace a 'Cartesian' and 'progressive hermeneutic'—the very thing they accuse their evangelical brothers and sisters of doing. And worse still, they claim that what they are teaching is what Christians have always believed, which is simply not true.

Finally, Giles discusses three elements vital to the work of Köstenberger, Schreiner and Baldwin. First, he analyzes their novel argument from "the order of creation." The phrase, "order of creation," can be understood to refer either 1) to the sequential order in which man and woman were brought into existence, without any necessary implication or inferiority or subordination, or 2) to a constitutive ordering of human relationships in the creation story. Brown[80] gives an insightful statement of the view of Köstenberger, Schreiner and Baldwin, saying that in creation God has established, "explicit *mandata Dei* (Divine mandates) that hold good for all time and in every place." This use of the phrase, "order of creation," dominates fundamentalist evangelical literature. However, Giles holds that, "this argument is completely novel. It is not found in any commentary or book prior to the Second World War" (196). The historic basis for defining womens' role in the church has been that God created woman second, and thus inferior to men.

Giles concludes that the "order of creation" argument does not stand exegetically or historically, and there is no basis for limiting it to the church and home.

---

[80]Brown, "The New Testament Against Itself" *Women in the Church: A Fresh Analysis of 1 Timothy 2:9-15*, 204.

Giles' second concluding observation deals with the usage of the word "role." He cannot find any evidence of Christian usage of this term prior to 1960, meaning that the hierarchal use of this term to argue the permanent subordination of women is something quite novel (200-01). Since Knight's book entitled, *The New Testament Teaching on the Role Relationship of Men and Women*,[81] "women's subordinate status has been redefined by hierarchalists in terms of role differentiation" (201). In fact, Neuer is the only hierarchalist Giles can find who has seen "'the inappropriateness of role theory' to interpret the Bible's teaching on the differences between men and women." Neuer[82] says, "In the cause of truth we should give up talking about the roles of the sexes."

Third, Giles observes that Köstenberger, Schreiner and Baldwin use language much differently than that found in the actual historic interpretation. Whereas "stark and unambiguous language" is characteristic of the historic view (women are inferior, born to obey, weak and fickle), that found in Köstenberger, Schreiner and Baldwin is characterized by ambiguous and evasive language (203). For instance, Giles notes that instead of saying that women are not to teach because they are prone to sin, we now hear in this new approach that, "they are less likely to draw the line on doctrinal non-negotiables."[83] Giles continues, "In politics making bad news sound good is called putting a 'spin' on things. The writers of *Women in the Church* are 'spin doctors' in this sense" (203).

This leads Giles to conclude that behind the thrust of the work of Köstenberger, Schreiner and Baldwin is the self-serving theology of male hegemony—the right of males to run the show. With this prejudice underlying their work, "it

---

[81]George Knight, *The New Testament Teaching on the Role Relationship of Men and Women* (Grand Rapids: Baker, 1977).

[82]Werner Neuer, *Man and Woman in Christian Perspective* (London: Hodder and Stoughton, 1990): 30.

[83]Schreiner, "An Interpretation of 1 Timothy 2:9-15," *Women in the Church: A Fresh Analysis of 1 Timothy 2:9-15*, 145.

is not surprising that language is distorted, evidence is ignored, and logic goes out the door" (204). Even Brown[84] says in his chapter, "'presuppositions', not 'exegetical assertions', determine the conclusions reached on this matter."

When this debate began in the early '70s the two sides were content to call themselves "egalitarians" and "hierarchalists." However, more recently hierarchalists began to reject this term, preferring to be called "complementarians," or "holders of the historic position." Giles concludes rightly that these so-called complementarians neither hold the historic position nor are they functionally complementarians. He notes, "The truth of the matter is that both sides in this debate are complementarians" (204). The real debate is,

> between those who want men and women to complement each other by standing side by side in the home, the church and the state and those who want men and women to complement one another with the men standing above the women. The contrast is thus between hierarchal complementarians and egalitarian complementarians. Honesty demands that this be acknowledged (204).

5. *Summary of Critiques of Köstenberger, Schreiner and Baldwin*

It is a shame that so much effort has resulted in a work that has no discernible value. Köstenberger, Schreiner and Baldwin have simply provided a hierarchal counterpart to the equally useless evangelical feminist writings on 1 Tim 2:9-15 by the Kroegers. Both of these attempts are examples of prejudicial exegesis in addressing the important topic of women in the church. Both are examples of what not to do in biblical scholarship. Neither has any significant contribution to make to the current discussion of women in the church.

---

[84]Brown, "The New Testament Against Itself" *Women in the Church: A Fresh Analysis of 1 Timothy 2:9-15*, 197.

2. *1 Tim 2:8-15: Exegetical Considerations*

It is evident in 1 Tim 2:9-15 that some women were teaching in the public assembly of the church in Ephesus or Paul would not have forbidden it.[85] Two basic questions emerge from this text.[86] What precisely is Paul forbidding? In what way should the injunction apply to churches today?

A. *The Context of 1 Tim 2:8-15*

The introduction to 1 Tim begins in 1:3-11 with a statement of the problem created by individuals wanting to teach who do not have adequate or appropriate information, and it concludes in vv. 18-20 with Paul's excommunication of two of these, Hymenaeus and Alexander. Chapter three presents detailed characteristics essential for church leaders, which contrast markedly with what is said in the epistle about the false teachers. 1 Tim 2 occurs between these concerns about church life in Ephesus, all in the context of the disruptive influence of false teaching.

"Therefore" in 2:1 is to be understood as beginning the body of the letter in which the introductory appeal to Timothy to remain in Ephesus and counter the sinister influence of these false teachers (1:3-7) is given fuller discussion. The opening section of the body of the epistle (2:1-8) demands cessation of an exclusivist mentality on the part of the males and the incorporation of a vigorous prayer life for rulers and all in authority, in fact for *all* people. This continues a standard custom common in Jewish synagogues. Jewish people had been exempted from having to pray *to* the

---

[85]Douglas Moo, "1 Timothy 2:11-15: Meaning and Significance," *Trinity Journal* 1 (1980): 62-83, esp. 82, however, curiously denies even the possibility that women were teaching at Ephesus.

[86]It is unacceptable either to dismiss this text from consideration, as does E. M. Tetlow, *Women and Ministry in the New Testament* (New York: Paulist, 1980), or to disregard it because it does not cohere with one's preconceived notion of what Paul must have thought, as does Robin Scroggs, "Paul and the Eschatological Woman," *Journal of the American Academy of Religion* 40 (1972): 283-303.

Roman emperor, but were expected to pray *for* him.[87] Such
prayer was expected to result in peaceful lives for the
Christians in Ephesus.[88] It is not unimportant in this
connection that the conclusion in v. 8 stipulates that men
ought to pray without wrath and dissension.

This paragraph on prayer in Ephesian worship also
establishes the context for the following paragraph on the
dress and conduct of women while in the worship. Both
sections in 1 Tim 2 address specific situations in the
Ephesian church.

B. *1 Tim 2:(8)9-10*

The Greek text does not have a main verb in v. 9, so
one must be supplied from v. 8. If "I wish to pray" is
brought over, as most understand to be the case, v. 9 would
be understood as a specific instruction to women at prayer.[89]
This would cohere with Paul's admonition in 1 Cor 11:3 that
women pray in the public worship. "Likewise," in 2:9,
suggests that, having instructed the men how to pray in
Ephesus, Paul now instructs the women in the same way. If
Schreiner is correct, that only "I wish" is to be brought over,
v. 9 would give general instruction on women's clothing and
adornment.[90] The matter may be incapable of resolution,
but what is clear is that the context is the worshipping church
in Ephesus, and it is probable that prayer is in focus in v. 9.

1 Tim 2:9-10 presents injunctions that are every bit as
serious as those in 2:11-12. Instructions in vv. 9-10 are
given without qualification and affirm acceptable standards
of decency, as opposed to those found in the false teaching.

---

[87]See A. M. Rabello, "The Legal Condition of the Jews in the
Roman Empire," *Aufstieg und Niedergang der römischen Welt* 2.13:
703-04.

[88]Hans Conzelmann, *History of Primitive Christianity* (trans. J.
Steely; Nashville: Abingdon, 1973): 133.

[89]This view is advocated by Keener, *Paul, Women & Wives*,
102-03; Fee, *1 and 2 Timothy, Titus*, 70-71.

[90]Schreiner, *Women in the Church*, 114.

Certainly, from 1:3-8 it is clear that Paul directs Timothy to counter the sinister effect of certain teachers in the congregation. Their influence surfaces in Paul's directives in 2:1-8 (men not to argue), 2:9-15 (women) and 5:11-15 (widows). The situation in Ephesus is that some Christian women have overstepped traditional roles held by society. Their fundamental attitudinal shift has two facets. 1) They dress in culturally unacceptable ways. 2) They forsake domestic roles, seeking visible, teaching roles in congregational life. In each instance, their attitude is assertive, insensitive, and out of line.

That these women in the Ephesian church are brazenly over-dressed is stated and not at all unrelated to the following context.[91] The prohibition against excessive adornment should be understood against its cultural background. Diodorus, *Hist..* 12.21, says that golden jewelry or a garment with a purple border was a sign of a prostitute. Ps.-Lucian, *Affairs of the Heart* 38-43, laments a husband's horrible experiences in living with a wife who spends her day before the mirror attempting to beautify herself with creams, powders, expensive jewels, earrings, bracelets, and necklaces. She then visits the various gods, and later returns home after being unfaithful to her husband. Philo, *On the Virtues* 39-40, says that such adornment was associated with visiting pagan temples and with sexual promiscuity, as well as with disrespect for the husband's authority. In the *Sentences of Sextus* 513 is a typical observation of the period that, "A wife who likes adornment is not faithful." In view of these, and many similar statements, the dress and adornment of a wife is certainly very closely related to her submission to her husband.

Such women, disdaining the accepted code of dress, are told in vv. 11-12 that they must *learn*. This certainly denotes inadequate information on their part. That they should learn in a *peaceable* and *deferential* manner suggests some sort of unruly, disquieting, tumultuous, autocratic, domineering, or

---

[91]Note the similar prohibition against excessive adornment in 1 Pet 3:1-6, also in a context addressing deferential attitude.

arrogant behavior on their part. Now some, such as Philo,[92] argued that women should take care of domestic matters and appear in public only to go to the market and to the temple. He also stressed that women did not need education.[93] However, not all women were so restricted. The education of women was common among Stoics and Pythagoreans, among others (note the false teaching typical of both these groups in 4:1-4; see p. 229 above).[94] Yet, this education had certain drawbacks. Musonius Rufus,[95] a first-century AD philosopher who favored the education of women, argued that,

> some say that it is inevitable that women who associate with philosophers will be self-willed for the most part and arrogant when they abandon their duties at home and spend their time with men practicing discourses, speaking subtly, and analyzing syllogisms. They ought to be home spinning! I would not expect that the women who practice philosophy—any more than the men— would abandon their appropriate tasks to deal only with discourses; rather, I maintain that whatever discourses they pursue ought to be about the deeds they pursue.

What Musonius Rufus said probably would not occur, did in fact occur among some of the Christian women in Ephesus. Interest in teaching resulted in arrogant attitudes and abandonment of various domestic tasks. Paul finds this unacceptable.

---

[92]Philo, *Special Laws* 3.169-71, "A woman, then, should not be a busybody, meddling with matters outside her household concerns, but should seek a life of seclusion."

[93]Philo, *Apology for the Jews* 7.14, "The husband seems competent to transmit knowledge of the laws to his wife, the father to his children, the master to his slaves." In certain rabbinic circles, women were seen as temptation and distraction from study. See Pirke Aboth 1.5.

[94]Sterling, "Women in the Hellenistic and Roman Worlds," *Essays on Women in Earliest Christianity*, 1.76-84.

[95]Musonius Rufus, F 3. See O. Hense, ed., *Musonii Rufi Reliquae* (Leipzig: B. G. Teubner, 1905).

In lieu of this situation, Paul stresses in v. 10 that these Christian women would do well to concentrate on healthy teaching conducive to genuinely Christian life-style. "Good works" here does not refer to works that might be done with the motive of acquiring merit, but to the sort of "good works which God designed long ago that we should walk in them" (Eph 2:10)—that is to say, works (life-style characteristics) such as goodness, kindness, patience, gentleness, modesty and the like. These things are just more "fitting" for these Ephesian women who "profess" the Christian faith than expressing a lack of respect for their husbands by wearing inappropriate clothing that sends distinctly wrong signals.

C. *1 Tim 2:11-12*

English translations of 1 Tim 2:12 vary somewhat.

I do not permit a woman to teach or to have authority over a man; she must be silent. NIV

I do not permit a woman to be a teacher, nor must woman domineer over man; she should be quiet. NEB

I am not giving permission for a woman to teach or to tell a man what to do. A woman ought not to speak. JerB

It must be kept in mind that the entire letter of 1 Timothy deals with the false teachers mentioned in 1:3ff and Timothy's role in quelling their influence. In 2:1-8, the men are admonished to pray for all people, without "getting involved in the quarrels and disputes engendered by the false teaching."[96]   In 2:9-15, the women are admonished to present and conduct themselves in a manner appropriate for godly women, without abandoning submission to their husbands and distorting their place among men in general.[97] In 2:11-12, Paul continues to address the problem of insubordination, moving from dress and demeanor to the realm of information.

---

[96]Fee, *Gospel and Spirit*, 57.

[97]Scholer, "1 Tim 2:9-15," *Women, Authority & the Bible*, 201.

Two principal views have emerged concerning the interpretation of 1 Tim 2:11-12. 1) One view holds that this text forbids women from teaching or exercising authority over men because of the order of creation. Proponents of this view maintain that the Genesis material in vv. 13-14 provides the reason for the prohibitions in vv. 11-12, and the conclusion is drawn that these sanctions are to be applied universally in all times and places. 2) The other view holds that this is a temporary restraint to curb the inordinate conduct of certain Ephesian women who were teaching the heresy mentioned in 1:3-7 as the reason for the epistle. In this view, the Genesis material in vv. 13-14 provides an example or explanation of how the deception of Eve having drastic consequences parallels that of the women at Ephesus.

To begin with, just as vv. 9-10 are to be understood in terms of ancient cultural values and are addressed to the threat of certain false teachers in Ephesus, so also are the admonitions to silence and submission in vv. 11-12. The stipulations in vv. 11-12 are well in line with first-century AD expectations for women, both in the Jewish and Greco-Roman worlds. Consequently, vv. 11-12 stipulates responsible action for women in response to the sinister teaching that forms the basis of the epistle from 1:3.

In this view, vv. 11-12 is a temporary stipulation intended for the particular situation at Ephesus. These injunctions were not intended as universal norms for all women in all times and places.[98] Instead, vv. 11-12 were intended to curtail the influence and involvement of certain women involved in the false teachings at Ephesus.

V. 11 states that "a woman must learn in a quiet spirit with all submissiveness." The term "learn" (*manthanéto*) is a present imperative in Greek, which means that the term is concerned with the ongoingness of their leaning, i.e., "a woman must go about this business of learning with a . . . ." Women were participating in worship and learning; but such learning was a relatively new thing for women at that time.

---

[98]With Fee, *Gospel and Spirit*, 61, and others.

Whereas some in Ephesus might oppose women learning, Paul underscores the right of women to learn. These women, though, have presented a problem in that regard and need to adopt an appropriate manner of learning, e.g., in a spirit of quietude which implies receptivity. They should learn adequate and correct information before challenging their teachers or even trying to teach it themselves. They should remember that they are novices, not "teachers." Silence was expected of students, both in Judaism and in the Greco-Roman world.[99]

The phrase, "with all submissiveness," describes the manner in which these women are to learn. The meaning of "submissiveness" must be determined by the context in which it occurs. Towner cautions that the term has a wide range of meanings, and that care must "be taken to avoid assigning the basic meaning of 'order *under*' indiscriminately."[100] The term is used at times when hierarchy is under discussion (Rom 8:20; 1 Cor 15:27-28; Phil 3:21), but in numerous other instances the term denotes a willing deference rather than hierarchy (Eph 5:21-22; Col 3:18; 1 Pet 3:1). Such "submissiveness" was intended to provide order and peace, but the text does not specify to whom they are to be submissive. Actually, the term simply signifies a basic attitude. As Ward puts it, "Paul's aim is to avoid 'disturbance'."[101] "Submissiveness" refers to a willingness to be taught and to be accountable to what is taught.

So certain Ephesian women have serious attitudinal problems relating to their dress and adornment and to the learning process going on in the assembly. Paul's counter in vv. 9-11 is that they should 1) dress in ways that show respect for their husbands and for males in general, 2) be more concerned with basic life-style characteristics that are appropriate for godly women, and 3) undertake the learning of accurate information in a receptive spirit.

---

[99]See Keener, *Paul, Women & Wives*, 107-08.

[100]Towner, *The Goal of Our Instruction*, 213.

[101]Ronald A. Ward, *Commentary on 1 and 2 Timothy and Titus*, 51.

It is easy to understand how 2:12 could be read in English with the conclusion that a woman is never to teach a man or be in a position of authority over a man. However, in the Greek text, the verb "domineer" [NEB; "have authority" RSV NIV] qualifies "teach" and specifies what kind of teaching is prohibited.[102] It is not that these women are "teaching" per se, but specifically that they are "teaching domineeringly" that annoys Paul.[103]

The term *authentein* is taken by some to mean "exercise authority" [RSV NIV], but stronger reasons exist for taking it to mean "domineer."[104] Instead of "domineering over a man," they are encouraged to be "deferential" (2:11). Instead, they should evidence an attitude of "peaceableness/ quietude."[105] This prohibition of "domineering" does not introduce a second prohibition, but qualifies the first—that is, they are "not to teach *in a domineering way*, but are to be in peaceableness/quietness." In this context, the term refers to the role the women were playing in teaching the erroneous information of the false teachers.[106]

The admonition at the end of v. 12 that these women are to "keep silent" [RSV] is not a mandate that women maintain absolute silence in worship. It rather specifies that an attitude of "peaceableness/quietness" be maintained instead of their current attitude of "domineering." Since in 1:7 Paul specified that "they want to be teachers of law, but they do not understand what things they so confidently affirm," it is

---

[102]When two Greek verbs are joined in this way, the nearer qualifies the farther, i.e., "domineer" qualifies "teach." See Herbert W. Smyth, *Greek Grammar* (rev. G. Messing; Cambridge: Harvard Univ. Press, 1956): 364-365.

[103]With J. N. D. Kelly, *The Pastoral Epistles* (London: A. & C. Black, 1963): 68, among others.

[104]See, among others, Scholer, "1 Tim 2:9-15," *Women, Authority & the Bible*, 205; Fee, *1 and 2 Timothy, Titus*, 73; Keener, *Pau, Women & Wives*, 108-09.

[105]See Carroll Osburn, "ΑΥΘΕΝΤΕΩ (1 Timothy 2:12)," *Restoration Quarterly* 25 (1982): 1-11.

[106]Keener, *Paul, Women & Wives*, 111-12.

clear that they need instruction. It follows that if they learn in a peaceable and gentle spirit (v. 11) and teach in a peaceable and gentle spirit (v. 12), Paul would have no problem with them.[107] This is not at all unlike the situation in 1 Cor 11, where Paul had no problem with the women praying and prophesying, only their bad attitude in disdaining social customs regarding appearance in public.

D. *1 Tim 2:13-15*

The Greek *gar* [for] in 2:13 indicates that the two following illustrations are intended to support the prohibition against domineering teaching by these women. Paul grounds his prohibition in the creation stories in Genesis. Now v. 13 is often taken to refer to an "order of creation" in which man has authority over woman because Adam came first,[108] and v. 14 is likewise taken to mean that Eve's gullibility illustrates why women should not teach.[109] Thus, heirarchalists view these as reasons from Genesis for the prohibitions. Alternatively, the Greek term *gar* is not used here in an illative sense [for, because], giving the reason for the prohibition, but simply introducing an example [for example].[110] In this view, vv. 13-14 are a short exposition on Gen 2:7ff and 3:1ff, texts commonly used by Jewish expositors to teach women a lesson.[111] At issue is whether the connective "for" [Greek, *gar*] relates vv. 13-14 to vv. 11-12 as giving the reason or examples. Taking *gar* to provide examples rather than reasons, Scholer argues that

---

[107]With Keener, *Paul, Women & Wives*, 112.

[108]Hurley, *Man and Woman in Biblical Perspective*, 207.

[109]Moo, "What Does It Mean Not to Teach or Have Authority Over Men?" *Rexocering Biblical Manhood and Womanhood*, 188-190.

[110]A. T. Robertson, *A Grammar of the Greek New Testament in the Light of Historical Research* (Nashville: Broadman, 1934): 1190, says that in Greek, *gar* "does not always give a reason. It may be merely explanatory."

[111]Witherington, *Women in the Earliest Churches*, 122-24.

there is no evidence that these allusions to Genesis give vv. 11-12 universal significance.[112]

Now 2:12-14 is a sentence in Greek. Within that sentence there are four thought-units: 1) not to teach, 2) not to domineer, 3) Adam first, 4) Eve deceived. V. 15, although a separate sentence, is closely linked to vv. 11-14. There exists here a literary structure in which the two items in v. 12 are followed by an analogy and an appeal. The analogy in vv. 13-14 comments on "not to teach" in v. 12a, and the appeal in v. 15 comments on "domineeringly" in v. 12b.

12 *a*   I am not permitting a woman to <u>teach</u>
    b   <u>domineeringly</u> a man,

13 *a'*   *for* Adam was formed first, <u>then Eve,</u>
14   Adam was not <u>deceived</u>, but the woman,
         when she was deceived, became a
         transgressor.
15 *b'*   She will be saved through
         childbearing, if they continue in faith,
         love, and holiness with propriety

From a linguistic point of view, the relationship of an example or illustration to a specific situation must be understood in terms of topic, image, and point of similarity. In this passage, the topic is the *domineering* teaching of certain women in Ephesus. The image is that Eve was created after Adam. What, then, is the point of similarity?

Well, Paul is certainly not engaging in exegesis of Gen 1-3.[113] Rather, he is using a common Jewish analogy in which Eve was caricatured as a deceived and bumbling fool who constantly led Adam into trouble. For example, we

---

[112]Scholer, "1 Tim 2:9-15," *Women, Authority & the Bible*, 208.

[113]See Rick R. Marrs, "In the Beginning: Male and Female (Gen 1-3)," *Essays on Women in Earliest Christianity* (ed. Carroll D. Osburn; Joplin, MO: College Press, 1995): 2.1-36.

have already quoted Sirach 25:24, "from a woman sin had its beginning, and because of her we all will die." In the *Life of Adam and Eve*, a first century expansion of Gen 1-4, Eve is assigned in 44:2 responsibility for sin in the world, and in *Apocalypse of Moses* 32:1-2, Eve acknowledges full responsibility for the human dilemma. As Chesnutt[114] says,

> the portrait of Eve as one constantly weeping, ignorant, perplexed, vulnerable to sin, and dependent upon the males around her for insight bears some relation to the way women were actually perceived and treated in the authors' and redactors' own times and places.

So, Paul does not draw from Gen 1-3 a universal principle from the historical Eve, but an ad hoc analogy from the later caricature of Eve in Jewish tradition. The point of similarity between v. 12 and v. 13 is that just as it is commonly remarked that Eve was deceived and led Adam astray, so certain women in the Ephesian church lack information and teach false information that leads people astray.

The reference in v. 14 to Eve's sin in Gen 3 comments on the analogy in v. 13. The image that Eve, rather than Adam, was deceived is drawn from traditional Jewish interpretation of Gen 3. It is important to remember that in Gen 3:1-7 the man and woman sin together, the serpent addresses the woman with the plural "you," and vv. 3 and 6 indicate that the man was with the woman at the time.[115] However, in Jewish tradition, Eve was deceived with unfortunately catastrophic results for all mankind.[116] The analogy is carried further in v. 14, specifying that these Ephesian women are not to teach because they have been deceived and transmit false information just as in Jewish tradition Eve was deceived and led Adam to sin.

---

[114]See Randall Chesnutt, "Jewish Women in the Greco-Roman Era," *Essays on Women in Earliest Christianity* (ed. Carroll D. Osburn; Joplin, MO: College Press, 1993): 1.93-130, esp. 102.

[115]See Scholer, "1 Tim 2:9-15," *Women, Authority & the Bible*, 210.

[116]See Philo, *Questions on Genesis* 33.

Paul's use of this illustration from Genesis underscores the fact that his prohibition against these women teaching was not done with reference to hierarchalism. Instead, where the original complementary relationship between men and women is destroyed, as in Ephesus, Paul mandates what is necessary in that particular setting to restore the original pattern. It is not necessary or advisable to take this as a general directive to all women everywhere.

In 2:15, Paul concludes the admonition to these Ephesian women with an observation that women are not saved through teaching (i.e., domineering), but by attention to their traditional roles, represented here by bearing children.[117] Porter notes that the passage should be understood contextually:

> The author of 1 Timothy seems to be fighting against a group distinguished by several characteristics. They were promoting doctrine (1 Tim. 1.3) that resulted in the telling of all sorts of silly myths and the emphasizing of genealogies (1.4), holding to stories about deceitful spirits and demons (4.1), and forbidding marriage and other practices (4.3). . . . It is easy to conclude that the encouraging of ascetic practices, combined with shunning of the women's domestic roles, resulted in sexual abstinence or similar practices which were considered by the author to have missed the mark (cf. 1.3-7; 6.20-21). In the light of this ascetic tendency, the author endorses the resumption of normal practices between men and women, including sexual relations that result in giving birth to children.[118]

---

[117]See J. N. D. Kelly, *A Commentary on the Pastoral Epistles* (New York: Harper & Row, 1963): 69; and Krijn A. Van der Jagt, "Women are Saved Through Bearing Children (1 Timothy 2.11-15," *The Bible Translator* 39 (1988): 201-08. Thomas Geer, "Admonitions to Women in 1 Tim 2:8-15," *Essays on Women in Earliest Christianity*, 1.297, mentions three other views: 1) despite Eve's transgression, Christian women will be saved through *the* childbirth, i.e., Christ, 2) despite the curse (Gen 3:16), Christian women are brought safely through the birth experience, and 3) in their proper submissive role, Christian women disdain teaching and domineering over men.

[118]Stanley E. Porter, "What Does It Mean to be 'Saved By Childbirth' (1 Timothy 2.15)?" in *New Testament Text and Language*

V. 15 is the climax of the entire unit of text that began in v. 9 with, *"likewise women."* This verse was written as a positive alternative for these women to the negative critiques in vv. 11-14.

One grammatical problem with v. 15 is that the first verb is singular (she will be saved) and the second is plural (they continue). This is due to the fact that womankind is in focus with "she" (as with Eve), whereas the latter reference shifts to the plural with the Ephesian women in mind (they).

The statement that "the woman will be saved through childbirth," is translated incorrectly in NIV as, "women will be kept safe through childbirth." Not only does experience show that this statement is incorrect, but "safe (saved)" is shown to refer to Christian salvation by the following phrase, "if they continue in faith, love, and holiness with propriety" (NIV). The point is that just as ancient (post fall) Eve was to find her place in society as a mother with domestic roles, so these women should find their place in society by fitting into "the maternal and domestic roles that were clearly understood to constitute propriety in the Greco-Roman culture of Paul's day."[119]

3. *Conclusion.*

It may be concluded, then, that 1 Tim 2:9-15 was directed to a specific group of troublesome women in a particular place in the early church. Their particular problem was specifically that of being misinformed and domineering teachers. In overstepping traditional roles, some Ephesian Christian women demonstrate a fundamental attitudinal shift which evidences itself in their dress and in forsaking traditionally domestic roles in a quest for visible roles in congregational life. Such domineering and assertive

---

(ed. by Porter and C. A. Evans; Sheffield: Sheffield Academic Press, 1996): 160-175 [originally published in *JSNT* 49 (1993): 87-102].

[119]Scholer, "1 Tim 2:9-15," *Women, Authority & the Bible*, 197.

behavior, coupled with such scandalous behavior as
overdressing in public, certainly sent the wrong signals to
Ephesus about the real nature of Christianity. Hence,
Timothy is admonished forthrightly to counter this sinister
development in the Ephesian congregation.

So, wherever there are misinformed, unreliable, and
domineering women attempting to teach Christian truth, the
ancient admonition of Paul to Timothy has direct application.
However, nothing is said in this text about informed,
reliable, and gentle women teaching—either in church or
out, either on religion or not, either to men or women, either
to young or old. No biblical text has been so misused to
legislate so many prohibitions that stifle so much service by
so many people. Put simply, any female who has sufficient
and accurate information may teach that information in a
gentle spirit to whomever in whatever situation they may be.

While the particular situation Paul addresses in
1 Tim arose due to particular *women* who were misinformed
and domineering, the point of the text would be equally
applicable to any *men* who might be acting similarly.

13

CONCLUSION

The question of the role of women in the church must be refocused in terms of the view of women we are to have in the church. Christians certainly have no right to bind as biblically imperative that which is merely cultural. So, it becomes necessary for Christians to sort out what is distinctly biblical in their religion from what is cultural.[1]

1. *Assessment of Current Options*

A. *Radical Extremes*

Radical feminism and patriarchalism are both rejected as viable options. While both have some commendable questions and answers, each proceeds in reactionary ways from basically cultural agendas. It is unlikely that human relations will profit significantly from either perspective.

Both of these extreme views are steeped in prejudice, both are essentially isolationist, and both are influenced tremendously by cultural bias. Both views tend to ignore

---

[1]Unfortunately some books on maleness are based upon negative experience and hurt. See Robert Bly, *Iron John* (New York: Random House, 1992), and Sam Keen, *Fire in the Belly: On Being a Man* (New York: Bantam, 1991). See also Victor Seidler, *Recovering Masculinity: Reason, Language and Sexuality* (London: Routledge, 1989). For a growing literature on biblical manhood that promotes positive views of both men and women, see, among others, Don Welch, *Macho Isn't Enough!—Family Man in a Liberated World* (Atlanta: John Knox Press, 1985), and Mary Stewart Van Leeuwen, *Gender and Grace: Love, Work & Parenting in a Changing World* (Downers Grove, IL: InterVarsity Press, 1990).

biblical passages that do not support their presuppositions.
Both views tend to overstate their cases. Both work in
emotionally-charged atmospheres in which objectivity seems
impossible and honest evaluation entirely avoidable.

While neither radical feminism nor patriarchalism
provides the needed balance and perspective, those who hold
one or the other view should be incorporated into the
discussion to the extent possible. However, to continue to
permit these extreme views to couch the questions or to
dominate the discussion is to fail. We must look elsewhere
for a responsible Christian view of women.

B. *Moderate Views*

Although the views of evangelical feminism and
hierarchal complementarianism have significant differences,
they have some major matters in common. This means that
actually they are more compatible with one another than with
either extreme.

It is significant that both views accept the existence of
the supernatural. Both are committed to working out a view
of women within the historic Christian faith. Both view the
Bible as authoritative. Both work in terms of the ancient
manuscript tradition lying behind the biblical text, and both
approach exegetical work in terms of literary and historical
controls on interpretation. Both attempt to understand the
Bible in terms of its cultural milieu. Both understand that
past and present cultures have influenced the church. Both
presuppose the equal value of the sexes. Both acknowledge
discrimination and oppression of women in society as well
as in the church. Theoretically, both find radical feminism
and male domination unacceptable. And, theoretically, both
have a willingness to evaluate their own view and to interact
with other views.

Even so, considerable tension has resulted from major
differences between evangelical feminism and complementarianism. For instance, the presuppositions of a "God-
ordained hierarchalism" among complementarians and of

"God-ordained egalitarianism" among evangelical feminists undoubtedly influence both the selection of texts used to support arguments and the exegetical conclusions of each group.

Another significant difference between these views involves the inerrancy of Scripture. Some complementarians have accused some evangelical feminists of abandoning the inerrancy of Scripture and of being unregenerate. Some evangelical feminists, as might be expected, have responded tersely. Whether or not one agrees with the view of Dunn,[2] that biblical inerrancy is "exegetically improbable, hermeneutically defective, theologically dangerous, and educationally disastrous," one does need to avoid premature judgments, hardening of attitudes, drawing lines of fellowship, and questioning the motives of others. A clear understanding of and appreciation for the authority of Scripture does not necessitate a hierarchal stance. In fact, a high view of Scripture might just lead one to be an egalitarian.

As we saw in chapter four, some of the current literature on biblical texts is so biased in terms of prejudices that it is unacceptable. Now, presuppositions are important, but presuppositions that harden into prejudices which in turn become non-negotiable canons of interpretation present a problem. This, I think, is basically where the battle is being fought, and this is why I appeal for a refocusing of the discussion. Of course, canons other than the Bible have been in process for years—tradition and feeling, for example. While all of these must be thrown into the mix, the biblical text must be authoritative—and that demands that responsible method and procedure be followed, even when presuppositions are challenged.

---

[2]J. D. G. Dunn, "The Authority of Scripture According to Scripture," *Churchman* 96 (1982): 118. See also John Stott, "The Authority of the Scriptures: A Response," *Evangelical Essentials: A Liberal-Evangelical Debate* (Downers Grove, IL: InterVarsity Press, 1989): 101, that inerrancy cannot be made an indispensable criterion of evangelical orthodoxy.

2. *Biblical Texts on Women*

A. *Texts at the Heart of the Discussion*

It is often thought that the crucial texts on which the debate hinges are Gal 3:28 on the one side and 1 Cor 14:34-35 and 1 Tim 2:9-15 on the other. However, I have come to view Gen 1-3 and 1 Cor 11 as being the crucial texts at the heart of the discussion.

1) *Gen 1-3.* Hierarchal complementarians urge strongly that hierarchalism exists in Gen 1-2, even though they admit that it cannot actually be found in the biblical text. Careful analysis of the text of Gen 1-2 makes it clear that in the pre-Fall era man and woman were equal, but different. The Fall in Gen 3 shattered this equity and began a long history of gender conflict based upon male hierarchy. Patriarchy is an unfortunate result of the Fall, not something designed by God at the outset but part of the curse. The so-called "order of creation" is only a figment of the hierarchal imagination.

2) *1 Cor 11:2-16.* The oft-cited appeal to "God-Christ-man-woman" in 1 Cor 11:3 reads hierarchalism into the text. Paul's frustration with Christians in Corinth flouting commonly-accepted cultural norms and showing disrespect and lack of unity leads him to stipulate that they should pray and prophesy in public worship in a manner that would not disgrace or dishonor others.   1 Cor 11:2-16 deals with the interdependence of males and females "in Christ." Here Paul stresses that each is equally dependent upon the other. No doubt, women prayed and prophesied in public worship.

3) *Gal 3:28.* Gal 3:28 emphasizes what it means to be "in Christ." The three groups in v. 28 underscore that social, cultural and gender distinctions should not affect unity with Christ. As part of a unified diversity, unnecessary barriers and distinctions are to be replaced with reconciliation and mutual responsibility. "In Christ" does not mandate doing away with cultural categories.

4) *1 Cor 14:34-35.*   There is no evidence that Paul contradicts in 1 Cor 14:34-35 what he had taught earlier in 11:2-16. The real issue is not the *extent* to which a woman may participate in the work and worship of the church, but the *manner*. Paul's corrective does not ban women from speaking in worship, but it does stop the disruptive verbal misconduct of certain wives who are giving free rein to "irresistible impulses" to "pipe up" at will with questions in the assembly by redirecting these questions to another setting where they can have access to information without causing verbal chaos. 1 Cor 14:34-35 teaches that these particular wives, like the uncontrolled tongue-speakers and prophets at Corinth, must *defer* to the assembly by voluntarily yielding to orderliness. Neither in this nor in any other biblical text is there a prohibition against women speaking in public.

5) *1 Tim 2:8-15.*   1 Tim 2 was directed to a specific group of troublesome women in a particular place in the early church.   Overstepping traditional roles, some Ephesian women demonstrate a fundamental attitudinal shift that evidences itself in their dress and in forsaking traditionally domestic roles, seeking visible roles in congregational life. Some of them were misinformed and domineering teachers. Such domineering and assertive behavior, coupled with the scandalous behavior created by dressing inappropriately in public, certainly sent wrong signals to Ephesus regarding what Christianity was all about.   Nothing in the text of 1 Tim 2 demands a hierarchal view of women, nor is there even a hint that a woman is not to teach men simply because she is female.   That which is prohibited is dressing immodestly, teaching without adequate information in hand, and/or teaching with a domineering attitude.

B. *Other Important Texts on Women*

1) *Jesus' View of Women in the Gospels.* Jesus did not address directly the status of women, but held a high view of women in a world in which they were often viewed as second-class. In his life and teachings, Jesus redefined "power." Rather than use power to control others, Jesus advocated using power to serve, forgive, and encourage

others in a context of mutual deference. Jesus insisted upon equity for both men and women regarding laws of marriage and divorce. This is exemplary of his understanding of power and is a direct application of that teaching to husband-wife relationships. Jesus' openness to women made it possible for a mixed group of male and female followers to travel along with him.

Later, Paul applies Jesus' view of power as service rather than control to the Corinthian situation. Paul states that the husband belongs to the wife in the very same way that the wife belongs to the husband. This principle of mutuality holds true when Paul discusses divorce and remarriage. Paul applies Jesus' view of power in Eph 5, where mutual deference is presented as characteristic of Christ's life and of the Christian life. Many think that power is "over" some-one, but Paul's point is that Christ's relationship to the church was *service*. This comparison of a husband's love with Christ's sacrifice challenged the long-standing tradition of male-dominance in existence since Gen 3. It presented men with a new basis for relating to their wives and wives with a new basis for relating to their husbands—voluntary mutual deference. Nothing is said about decision-making roles or of division of gender roles—only that for Jesus the recovery of the pre-Fall ideal of human equity is desirable.

2) *Phoebe (Rom 16:1-2)*   A Christian lady named Phoebe, from Cenchrea near Corinth, is mentioned as a "deacon" in Rom 16:1. She is also called a "patron" of Paul. To suggest that she served only women is to make a distinction that the biblical text does not make. On the other hand, nothing supports the notion that Phoebe served as governing officer or president of the congregation, nor that she served as an official of any kind. Phoebe was a "deacon in the church" in the sense of "designated servant" and a "patron" of Paul and many others. Whatever the "deacons" were at Philippi, that is what Phoebe was at Cenchrea. Whatever the "female deacons" were in 1 Tim 3:11, that is what Phoebe was at Cenchrea.

3) *Female Deacons.* In 1 Tim 3:11, Paul observes that, "Women likewise must be serious, not slanderers, but temperate, faithful in all things." "Women" of the category under discussion in the context are in mind. The evident parallelism between the four items in vv. 8-10 dealing with males and the four in v. 11 that treat females is unmistakable. Characteristics vital to "service" for males are given similar specificity concerning the females who also engage in such "service." We should view 1 Tim 3:8-10 as treating selected characteristics of male deacons, and v. 11 as treating similar characteristics of female deacons.

4) *Prisca (Priscilla).* Prisca and her husband Aquila are mentioned as outstanding workers in the early church. Hierarchalists view her as a "helper" of Aquila, but feminists view her as one of the most prominent women in the early church. The primacy of Prisca hinges on the fact that her name is mentioned before his in a few texts. However, it is only a guess that the order of their names signifies that Prisca was the dominant of the two. In Acts 18:24-28, Prisca and Aquila are viewed as equals, highly-respected workers, and competent in instructing Apollos on Christian baptism. She is illustrative of the important and energetic service rendered by women in the earliest churches.

5) *Eph 5:21-33—Submission.* Realizing that the term "subject" carries with it substantial negative meaning, the term "submit" is currently used to describe Christian relationships. The form of the verb used of Christian submission necessitates a voluntary action (1 Pet 1:13; Heb 12:9). In Eph 5:21-24 Paul stipulates a mutual submission, a voluntary deference for all Christians, whatever their roles in life. The "mutual submission" that is the focus of Eph 5:21 is typical of NT teaching elsewhere (Matt 20:26-28; Phil 2:3; 1 Pet 5:4-5). This is one important way, Paul says, that Christians can "be filled with spirit" rather than "drunken with wine" (Eph 5:18). To say that "the husband is head of the wife as Christ is head of the church" is not to stress the husband's authority or position, but his service— as Christ loved, served and died for the church, so the husband is to love, serve and give himself for his wife.

3. *An Assessment of Moderate Views*

A. *The Complementarian View.*

My studies lead me to conclude that there is no biblical mandate for hierarchalism in either the church or society. Hierarchalism is a legacy from remote antiquity, originating in the post-Fall era of Gen 3. It was not designed by God, but was the result of human frailty. Jesus did not overthrow hierarchalism, as some feminists suggest. Instead, he worked within the hierarchal society of his time. He gave women greater respect, freedom, recognition, involvement, and responsibilities. This view of Jesus continued in the earliest churches for a limited time before patristic churches reverted to the patriarchalism that has become a dominant part of our Christian heritage for centuries.

Still we must ask, is hierarchalism necessarily evil? Is it inherently sinful? I think not. Certainly it often takes evil forms, but hierarchalism can be made workable. How so?

Complementarians have attempted to provide guidance for how their view plays out in daily life. Knight,[3] for instance, works from his view of distinctive roles of husband and wife in Genesis 3 to address matters such as wives and mothers working outside the home, how husbands and wives make decisions (especially regarding job changes and relocations), caring for the children, allocating duties and responsibilities, and how male leadership and female submission play out in church life.

Similarly, Farrar[4] emphasizes the partnership of man and wife and calls for sensitivity to gender differences. Urging men to take responsibility for leadership, he calls them to avoid "spiritual anorexia" and to develop spiritual

---

[3]George W. Knight III, "The Family and the Church: How Should Biblical Manhood and Womanhood Work Out in Practice?" *Recovering Biblical Manhood and Womanhood*, 345-357.

[4]Steven Farrar, *Point Man: How a Man Can Lead a Family* (Portland: Multnomah, 1990).

endurance. Real men, he says, do not commit adultery, but maintain fidelity to their wives and develop a spirit of teamwork. He stresses the need to develop masculine sons and feminine daughters by being both a role model and an instructor of life-style basics.[5] Following Piper's definition of *kephale* (headship; p. 261), Farrar urges men to view their wives with respect and sensitivity, aware that they are also made in the image of God, but to assume God-given responsibilities of leadership.

How this plays out for women involves also a much-improved view over that of *Fascinating Womanhood* and *Total Woman*. Emphasis is upon reviving the categories of *manhood* and *womanhood*, viewed in terms of woman being a complement to man and respecting his leadership.[6] Maintaining an emphasis upon the home, hierarchal complementarians urge that homemaking be recovered as the principal task of a Christian mother.[7] It is held that women must not exercise spiritual authority over men. However, numerous ministries are available to women, such as teaching women and children, writing, personal evangelism, and other public functions such as reading Scripture, offering prayer, making announcements, or leading songs— none of which involve authority over men.[8]

Hierarchal complementarianism cannot be said to be the biblical ideal, but in stressing that males be kind, loving and respectful instead of domineering and in working to ensure that women are able to develop their capabilities it is certainly much more workable than patriarchalism.

---

[5]See also George Alan Rekers, "Psychological Foundations for Rearing Masculine Boys and Feminine Girls," *Recovering Biblical Manhood and Womanhood*, 294-311.

[6]Elisabeth Eliot, "The Essence of Femininity: A Personal Perspective," *Recovering Biblical Manhood and Womanhood*, 394-399.

[7]Dorothy Patterson, "The High Calling of Wife and Mother in Biblical Perspective," *Recovering Biblical Manhood and Womanhood*, 364-377.

[8]H. Wayne House, *The Role of Women in Ministry* (Nashville: T. Nelson, 1990): 148-158.

B. *The Egalitarian View.*

On the other hand, egalitarianism is certainly preferable as far as the ideals of the kingdom are concerned. My studies have led me to conclude, however, that there is no biblical mandate for egalitarianism either, although it was the pristine ideal in the pre-Fall era of Gen 1-2. It is recovered in the thinking of Jesus and is behind much of the practice of the earliest churches, but was later lost again in the strongly patriarchal world of the eastern Mediterranean.

However, is egalitarianism so necessary that all forms of hierarchalism must be obliterated? Feminists certainly want one to think so! However, neither Jesus nor the earliest churches took this radical view. Just as they did not overthrow slavery, but worked with that system and the evil sometimes present, so they did not overthrow hierarchalism, but worked within the system and the evil sometimes there.

In our changing world, however, cultural hierarchalism is receding. The current focus, however, should not be on cultural change but on basic elements of the Christian mind-set, such as justice, mercy, peace, love, patience, unity, and tolerance. Evangelical feminists should abandon feminist "soap boxes" and recover an emphasis on these traditional Judeo-Christian attitudes.[9]

Bias against women in our culture[10] from birth to old age has created tremendous desire for a new image for women and also a new image for men.[11] Maintaining

---

[9] For current views of feminist ethics, see the essays in Lois K. Daly, ed, *Feminist Theological Ethics* (Louisville: Westminster/John Knox, 1994); Margaret A. Farley, "Ethics and Moral Theologies," *Dictionary of Feminist Theologies* (ed. L. M. Russell and J. S. Clarkson; Louisville: Westminster/John Knox, 1996): 88-91.

[10] See Rhoda K. Unger, *Female and Male: Psychological Perspectives* (New York: Harper and Row, 1979): 26-52.

[11] David C. McClelland, "Wanted: A New Self-Image for Women," *The Woman in America* (ed. Robert Lifton; Boston: Houghton Mifflin, 1965): 173-192.

emphasis on the differences in the sexes, yet stressing mutuality, some are now calling also for a new image of maleness.[12] Spencer,[13] frustrated that men seem to have only two rather poor options (to be God or the Devil), suggests ways equality can be achieved in relationships regarding shared parenting and other common tasks. Control must be replaced with love. Manipulation must be replaced with service. He concludes (pp. 177-179),

> If we males are to assume our God-given responsibility to enable our wives to reach full splendor in the gifts God has given them as they will help us reach ours, we ought to go out of our way to provide them with the time, encouragement, and opportunity to discover and exercise those gifts. If we are to take our family responsibility seriously, we have to make our home, our spouses, our children, and at times our extended family, along with ourselves, the earthly priority for our concerns and actions. . . . If the scriptural imagery is true, if women express half the image of God, if they are, indeed, in the image of God, if they are, therefore, called by God to God's service, then we mutually complement one another.

An interesting work along this line is that of Welch,[14] who stresses equity between male and female in achieving a working partnership in marriage. "The basic principle of equity means that we must allow all persons the opportunity to fashion their own lives, free from existing stereotypes," yet "equity implies certain things about the way we should live our lives together" (14). Traditional myths of what constitutes masculinity and femininity should be rethought with equity in mind. Both are useful concepts, but when employed carelessly can create harmful notions:

---

[12]Among others, Gilbert Bilezikian, *Beyond Sex Roles* (2nd ed.; Grand Rapids: Baker, 1985); and Gretchen Gaebelein Hull, *Equal to Serve: Women and Men in the Church and Home* (Old Tappan, NJ: F. H. Revell, 1987).

[13]William David Spencer, "Equaling Eden: A Practical Male Afterword," in Aída Besançon Spencer, *Beyond the Curse: Women Called to Ministry* (Nashville: T. Nelson, 1985).

[14]Don Welch, *Macho Isn't Enough!—Family Man in a Liberated World* (Atlanta: John Knox Press, 1985).

Traditionally male	_Traditionally Female_
rational	emotional
strong	weak
independent	dependent
vigorous	frail
public	private
conquering	nurturing

Several virtues have come to be attributed to females that are not female characteristics at all, but basic human characteristics: i.e., love, kindness, patience, self-control, humility. The same can be said for certain traditionally male characteristics. In any redefinition of male and female roles, attributes vital to the Christian mind-set must be recovered as foundational for society, not just for women (or for men).

Further, Welch argues for "*equity* for both sexes, rather than *equality* of the sexes" (p. 30). Required for equal partnership are consent, respect, trust, love, and sharing responsibilities. Matters are to be discussed as peers. Authority is held in common. The resolution of differences is more difficult when one person does not have the "right" to "run" the family, but equity demands that this more difficult way be taken. The devaluation of careers is the almost inevitable outcome of a truly equal two-career arrangement; each partner's career must be tempered by the career interest of the other. Sometimes partners may be asked to interrupt their own career for the sake of the other.

A responsible theology of women in the church for these changing times is surely to be found in terms of egalitarian principles and practice that are integral to core NT theology.

4. *Conclusion*

In our survey of views, it is apparent that evangelical feminism and hierarchal complementarianism have much in common, yet they differ radically in some ways from one another. Each has addressed significant problems regarding women in our churches and in society and each has made major advances leading away from the unproductive extremes that control so much discussion of women today.

However, it is mandatory that participants in this discussion be aware that what is at stake is not egalitarian or hierarchical presuppositions for which some in each group seem determined to die, but the achieving of an understanding that will permit men and women alike to become whatever it is that God intended in the beginning. While neither hierarchalism nor egalitarianism is biblically mandated, egalitarianism is preferable in terms of biblical exegesis and the ideals of the kingdom. Christian ideals indicate that woman is not, and never was intended to be, man's servant—owned, dominated, with no life of her own. It is regrettable that many hierarchalists restrict woman's development of capabilities and exercise of abilities. It is regrettable that some egalitarians are involved in change for change's sake—rude, brash, impatient, unwilling to wait for people to come to an understanding.

In conclusion, my quest for a responsible biblical view of women has led me to abandon the hierarchal stance with which I began this study, and to accept egalitarian ideals concerning women in the church while avoiding the radical feminism behind much of today's ferment in society and consternation in the churches.

This means that the search for biblical truth is vital, that God is Father and Christ is Lord, that traditional Christian values remain supreme, that man and woman are equal in the sight of God, that the family is still central to God's plan, that there is no such thing as an "order of creation," that mutual submission is basic to male/female relationships and that women should have the same opportunities to develop as do men.

This means that discrimination and oppression of women should cease, that feminist "pushing and shoving" is out of place and that undue restrictions on women are wrong.

This means that there are significant differences between men and women, and that "masculine" and "feminine" qualities should be ascertained in terms of Christian values and principles rather than merely by traditional acceptance.

This means that certain paternalist restrictions have no biblical basis. For instance, those who hold that females cannot teach young boys who are past the age of 12, or that they cannot pray aloud with men in the room, or that they cannot speak in a worship assembly, etc., have absolutely no basis for such peculiar restrictions.

This means that women should be able to do anything of which they are capable and in which they are trained, such as, conduct personal evangelism, give greetings, make announcements, lead singing, read Scripture and write. It is imperative that women do these things, as all men should, in a spirit of helpfulness, genuineness, gentleness—in the spirit of Christ. Hierarchal complementarians are correct in removing many burdensome and unnecessary patriarchal restrictions and opening these wider arenas of service and opportunity to women. However, maintaining restrictions in the areas of church and home has no biblical basis.

This means that whatever women did in NT times, women should be able to do today. For instance, women served as deacons. Women led prayer and taught in the public worship. These do not seem right to hierarchal complementarians, but as they are plainly approved in the biblical text they should be options for women in churches today. The NT nowhere restricts the conduct of baptism or the Lord's Supper to males. Egalitarians are correct to have women serve on committees and speak publicly.

The NT does not speak regarding women in leadership or preaching capacities. All named evangelists in the NT are male, as are all elders. However, as there is no validity to the "order of creation" argument, this situation should not be viewed as a "pattern" mandatory for all times and places, but merely as reflecting the culture in which the NT events were played out. Scripture does not teach that it is sinful for a woman to preach or serve in a leadership capacity. Deborah (Judges 4-5) is instructive here. The leadership role she played in Israel's military victory over the Canaanites was not common, but it did occur and was approved by God. Restrictions against women in leadership or public ministry roles then, as now, are dictated by culture and custom rather than biblical necessity. In fact, there will probably be an increasing number of Christ-like women who will undertake appropriate training for various ministries, thus recovering an early nineteenth century practice.

Finally, though many are bothered by questions about the "role" of women in the church, we must remember that reservations about the "role" of women in worship and leadership are not really the main issue. Instead, the principal concern should be the recovery of the egalitarian view of women that God had in mind in the creation. This means that the recovery of the biblical ideal of women should evidence itself in all areas of life. A recovery of this view would permit the church to demonstrate a biblically and theologically solid understanding of male/female relationships to a confused and troubled world.

Abbott, S.: 16
Achtemeier, E.: 55
Alexander, J.: 97
Allen, B.: 71
Allen, R.: 71
Amatniek, K.: 15
Andelin, H. B.: 38, 39, 40
Anderson, B.W.: 119
Andolsen, B. H.: 26
Anthony, S. B.: 7
Appian: 183
Aquinas, T.: 158
Armstrong, J. N.: 10
Arndt: W. F.: 140
Athenaeus: 181
Aune, D. : 66, 195
Bachmann, P. : 197
Baird, W. : 198
Baldwin, S.: 83, 207, 213, 216, 234
Barclay, W. : 188, 196
Barrett, C.K.: 190, 196, 198, 201
Barr, J.: 58, 78, 89, 108, 152, 209
Bartchy, S.: 129
Barth, M.: 156, 169
Barton, B.: 9
Bauer, W.: 57, 183, 208
Bendroth, M. L.: 16, 17, 33, 91, 94, 108
Berg, B.: 5
Bergmann, B.: 22
Best, E.: 140
Bilezikian, G.: 60, 157, 159, 163, 165, 168 177, 191, 192, 194, 263
Black, M.: 173
Blackburn, B. L.: 144
Blass, F.: 146, 199, 215, 221
Bly, R.: 253
Bordin, R.: 7
Borland, J. A.: 126, 127
Bozeman, T. D.: 11
Braaten, C. E.: 98

Brereton, V. L.: 7
Bright, J.: 193
Brinsmead, B. H.: 134, 135
Brooten, B.: 29
Brown, H.: 232, 234, 238
Brown, K. M.: 44
Bruce, F. F.: 53, 79, 98, 136, 196, 199, 201, 205
Bruland, E. B.: 52, 95
Brumberg, J. J.: 7
Bruner, F. : 197
Budé, G.: 58, 210
Bultmann, R.: 98
Busenitz, I. A.: 123
Bush, P.G.: 207
Bushnell, K.: 191
Calvin, J.: 158
Campbell, J.: 23
Carlson, D.: 6, 14, 18
Carmody, D. L.: 28, 148, 151, 170
Carpenter, J. A.: 33
Carroll, J. W.: 7
Carson, D. A.: 61, 192, 195
Casey, M. W.: 105
Cassuto, U.: 185
Cervin, R.: 165
Chafe, W.: 5
Chesnutt, R.: 249
Chisholm, S.: 25
Chopp, R. S.: 24
Christ, C. P.: 26
Christensen, L.: 17, 34, 35
Chrysostom, J.: 217
Clark, E.: 22
Clark, S. B.: 126
Clement of Alexandria : 140, 153, 182
Coats, G.: 121
Cobb, J. B.: 87
Coffman, B.: 144, 175
Collier, G.D.: 47
Collins, A. Y.: 29, 30
Collins, J. N.: 140
Conn, H. M.: 70

Conzelman, H.: 190, 240
Cotterell, P.: 99, 177, 178
Cottrell, J.: 28
Couper, S.: 21
Cranfield, C. E. B.: 140
Daly, L.K.: 262
Daly, M.: 24, 26, 28
Dana, H.E.: 215
Daniélou, J.: 140, 154
Dautzenburg, G.: 203
Davidson, R.M.: 118, 119, 120, 123
Davies, J. G.: 144
Dayton, D.: 94
Deaver, R. C.: 36
DeBerg, B. A.: 5, 11
Debrunner, A.: 146, 199, 215, 221
Deckard, B.: 7, 22, 23
DeHoff, G. W. : 175
Deist, F. E.: 117
Delling, G.: 201, 202
DeWolf, L. H.: 92
Dex, S.: 49
Dibelius, M.: 186
Dickson, E.: 6
Diodorus Siclulus: 183
Dixon, A. C.: 102
Dodd, C. H.: 144
Dollar, G. W.: 32
Donaldson, J.: 218
Donovan, J.: 50, 96
Doriani, D,: 232,235
Douban, E.: 15
Douglas, J.D.: 233
Dunn, J. D. G.: 85, 141, 255
Ebeling, G.: 98
Elliot, E.: 36, 261
Elliot, J. H.: 143
Engelsman, J. C.: 30
Evans, M. J.: 111, 129
Farley, M.A.: 262
Farrar, S.: 260
Fee, G. D.: 101, 109, 131, 145, 147, 163, 165, 175, 177, 183, 190, 201-203, 225-27, 229, 240, 243, 244
Ferguson, E.: 174, 185
Findlay, G.G.: 194
Fiorenza, E.: 23, 25, 29, 30, 139, 143, 149, 153
Fitzmyer, J.A.: 163, 186
Flanagan,N.: 191
Flatt, B.: 98
Fletcher, J.: 14, 102
Flexner, E.: 6
Foh, S.: 63, 69, 113, 114, 115, 122, 230
Ford, J. M.: 154, 200
Frank, D.: 9
Friedan, B.: 15, 23
Funderburk, A. R.: 11
Gage, M. J.: 7
Gardner, A.: 119
Gasque, W. W.: 131, 132
Gifford, C. D. S.: 51
Giles,K.: 212, 230, 234
Gingrich, F. W.: 140
Girvetz, H.: 15
Goldenberg, N.: 29
Goldstein, V. S.: 26
Gornick, V.: 22
Goodwin, W.W.: 215
Goudge, H.L.: 187
Green, M.: 147
Greer, T.: 250
Grimké, A.: 6
Grimstad, K.: 16
Gritz, S.H.: 224, 225
Grosheide, F. W. : 196, 204
Grudem, W.: 75, 76, 163, 164, 165, 177
Gudorf, C. E.: 26
Gulick, C.B.: 215
Gutek, B.: 22
Haenchen, E.: 152
Hailey, J. F.: 138
Haldane, R.: 141
Halkes, C.: 28

Hall, B.: 50
Hammond, G. B.: 32
Haney, E. H.: 25
Hanson, A.T.: 207
Hardesty, N. A.: 52, 125, 156
Hargrove, B.: 7
Harland, G.: 92
Harrill, J.A.: 232
Harris, B.: 1
Harrison, B. W.: 6
Hatch, N.: 12
Hawley, J. S.: 1
Hawley, M.: 88
Headlam, A. C.: 141, 150
Heine, S.: 26, 27, 62
Hennessey, L.: 141
Hense, O.: 242
Henry, C. F. H.: 53
Héring, J.: 186, 187, 194, 204
Hess, R.: 122
Heyward, I. C.: 28
Hirsch, E. D.: 99, 103
Hoch, C. B.: 25
Hodge, C.: 201
Hole, J.: 6
Hooker, M.D.: 186
Hooks, B.: 21, 22
House, H.W.: 114, 127, 133,
    148, 152, 261
Howard, C.J. : 199
Hugenberger, G.: 225
Hull, G.G.: 111, 129, 263
Hurley, J. B.: 65, 72, 73, 74,
    113, 114, 126, 133, 160,
    168, 197, 229
Hyppolytus: 218
Isbell, C.: 193
Jannaris, A.N.: 215
Jewett, P. K.: 52, 53, 54, 76,
    79, 110, 111, 131, 201
Johanson, B.: 194
Johnson, L. T.: 134, 135, 150
Johnson, S. L.: 79, 133
Johnston, R. K.: 103
Jones, P. R.: 104

Joreen: 20, 21
Josephus: 201
Keck, L. E.: 46
Keen, S.: 253
Keener, C.: 62, 226, 230, 240,
    245-47
Kelly, J. N. D.: 145, 147,
    246, 250
Keniston, K.: 15
Kirkpatrick, C.: 35
Kistemaker, S.: 151
Klein, C. R.: 7
Knight, G. W.: 65, 67, 68,
    85, 114, 115, 133, 161,
    162, 168, 170, 201, 213,
    230, 237, 260
Köstenberger, A.: 83, 207,
    219, 220, 223, 234
Krentz, E.: 104
Kroeger, C. C.: 57, 58, 163,
    166, 177, 196, 207, 209,
    210, 224
Kroeger, R. C.: 57, 58, 196,
    207, 209, 210, 224
Kulka, R.: 15
Kümmel, W. G.: 101
Kurfees, M. C.: 9, 35, 189
Lafferty, J.: 22
LaHaye, B.: 36
LaHaye, T.: 17, 36
Lampe, G.W.H.: 217
LaPorte, J.: 140
Lathrop, N.: 8
Laws, J. L.: 22
Lenski, R. : 199
Lerner, G.: 6
Levine, A. J.: 31
Levine, E.: 6
Levinson, R.: 22
Lewis, J. P.: 122
Liddell, H.G,: 183
Liefeld, W.: 125, 192, 200,
    201
Lietzmann, H.: 190
Liftin, A. D.: 97

Lindsell, H.: 53, 102
Lipscomb, D.: 174, 189, 200, 201
Loades, A.: 29
Longenecker, R.: 132, 136
Louw, J. P.: 57, 208
Love, B.: 16
Lucian: 182
Lummis, A. T.: 7
MacGorman, J.W. : 197
Machen, J. G.: 102
MacMullen, R.: 143, 180
Macquarrie, J.: 102
Malcolm, K. T.: 57, 209
Malherbe, A.: 153
Mantey, J.R.: 215
Mare, W.H. : 199
Marrs, R.R.: 117, 118, 121, 122, 248
Marsden, G.: 13, 32, 33, 51, 92, 94
Marshall, A. J.: 143
Marshall, I. H.: 101
Martimort, A.: 140
Martin, R.: 200
Marty, M. E.: 33
Matalin, M.: 27
McClelland, D. C.: 22, 262
McClelland, S. E.: 111, 112, 125
McGarvey, J.W. : 174, 179
McGlone, L.: 121
McKim, D. K.: 105
McNamara, J.: 1
Mercadante, L.: 74
Metzger, B.: 191
Michaels, J. R.: 101
Mickelsen, A.: 110, 163, 165, 177
Mickelsen, B.: 110, 163, 165, 177
Migne, J.P.: 217
Mitchell, M. M. : 176
Mitchell, L.: 45
Moffatt. J.: 146, 196

Mollenkott, V. R.: 54, 55, 84, 133
Moo, D.: 80, 81, 82, 83, 220, 228, 229, 231
Moore, R. L.: 11
Moran, B.: 22
Morgan, C.: 8
Morgan, M.: 38
Morgan, R.: 15
Morris, L.: 178-180, 185, 187, 194
Moule, C. F. D.: 126
Murphey, C.: 24
Musès, C.: 23
Music, G.: 36, 37, 38
Neller, K.: 155, 169
Neuer, W.: 152, 197, 200, 237
Newsom, C.: 23, 29
Niccum, C.: 204
Nicole, R.: 101
Nida, E. A.: 57, 208
Niebuhr, R. G.: 28
Noll, M. A.: 12, 90, 95, 109
Nunn, H.P.V.: 215
O'Connor, J.M.: 183, 190
O'Neill, W.: 8
Odell-Scott, D. W.: 60, 192
Oepke, A.: 180, 182
Origen: 186
Orr, W.: 200
Ortlund, R. C.: 77, 113, 114
Osburn, C. D.: 4, 57, 61, 82, 83, 90, 109,175, 185, 189, 209, 246
Osiek, C.: 30,
Oster, R.: 59, 60, 181, 211, 224
Pallas, D.: 142
Panning, A. J.: 57, 209
Parker, J.: 217
Pate, B.: 6
Patterson, D.: 261
Payne, P. B.: 58, 80, 81, 163, 165, 210, 220, 222
Pellauer, M. D.: 26

Pendleton, P. Y.: 179
Perriman, A.C.: 62
Phillips, J.B. : 193
Philo: 228, 229, 242, 249
Philostratus: 182
Pierce, R.W.: 223
Pinnock, C.: 117
Piper, J.: 75, 76, 77, 78, 113, 114
Pirani, A.: 23
Pliny: 144
Plummer,A.: 187
Plutarch: 182
Polybius: 183
Pomeroy, S.: 230
Porter, S.E.: 250
Pryor, J.: 62
Pulley, K. J.: 5, 56, 93
Quebedeaux, R.: 91, 92, 97, 101
Rabello, A.M.: 240
Ramm, B.: 89
Ramsay, W.: 149
Ramsey, G. W.: 78
Reed, E.: 22, 24
Rekers, G. A.: 261
Rennie, S.: 16
Reuf, J.: 177, 179, 182, 190, 194
Rice, J. R.: 10, 13, 32, 33
Ringe, S.: 23, 29
Robb, C. S.: 24
Robbins, J.: 69
Roberts, A.: 218
Roberts, B. T.: 7
Roberts, M.D.: 223
Robertson, A.: 187
Robertson, A. T.: 61, 199, 202, 215, 227, 247
Robinson, T. A.: 60, 211
Robinson, T. S.: 16
Roloff, J.: 145
Rosenzweig, M.L.: 120
Rossi, A. S.: 1, 6

Ruether, R. R.: 25, 28, 30, 31, 56
Rufus, M.: 242
Ryrie, C.C. : 198
Sakenfeld, K. D.: 51
Saller, R.: 143
Sampley, J.P.: 156
Sanday, W.: 141, 150
Sarup, M.: 17
Sawyer, J. F. A.: 58, 78, 152, 209
Scanzoni, L. D.: 52, 125, 126 156
Schaberg, J.: 24
Schatzmann, S. : 195
Schechter, S.: 22
Schlatter, A.: 197
Schmithals, W.: 102, 197
Schmitt, J.J.: 124
Scholer, D. M.: 51, 63, 66, 104, 106, 107, 226, 228, 230, 243, 246, 248, 249, 251
Schreiner, T.R.: 83, 207, 223, 225, 234, 235, 237, 240
Schweizer, E.: 147
Schwyzer, E. 216
Scott, E. F.: 104
Scott, R.: 183
Scroggs, R.: 239
Scullion, J.J.: 122
Seidler, V.: 253
Sewell, E. G.: 9, 35
Shank, M.: 132
Sherwin-White, A. N.: 144
Sigountos, J. G.: 132
Sinclair, A.: 8
Sire, J.W.: 189
Smith, F. L.: 41, 42, 45, 47, 139, 200, 204
Smith, P. R.: 28
Smyth, H.W.: 215, 246
Snodgrass, K.: 79, 131, 132
Snyder,E.: 191
Spain, C.: 147

Spencer, A. B.: 56, 57, 110, 111, 152, 209
Spencer, W.D.: 263
Spender, D.: 23
Stagg, E.: 118
Stagg, F.: 118
Stanley, A.P.: 184
Stanton, E. C.: 7
Stanton, G. M.: 98, 99, 208
Steinem, G.: 23
Stearns, P.: 5
Sterling, G. E.: 153, 242
Stewart, D.: 101, 109
Stitzinger, M.F.: 118, 119, 120, 121
Storkey, E.: 54, 61, 95, 96
Stott, J.: 85, 91, 255
Stuhlmacher, P.: 104
Stuhlmueller, C.: 29
Sudhaus, S.: 82
Swartley, W. M.: 104, 105, 232
Swidler, A.: 29
Swidler, L.: 29
Talbert, C.: 192
Tertullian: 180
Tetlow, E. M.: 54, 231, 239
Thayer, J.H.: 202
Thiselton, A.: 99
Thompson, C.L.: 181
Thrall, M. : 197
Tolbert, M. A.: 31, 32
Torrey, R. A.: 102
Towner, P.: 224, 229, 245
Trible, P.: 30, 31, 74, 119
Tucker, R.A.: 125
Turner, M.: 99, 177, 178
Unger, R.K.: 262
Van der Jagt, K.A.: 250
Van Leeuwen, S.: 253
Vanauken, S.: 71
Vander Broek, L.: 106
Vermaseren, M. J.: 59, 211
Verner, D. C.: 153
Veroff, J.: 15

von Harnack, A.: 148, 149 150
Von Rad, G.: 121
Vööbus, A.: 140
Wacker, G.: 17
Waddle, R.: 28
Wallace, F. E.: 10
Walters, J.: 139
Walther, J.: 200
Ward, R.A.: 245
Washborne, P.: 25
Webber, R.: 51
Weber, T.: 12
Welch, D.: 253, 263
Welter, B.: 5, 6, 9
Wenger, R.: 10
Westermann, C.: 121
Wilfong, M. M.: 122
Willard, F.: 7
Williams, J. M.: 8
Willis, W. : 175
Wilshire, L. E.: 58, 210
Wire, A. C.: 181, 190
Witherington, B.: 151, 152, 201, 227, 229, 247
Wolf, N.: 26
Wolters, A.: 58, 59, 210, 224
Woods, G. N.: 154
Wright, D.: 89, 108
Wurtzel, E.: 20
Wuthnow, R.: 14, 15
Yarbrough, R.W.: 231
Young, E.J.: 122
Young, P. D.: 55

Genesis

1: *118, 119, 256*
1-2: *110, 112, 124, 256, 262*
1-3: *72, 74, 77-79, 110, 113-117, 241, 248, 249, 256*
1-4: *249*
1-11: *117*
1.26: *119*
1.26-27: *110*
1.26-30: *118*
1.26-31: *110*
1.27: *68, 71, 113, 115, 119, 126, 127, 131*
1.28-29: *119*
2: *72, 74, 78, 110, 114-116, 119, 123*
2-3: *113, 116, 120*
2.4b-25: *65*
2.7: *113, 227, 247*
2.11: *117*
2.15-17: *113*
2.17: *112*
2.18: *111, 120, 184*
2.18-25: *68*
2.19-20: *115*
2.20: *114, 120*
2.21-24: *201*
2.21-25: *120, 184*
2.23: *111, 114*
2.23-24: *121*
2.24: *123, 157, 159, 164, 168*
3: *110-112, 115, 124, 130, 228, 229, 249, 256, 258, 260*
3.1: *114, 227, 247*
3.1-7: *121, 123, 228, 249*
3.3: *249*
3.5: *112*
3.5-6: *112*
3.6: *112, 121, 228*
3.11: *112*

3.13: *229*
3.14-19: *122, 123*
3.16: *17, 33, 112, 114, 122-124, 201*
3.17: *114*
3.17-19: *122-124*
4: *122*
4.7: *114*
5.2: *110*
6: *185*
6.1-4: *185*
12.3-7: *136, 137*
12-50: *117*
15.6: *135*
17.7: *136*
50.26: *117*

Leviticus

18.5: *135*

Deuteronomy

21.23: *135*
27.26: *135*

Judges

4-5: *267*

Psalms

137.1: *186*

Isaiah

28.11-12: *193*

Jeremiah

2.11: *55*

Habakkuk

2.4: *135*

Matthew

5.28: *126*
5.31-32: *129*
5.32: *126*
7.6: *220*
8.15: *141*
9.11: *127*
10.5-6: *107*
12.42: *127*
19.1-12: *129*
19.4: *126*
19.9: *126*
20.26-28: *169, 259*
24.41: *127*
26.6-13: *125*
27.55: *125*
28.1-10: *125, 127*
28.16-20: *107*

Mark

1.21-27: *127*
5.25-34: *125*
10.1-12: *129*
10.19: *38*
16.11: *125*

Luke

3.14: *220*
7.1-17: *125*
7.2-5: *143*
7.36-50: *125*
7.37-38: *14*
8.1-3: *125*
8.3: *127, 142*
10.40: *142*
12.33: *107*
12.37: *142*
13.10-17: *125*
22.30: *127*
23.27-29: *125*

John

2.14-17: *127*
4.1-42: *125*
11.20: *127*
12.2: *142*
12.2-8: *127*
14.26: *127*
20.17: *127*

Acts

1.21: *127*
2.14: *127*
2.17: *174, 188*
4.18: *221*
5.12: *127*
5.18: *127*
5.40: *127*
5.42: *127*
6: *127*
6.1: *142*
15: *150*
16.14-15: *127*
16.21: *220, 221*
18: *148*
18.2: *150*
18.18: *149*
18.24-28: *151, 152, 259*
18.26: *149*
18.28: *151*

Romans

5.12-14: *112, 229*
8.20: *245*
12.10: *130*
13.1: *160, 167*
13.5: *160*
15.25: *141, 142*
16: *125, 127*
16.1: *140, 145*
16.1-2: *73, 139, 258*
16.2: *142, 143*
16.3: *148, 149*

Romans (cont.)

16.5: *153*
16.6: *141*

1 Corinthians

1-4: *192*
1.10-17: *176*
5-7: *193*
6.12: *82*
7.1: *191*
7.2-5: *129*
7.2-13: *129*
7.4: 82, *159*
7.14-16: *129*
8-11: *108, 193*
8.1: *175*
10.7: *184*
10.31-11.1: *175*
11: *73,173, 175, 197, 247, 256*
11-14: *175,176, 180, 202-204*
11.1-16: *62, 160*
11.2: *176, 180, 187 192, 198, 203*
11.2-16: *73, 173-175, 177, 178, 188, 190, 191, 193, 197, 198, 204, 256, 257*
11.2-14.40: *173, 176, 193*
11.3: *163-65, 176-179, 240, 256*
11.3-4: *73*
11.3-16: *76*
11.4-5: *180*
11.4-7: *182*
11.5: *174, 225*
11.6: *182*
11.7: *183, 184*
11.7-9: *178*
11.8-9: *76, 184*
11.10: *184*
11.11: *186*

11.12: *187*
11.12-13: *187*
11.14-15: *187*
11.16: *177, 180, 188*
11.17: *174, 198*
11.17- 34: *193, 198*
11.17-14.40: *198*
12: *203*
12-14: *175, 193, 195*
12.27-31: *154*
12.28-30: *81*
12.33ff: *203*
14: *73, 193, 194 197*
14.14: *194*
14.16: *193*
14.16-20: *193*
14.17: *193*
14.19: *193, 198*
14.21-22: *193*
14.23: *198*
14.23-25: *193, 194*
14.26: *194-196, 200*
14.26-32: *196*
14.26-36: *203*
14.26-40: *202*
14.27: *198*
14.27-29: *203*
14.27-33: *196*
14.27-36: *203*
14.28: *195, 198, 200, 203*
14.29: *195, 200*
14.29-33: *191, 197*
14.30: *200, 203*
14.31: *203*
14.32: *160, 195, 202, 203*
14.33: *190, 191, 196*
14.33-36: *73, 132, 195 204*
14.34: *160, 196, 200, 202, 232*
14.34-35: *8, 60-62, 110, 131, 132, 147, 189, 190-192, 195, 197, 198, 200, 202-205, 257*

1 Corinthians (cont.)

14.34-36: *173, 174, 178, 188, 205, 256*
14.35: *198, 199, 203, 205*
14.36: *60, 147, 190-192, 202-204*
14.36-40: *192*
14.37: *191*
14.37-40: *203*
14.40: *190-191, 203*
15.21-22: *112, 229*
15.27: *160*
15.27-28: *202, 245*
16.15: *141*
16.16: *167, 202*
16.19: *150, 153*

2 Corinthians

8.4: *142*
9.1: *144*

Galatians

1-2: *134*
1.16-17: *221*
1.17: *127*
2.4: *134*
2.12: *134*
2.15-21: *134*
3: *134, 135*
3.1-5: *134*
3.2: *135*
3.5: *135*
3.6-9: *135*
3.6-20: *135*
3.10-14: *135*
3.12: *135*
3.15-20: *136*
3.17: *136*
3.21: *136*
3.21-23: *136*
3.26: *136, 137*
3.26-29: *136*

3.28: *31, 56, 71, 79, 84, 110, 131-134, 137, 138, 212, 231, 232, 256*
3.28-29: *137*
4.1-7: *137*
4.8-11: *137*
4.12-20: *137*
4.21-5.1: *137*
4.31-5.1: *137*
5.1: *134*

Ephesians

1.22: *165*
1:20-23: *164*
2:10: *243*
4.1: *156*
4.1-3: *169*
4.11-13: *154*
4.15: *163, 165*
4.15-16: *129*
4.17-24: *156*
5: *73,130, 157, 258*
5.15-18: *156*
5.15-21: *156, 168*
5.15-6.9: *168*
5.18: *259*
5.18-6.9: *62, 63*
5.18-20: *157, 161, 168*
5.19-21: *156, 161*
5.21: *73, 129, 130, 155-57 160-62, 164, 168, 169, 259*
5.21-22: *245*
5.21-24: *158, 167, 171, 259*
5.21-33: *76, 155, 160, 170, 259*
5.22: *37, 130, 156, 158, 161, 162, 164, 168*
5.22-23: *115, 157, 168*
5.22-24: *34, 155, 160, 161, 165, 170*
5.22-33: *157*

Ephesians (cont.)

5.22-6.9: *156, 160, 161, 167, 168*
5.23: *158, 163, 164*
5.24: *158, 162*
5.25: *159*
5.25-33a: *130*
5.28: *159*
5.29-33: *159*
5.31-32: *76, 157, 164, 168*

Philippians

1.1: *141*
2.3: *162, 169, 259*
2.3-5: *130*
3.21: *166, 245*

Colossians

1.18: *164, 165*
2.10: *164, 165*
2.18-19: *165*
2.19: *163*
3.16: *81*
3.18: *162, 245*

1 Timothy

1.3: *64, 222, 243, 250*
1.3-4: *221*
1.3-7: *65, 66, 239, 244*
1.3-8: *241*
1.3-11: *224, 239*
1.4-6: *80*
1.7: *246*
1.18-20: *65, 239, 224*
2: *214, 217, 235, 239, 240, 257*
2.1: *224, 239*
2.1-7: *225*
2.1-8: *239, 241*
2.8: *225, 240, 243*
2.8-15: *73, 74, 257*

2.9: *11, 63, 64, 225, 230, 240, 251*
2.9-10: *63, 65, 66, 225, 226, 240, 244*
2.9-11: *245*
2.9-15: *62, 63, 65, 72, 83 146, 207, 212, 223-225, 231, 232, 234, 236, 238, 239, 241, 243, 251, 256*
2.11: *80, 226, 233, 234, 246, 247*
2.11-12: *63, 65, 66, 74, 81, 132, 208, 225-228, 241, 243, 244, 247, 248*
2.11-14: *76, 230, 248, 251*
2.11-15: *8, 13, 57, 60, 80, 132, 211, 229*
2.12: *37, 56, 57, 59, 65, 81, 208, 211- 214, 217, 219-222, 223, 228, 243, 246-49*
2.12-14: *248*
2.13: *113, 227, 228, 233- 35, 247, 249*
2.13-14: *66, 76, 110, 227, 244, 247, 248*
2.14: *13, 228, 229, 234, 235 239, 247, 249*
2.15: *63-66, 227, 230, 234, 235, 248, 250, 251*
3.1-7: *146*
3.1-13: *73, 146*
3.2: *146*
3.4-5: *64*
3.7: *64*
3.8: *145-47*
3.8-10: *146, 147, 259*
3.11: *144-47, 258, 259*
3.12: *64, 145-47*
3.13: *146*
3.14-15: *65*
4.1-3: *80*
4.1-4: *229, 242*
4.1-8: *65*

1 Timothy (cont.)

4.1-10: *224*
4.3: *64, 230, 250*
5.9-13: *146*
5.9-15: *64*
5.11-15: *224, 241*
5.14: *64*
5.15: *80*
5.16: *65*
6.3-10: *65, 224*
6.4-5: *80*
6.20-21: *65, 224*

2 Timothy

4.19: *148, 149*

Titus

2.3-5: 34, 37, 70
2.4: *162*

Hebrews

12:9. *167, 259*

1 Peter

1.13: *167, 259*
2.18-21: *107*
3.1: *162, 245*
3.1-2: *34*
3.4-6: *37*
5.4-5: *169, 259*
5.5: *162*

1 John

3.17: *107*

Jude

3: *10*